T0159664

"Thanks to shows like *The Big Bang Theory*, being awkward has become cool. But for the millions of awkward people out there, navigating the maze of social life can be paralyzing and terrifying, as Ty Tashiro shows in his touching new book. Full of moving stories and chock-full of research, Tashiro's book offers awkward and non-awkward people alike insight into how to have better relationships and, ultimately, lead a richer life. A thoroughly enjoyable read."

—Emily Esfahani Smith, author of *The Power of Meaning: Crafting a Life That Matters*

"This book is a refreshing reminder that uniqueness and eccentricities are strengths, not liabilities. A gift for everyone who has worried about fitting in and being judged by other people. Entertaining and practical."

—Dr. Todd Kashdan, author of *The Upside of Your Dark Side* and *Curious?*

"In *Awkward*, Ty Tashiro expertly blends humorous anecdotes with the latest research findings to illustrate the unique skills often associated with awkwardness. It is a must-read for anyone who is awkward or knows someone awkward."

—Patricia Frazier, PhD, associate chair of the Department of Psychology and Distinguished McKnight University Professor, University of Minnesota

"*Awkward* contains many useful and resonant observations about everyday interactions."

—*New York Times Book Review*

"Tashiro has become an evangelist for his kind . . . positing that there's an upside to all this nerding out. . . . In many ways *Awkward* is a memoir. . . . Packed with vignettes from the author's childhood, even as it loops in scientific studies and Darwinian theory."

—*Washington Post*

"An academic and psychologist examines the 'quirks and unique talents of awkward individuals' and why it's not so bad to be awkward. . . . The author assures that awkwardness can be a gift and that one can be grateful for it."

—*Kirkus Reviews*

"Mixing personal anecdotes with summaries of psychological studies, Tashiro effectively delivers an informative and engaging pop psychology piece on what it's like to be socially challenged."

—*Library Journal*

"Illustrating his points with fascinating examples, Tashiro discusses the way awkward people deal with emotional situations . . . and, finally, how we can learn to love our own awkwardness to bring out the best in ourselves. An entertaining mix of social science and pop psychology."

—*Booklist*

AWKWARD

AWKWARD

THE SCIENCE OF WHY WE'RE
SOCIALLY AWKWARD
AND WHY THAT'S
AWESOME

TY TASHIRO, PhD

wm

WILLIAM MORROW
An Imprint of HarperCollins*Publishers*

HarperCollins books may be purchased for educational, business, or sales promotional use. For information, please e-mail the Special Markets Department at SPsales@harpercollins.com.

A hardcover edition of this book was published in 2017 by William Morrow, an imprint of HarperCollins Publishers.

FIRST WILLIAM MORROW PAPERBACK EDITION PUBLISHED 2018.

Designed by Fritz Metsch

Library of Congress Cataloging-in-Publication Data has been applied for.

ISBN 978-0-06-242916-2

18 19 20 21 22 RS/LSC 10 9 8 7 6 5 4 3 2 1

For my brother and sister,
who illuminated a better way

CONTENTS

PART II: THIS IS GETTING AWKWARD

HOW MODERN SOCIETAL SHIFTS ARE MAKING EVERYONE

FEEL MORE AWKWARD

I can feel everyone staring. The sharply dressed guests, all sipping their cocktails a safe distance from the pool, are surely wondering what I plan to do about the frail six-year-old struggling to stay afloat in front of me. I'm wondering the same thing.

Every time I extend my arms toward the flailing child to offer help, my gesture is refused by his grating scream: "Let me do it!" I feel an uneasy sense of responsibility, but I want to respect his efforts, so I continue to let him struggle. The tension between the adults' judging glances and this scrappy kid's determination to persist has me caught in a seriously awkward position. And he's not even my kid.

Spencer was the son of my friend Zak, whom I had met in graduate school at the University of Minnesota. Zak and I had kept in touch and in the fall of 2013 I had a chance to stay with him and his wife, Lydia, while I attended a psychology conference in Florida. The day I arrived in Florida they happened to be throwing a birthday party for Lydia in their backyard. For some reason, Spencer instantly latched on to me as his new buddy, which was apparently a departure from his normally aloof disposition.

As people arrived at the party, they did the typical things adults do with six-year-olds. In their best "kid voice" they asked

Spencer his age, gave him extra-cuddly hugs, or wondered aloud, "Do you remember me, Spencer?" They were being lovely, but this small talk in a party setting was like kryptonite for Spencer. I watched his body language slowly shrink while a palpable sense of anxiety began to overcome him. After a well-intentioned guest asked Spencer, "Well, how did you get so handsome, young man?" he abruptly turned toward me and said, "I want you to help me with my swimming."

When Spencer and I looked toward Zak and Lydia for permission, they said it would be great if I could occupy Spencer while they attended to their arriving guests. As we prepared to get into the pool, Spencer told me, "Yesterday, at my swim lesson, I practiced jumping into the pool and swimming back to the side." He demonstrated this feat two or three times, but then grew bored with his success. As he adjusted his Spiderman goggles, he proclaimed that he would try to swim the entire sixteen-foot width of the pool.

Spencer directed me to stay two feet in front of him while he dog-paddled his way toward the other side. During his initial attempts, he was having trouble making it past the midway point, and each time he began to flounder he rejected my attempts to help. Eventually he would relent, ask me for help, and I would carry him back to the ledge. After a minute of rest, he would say, "Let's try again."

I'm no Olympian, but even for a six-year-old Spencer did not appear to be gifted with much strength or coordination. His swimming had a decidedly spastic vibe and seeing it gave one a visceral sense of discomfort, which was accentuated by his loud gasps. I appreciated his chutzpah, but also worried about his ability to stay afloat. I looked to Zak and Lydia for some guidance; they nodded their heads as if this spectacular struggle was completely normal.

With each failure to reach the opposite ledge, Spencer became more agitated, and after his fourth failure he appeared to be on the brink of tears. When I sat him on the ledge I pointed out the tremendous progress he had already made and suggested that we try again tomorrow. But he was not looking me in the eye and in fact I don't think that he heard much of the easy out I provided for him. He appeared lost in his mind, replaying the causes for his failures and trying to think of better ways to approach the problem. He looked at me intently, though not quite in my eyes, and in a matter-of-fact tone said, "One more try . . ."

To understand Spencer's ambition, it helps to know a little about his parents. During graduate school, Zak was one of the star students in applied mathematics. When he graduated, he took a job at NASA, where he was technically a rocket scientist. Lydia was one of the top intellectual-property attorneys in the country. Together they were a remarkable couple with high-powered intellects and ambitions, but they were also humble and generous people who had always been loyal friends to me.

While Zak was driving me back to their house from the airport, he told me that he had been deeply concerned about Spencer. During kindergarten, he showed little interest in playing with other kids, but when he did try to interact with his peers his efforts came across as overly intense and other kids found him to be odd. It's not unusual for children to be interested in space travel or trains, but Spencer was obsessed with questions such as planetary orbits and the mechanisms of combustion in different types of engines. The combination of his unusual interests and intense manner made it hard for him to play very well with others. Spencer was bored by his schoolwork and his teachers described him in terms usually applied to much older children, including "bright, but disengaged" and "underachieving."

When Spencer launched into a monologue on planetary orbits or explained the mechanisms of steam engines, he sparkled in a brilliance that fascinated adults. His mind was always at work, generating observations by combining information from his large catalog of facts. Spencer was like a forty-year-old professor caught in a six-year-old boy's life. But his social skills deficits were just as glaring as his precocious ability. His eye contact was erratic, his nonverbal behaviors were muted, and he generally played alone during recess.

The school counselor suggested that a child psychologist should evaluate Spencer for a disorder like attention-deficit hyperactivity disorder or a learning disability. One night after Spencer had gone to bed, Zak asked if I would take a look at the report, which had come back with nebulous recommendations. He knew that I couldn't act as Spencer's psychologist, but he was desperate to get some insight into his son's mind and hoped that as a psychology professor I might have some advice on how to best support him.

The school psychologist found that Spencer's IQ scores put him well into the top 1 percent of kids his age. His psychopathology test scores never crossed into the diagnosable range for disorders including ADHD or oppositional defiant disorder, but I saw a pattern of unevenness in his profile. His scores for self-control were in the bottom tenth percentile compared to those for kids his age, and his scores for obsessive tendencies were in the top fifth percentile. Spencer was a boy who did not fit neatly into a diagnosable category, but instead seemed to occupy a limbo in between normal and diagnosable. The psychologist gave Spencer a diagnosis of "Pervasive Developmental Disorder—Not Otherwise Specified," which I usually read as psychologist speak for, "Something is socially problematic, but I'm not sure what."

After we discussed the report, Zak and Lydia asked me a perfectly logical follow-up question, "So what should we do?" After a long pause, I replied, "I'm sorry, I don't know." My reply activated Lydia's litigation mode and she began marching down a line of interrogation:

Why is he awkward? What makes him awkward?

Well, Lydia, there's not yet data to—

How many kids feel socially awkward?

I don't know that anybody has investigated—

Can you be awkward and happy? Do awkward people make
   friends?

Sure, but—

How did you make friends? You're so awkward.

Lydia's face flushed with embarrassment. She launched into an apology for her last question, but I told her there was no need to apologize. For me, it was a refreshing realization that I had been happy with my life even though there were still discernible traces of awkwardness on display. The urgency in Lydia's voice was a familiar tone, a near-panicked feeling that had once pervaded my private deliberations about how I could navigate a social world that seemed like it moved too fast for me to decipher its secrets. That panic had left me years ago, but I could not articulate how that change occurred or even what the change had been.

As a guy who spends his days reviewing social science research, I was disappointed that I could not provide sound answers. I knew that research must be out there that explains why some people are prone to being awkward and why so many awkward people I knew had managed to forge meaningful social ties. Yet I was unaware of anyone who had put forth a coherent, evidence-based set of answers to the kinds of questions Lydia needed answers to.

After that trip to Florida, I became obsessed with finding answers about why some people feel awkward and how they can navigate an increasingly complex social world. While I scoured hundreds of research papers for answers, I found sociological research to suggest that modern social life has made all of us feel more awkward. We can all relate to having an awkward moment, but I also found compelling psychological research to explain why some people experience awkward moments not as an exception to the rule, but as a way of life.

Awkward people see the world differently from non-awkward people. When non-awkward people walk into a room full of people, they naturally see the big social picture. They intuitively understand things like the emotional tone in the room or how formally they should act. By comparison, awkward people tend to see social situations in a fragmented way. It's as if they see the world with a narrow spotlight that makes it hard to see the big social picture all at once, but their spotlighted view means that they see some things with an intense clarity.

Their spotlighted attention gravitates toward nonsocial areas that are systematic in nature, which is why they like the rules of math or the logic of coding and leisure activities like games or collecting. Although they are more likely to choose Silicon Valley or physics theory over sales or customer relations, they can be found across a wide range of vocations. Regardless of their specific interests, what awkward individuals have in common is a spotlighted view of the world and an obsessive drive to understand their interests, and this drive helps them see unusual details and configurations among details.

Awkward people are a passionate bunch, who tend to be obsessive about the things that interest them. Their obsessive interest to learn everything they can about a topic mirrors the "rage to master" that researchers observe in high-achieving people. Researchers who study prodigious achievement find that high-achieving people share some psychological traits, including a razor-sharp focus, a willingness to search for unusual questions or solutions, and an obsessive drive to master their craft, regardless of whether that occurs in technology, the arts, or entertainment. Awkward people's obsessive interest helps a scientist persist through the drudgery of repeating procedures hundreds of times in her laboratory, drives a dancer to spend hours fussing over the mechanics of a plié, and allows a comedian the ability to bomb in front of audiences while perfecting new jokes.

However, awkward individuals' intense and obsessive focus on specific interests comes with an opportunity cost, which is that they are more likely to miss social cues and cultural expectations that others see easily and that are integral for smoothly navigating social life. Their spotlighted view explains some of their common behaviors, including why they have trouble remembering to attend to routine social expectations such as greetings, social graces, and understanding nonverbal cues. They can also appear lost in their heads instead of present in their interactions with others. To the awkward, their social world is a Goldilocks tale of living in a world that feels too big or too small, too hot or too cold, but their trial-and-error search for "just right" comes with some painful social missteps and, at times, a sense of feeling alone.

Awkward people can feel like social interactions are chaotic, which makes it hard for them to calmly predict how to navigate new social situations. This makes a scientific approach a good tool for awkward people to understand how social interactions work. The broad aims of science are to describe complex phenomena, organize information, and predict seemingly random outcomes. Awkward people's minds tend to make them natural scientists because they are good at seeing details, picking up on patterns in those details, and taking a systematic approach to problems.

As kids they do unusual things like take the toaster apart to see how it works or ask incessant questions about how birds know to fly south for the winter or become fascinated with how hybrid engines work. They are not so much interested in toast, pretty birds, or fast cars, but in the hidden mechanisms that make those things tick. So a good approach for awkward people to build their sociability is to methodically take apart social interactions, examine how component parts work, and then reassemble those parts in a way that works for them. But they cannot be satisfied with the intellectual exercise of studying social life, they also need to translate their observations into repeatable actions that become habit-like. It's the difference between discovering combustion in the laboratory versus building a car engine that can run reliably for thousands of miles.

There is a wealth of self-help advice about how to be more charismatic or gregarious, but that's not really what awkward people are looking for, at least not at first. Awkward people are often given well-intentioned advice such as, "Just put yourself out there," or "Just be yourself," or parents might tell their children after a rough day at school, "They're just jealous of you." But for awkward individuals, none of this advice makes much sense. When they hear it, they think, "I have trouble handling what's out there," or "Being myself means being awkward," and "I highly doubt that kids are jealous about my social life." Most awkward people are not thinking about how to be charismatic or wildly popular; they would be happy to start with figuring out how to manage routine social situations and fitting in at school or work.

I wrote this book for awkward people who want insight into the vague rules of social life that govern things like the ingredients that go into a good first impression, the function of emotion, and the rationale behind social formalities. But I also wrote for non-awkward people who hope to understand how modern social life has become more awkward for all of us, as well as those parents, teachers, counselors, managers, and even spouses of awkward people who wonder what makes awkward people tick and how they can support their tremendous potential. Although awkward people share some psychological commonalities, it's also important to note that not all awkward people are alike. They possess different combinations of awkward characteristics, and those characteristics can combine with other personality traits to create different styles of awkwardness.

When non-awkward people look past an awkward person's social clumsiness and take the time to really get to know them, they often discover good people who simply have a different view of the world. Awkward people often tell me, "I wish that people would give me a chance because I think that they would like me." This wish is congruent with studies we will review that show awkward people's difficulty handling routine social interactions can prevent others from getting to know what they are really like, but awkward people often have less obvious characteristics that are interesting and valuable. So awkward people can benefit from understanding what is expected in routine social situations, why they tend to miss what is expected, and find a way to humbly make the characteristics they want people to see readily apparent.

There are a few things that this book is not. My goal was not to create any excuses for awkward people or the impression they have it worse than anyone else. Social expectations and cultural rules sometimes exist for a good reason, especially when those rules are rooted in ensuring that everyone gets a fair shot or feels respected. I think that awkward people could use a little extra patience from others, but they also have to do their best to improve their ability to manage social interactions.

I have given careful consideration to striking a balance between a healthy sense of humor about awkward situations while never intending to make light of someone's social struggles. When awkward stories are about someone besides myself, I have created composite characters and mixed up some of the details in each of those stories. But I think it's healthy to have a good laugh at some point about our awkward moments. A sense of levity about our social missteps can be a great antidote to the feelings of embarrassment or blows to our self-esteem.

I have been encouraged by the wealth of quality research about social awkwardness, but like any area of scientific inquiry, I sometimes found mixed results. Some research findings were steeped in jargon or complicated statistical analyses. I had to keep in mind that awkward people are prone to becoming so enthused by an area of interest that we can easily begin lecturing others about uninteresting minutiae. I have done my best to be fair about summarizing the theories and research findings in the book, but I felt a constant tension between complexity versus clarity and breadth versus brevity. Although I have done my best to highlight robust research findings, readers will find that not all findings apply to their particular situation. For the reader interested in more details about some of the original sources, the bibliography contains references to selected studies about key topics in each chapter.

In the end, an unexpected pattern of nuanced results emerged from the hundreds of scientific studies I reviewed and revealed surprising insights about why we're awkward and why the psychological characteristics that make people awkward can also position them for prodigious achievements in other contexts. I hope that you find this wealth of scientific insight as helpful as I did for understanding why being awkward can be awesome.

Spencer was not one for semi-emotional rituals such as good-byes, and after I exchanged hugs with his parents by the front door, I waved good-bye from afar so as not to interrupt his *Thomas the Tank Engine* episode. But he leapt from the couch, ran toward the door, and gave me an awkward but enthusiastic side hug. He said, "It was nice to be your friend."

Later that day on my plane ride back to New York City, I felt determined to find some answers about awesome people who also happen to be awkward. I opened my laptop and started on a document titled:

AWKWARD: The Science of Why We're Socially Awkward and Why That's Awesome

PART I

SO THIS IS AWKWARD

———

1

WHAT DOES IT MEAN TO BE AWKWARD?

My first discovery in graduate school was that I was almost normal. It was the fall of 1999 when I began my graduate studies in psychology at the University of Minnesota. New students were given the option to go through a rigorous psychological assessment that would give us feedback about our personality characteristics, intellectual abilities, and vocational interests. I figured the assessment would be a fun exercise in self-exploration, but after the testing sessions I realized these detailed test results might reveal that I possessed abnormal characteristics that had never troubled me before, in part because I had been blissfully ignorant about their existence.

Two weeks later, I found a yellow envelope in my mailbox with CONFIDENTIAL REPORTS scribbled across the seal. I cautiously pulled open the report feeling nervous about what I might discover, like someone opening the door to a long-neglected attic. There were dozens of charts showing where my scores fell on a bell curve for traits such as introversion, kindness, orderliness, and various forms of intelligence. Each chart was accompanied by a written summary that explained whether I was in a "normal range of functioning" or crossed into a diagnosable range of pathology.

Like Spencer's psychological testing profiles, my personality and pathology scores never crossed into a clearly diagnosable range, but my scores were uneven. For example, my scores on personality traits such as kindness and curiosity were significantly higher than the average person's but my scores on patience and orderliness were much lower than average. I wondered for a second what it was like for other people to make sense of someone who was kindly impatient or who possessed a disorderly sense of curiosity.

Overall, the first few pages painted a picture of someone who was relatively normal, but some unusual patterns began to emerge in a section toward the middle of the report titled "Social Development." This section included interviews with some of my family members, and the testing psychologist had highlighted responses to one particular question: "What is your most prominent memory of Ty before he was twelve years old?" The interviews had been conducted separately, but all of the respondents provided the same answer: "Ty's mother telling him to concentrate."

Some interviewees elaborated with a recurring incident that involved pouring a glass of milk. Interviewees reported that this incident began early in childhood and they reported that it continued "for much longer than you would expect." I would be seated at the kitchen table, my bowl-cut hair framing my brown eyes that were locked onto a milk carton. My mother would stand behind me in one of her tailored suits, her intent eyes locked on the same milk carton and the empty glass to its side. Eventually, I would grip the milk carton and slowly begin to raise it from the table. My mother would start repeating a hyper-enunciated directive, "CON-cen-trate . . . CON-cen-trate . . ." The chant had a Zen-like rhythm, a calming tone, then—

An abrupt action. All of my intent and determination was concentrated into a thrashing movement that looked like someone trying to dislodge ketchup from a glass bottle. The physics of this overly eager motion blasted into the edge of the glass, which went skittering across the table with a generous stream of milk chasing after it. Witnesses recalled that these quart-size debacles were followed by a stunned silence that Ty had had yet another one of his "accidents."

As the remaining syllable from my mother's wishful chant fell on to the hopeless situation, she would slowly shutter her eyes to take pause, and maintain her composure. My mother is an elegant and tidy woman. Witnesses of these spilling accidents found the mismatch between my mother's graceful demeanor and my haphazard nature to be unbearably amusing, but expressing their amusement would have been ill-timed in the immediate aftermath of these incidents. So onlookers quickly averted their eyes and wiped already dried dishes or mixed well-stirred pots. Clearly, a boy who is eight or ten or twelve years old should be able to pour his own drink with more than a 50 percent chance of success. Yet, my mother found a way to say the best thing possible after these public blunders, "That's all right, Ty, we just need more practice . . ."

"Practice" was a word that was in heavy rotation in our household, especially as it applied to "life skills," which was also in heavy rotation. My parents were remarkably patient with my clumsiness during routine social situations, but they must have privately felt a growing concern as they watched dozens of my life skills fall further into the "developmentally delayed" range with each passing year. They knew the social immunity I had been afforded as a young child was due to expire when I entered the ruthless world of junior high school.

Yet some of my nonsocial abilities were advanced for my age. I had a propensity for doing long division and multiplication problems in my head. I found it easy to memorize random facts such as the earned-run averages of National League starting pitchers. Although I was a walking baseball statistics encyclopedia, I routinely forgot to bring my baseball mitt to Little League games or remember that it was my turn to bring the snacks and drinks. As I got older, my parents observed that my peers were starting to cast quizzical glances my way when I stood empty-handed when it was time for the post-game refreshments.

My social missteps never arose from malicious intent and they were generally innocuous mistakes, but around ten years old most children make leaps in their ability to form more complex social expectations and begin to judge other kids' social value based on their ability to meet these expectations. They begin to care more about whether a classmate paints weird things in art class or wears clothing that is not part of the canon of fifth-grade fashion. As my peers' social thoughts became more sophisticated, my quirks that previously went unnoticed were now as evident as lint under a black light. I had a sense about the social expectations around me morphing, but I did not fully understand the new rules of engagement or how to stop my growing feeling of social awkwardness.

My parents knew that there would be no easy answers when it came to helping their chronically awkward kid navigate social life. Like many awkward kids, I was aloof and very stubborn, which meant that my parents had to work with less information than most parents and they had to choose their battles. They must have been tempted to concentrate their efforts on making me less awkward, but my father was a high school teacher and my mother ran a clinic for kids with learning disabilities. Both of them had seen well-intended parents or teachers inadvertently discourage children's passionate interests in their pursuit to make them closer to normal.

My parents did a remarkable job throughout my life dealing with the unusual challenges they faced with a kid who was awkward, stubborn, and very private. In hindsight, I can see that my parents decided to take an ambitious approach to my socialization. They instilled a mindset in me that still guides my social deliberations in adulthood and that is best phrased as a question: How do you fit in without losing yourself?

It's an age-old question worthy of everyone's consideration and it has been at the forefront of my mind as I wrote this book, considering what I would say about how people can be less socially awkward. In the pages to come, I'll distill the results from a vast array of research areas, including personality, clinical psychology, neuroscience, and developmental psychology studies of giftedness. My hope is that whether you are an awkward adult, the concerned parent of an awkward kid, or a boss wondering how to connect with an awkward employee with tremendous potential, the chapters to come will provide useful insights into the quirks and unique talents of awkward individuals. To accomplish these ends, the book is divided into three sections:

1. In Part I, I will examine what it means to be awkward and how people can find guidance in navigating social life.
2. In Part II, I will look at how rapidly shifting social norms have made modern social life feel more awkward for all of us, and what we can do to adapt to them.
3. In Part III, I explain why the traits that make someone awkward can also help them strive toward remarkable achievements.

Chronically awkward people can feel like everyone else received a secret instruction manual at birth titled *How to Be Socially Competent*. For the awkward person, this dreamy manual would provide easy-to-understand, step-by-step instructions on how to gracefully navigate social life, avoid embarrassing faux pas, and rid oneself of the persistent anxiety that comes with being awkward. Of course there is no magic wand for social life, no listicle with ten easy steps to achieve instant popularity. But we will see that there are helpful research findings available for those of us trying to navigate the complexities of social life.

We will discover that the answers to these questions can be counterintuitive and nuanced, but eventually they coalesce into a story about how to find the social belonging we all yearn for while not sacrificing the wonderful quirks that make us unique. To begin our awkward investigation, let's examine how the evolution of social expectations set the stage for our awkward moments.

Our Fundamental Need to Belong

ONE OF THE few books that captured my attention in junior high school was *Lord of the Flies*. Like many students, I was fascinated by what would happen if I found myself in the same position as the main characters who were a group of boys trying to survive on an uninhabited island with no adults to govern them. Although some of the tension in this book comes from the characters' urgency to find food, water, or shelter, the greatest tension is generated by protagonists like Ralph, who struggles to forge alliances that are necessary to survive. He feels a constant concern about others doing their part and remaining loyal.

In real life, much of human history has been about a desperate fight to survive. Although this picture of tenuous survival seems like something far removed from modern life, as recently as the early 1800s more than a third of the deaths in Western Europe were due to lack of access to drinkable water, and malnourishment or death from starvation was much more common. For thousands of years the average life expectancy worldwide was under forty years old, and it's only in the past two hundred years that life expectancies grew longer.

In the 1950s, psychologist Abraham Maslow proposed that human motivations could be organized in a hierarchy of needs. Maslow thought physical needs like food and water were the most essential, whereas other needs like social belonging and self-esteem were of secondary importance. But recent evidence has challenged this assumption. In 1995, social psychologists Roy Baumeister and Mark Leary published a paper titled "The Fundamental Need to Belong," in which they reviewed hundreds of studies related to where the drive for social belonging fell in the hierarchy of needs. From their review, they found that humans' psychological drive to maintain a few gratifying relationships was as fundamental as physical needs such as food or water. In some instances people will forego opportunities to meet their physical needs in the interest of meeting their social needs.

At first glance, the notion that the need to belong is as fundamental as physical needs such as hunger or thirst appears implausible. But for thousands of years, people lived in hunter-gatherer groups of less than fifty people that were tightly bound by collective goals related to survival. The evolutionary bet that humans and other social animals made was to sacrifice their short-term self-interests and cooperate in mutually agreed-upon ways for food gathering, shelter, and protection. Well-coordinated groups divided labor into specialized duties. Some people farmed, others hunted, while some attended to rearing children. For tasks such as harvesting crops or defending against hostile invaders, groups could shift people to these time-sensitive tasks, which greatly increased the resources and protection afforded to each individual and improved all members' chances of survival.

The survival advantages conferred by a cooperative attitude have been reinforced by the psychological mechanisms that kick in to motivate us to forge mutually gratifying relationships. Like a drink of water when we're thirsty or a good meal when we're hungry, when we satiate our need to belong we feel a surge of positive emotion. Ed Diener from the University of Illinois has spent more than three decades studying happiness. Among dozens of possible predictors, Diener and others have found the strongest predictor of happiness is not our job, income, or attaining our fitness goals, but rather the presence of gratifying social relationships. Diener has also found that even in wealthy nations, where food is more abundant and life expectancies have almost doubled, there are still significant benefits associated with a sense of belonging. People with gratifying interpersonal relationships have better physical health and longer life expectancies.

Conversely, there are few things more psychologically devastating than the feeling of social exclusion. Janice Kiecolt-Glaser, the chairperson of the College of Medicine at Ohio State University, has found through decades of research that chronic loneliness is a significant risk factor for compromised immune functioning, cardiac disease, and many other serious medical conditions. These cumulative health risks can create a significant increase in mortality risk.

We not only *want* to belong to a social group, we *need* to belong to a social group. And for most of human history, belonging was relatively more straightforward. Groups struggling for survival had little choice but to take every man, woman, and child available. People needed the group, but the group also needed every individual to make meaningful contributions toward the group's collective goals.

Mary Douglas, an influential anthropologist, noted in her 1966 book *Purity and Danger* that hunter-gatherer groups needed a mechanism to frequently assess whether individuals were committed and doing their part to contribute to the group's collective goals. Groups could ill-afford to discover greedy members stealing food while other members were dying of starvation, and groups did not want to discover rogue members who planned to betray them in the midst of a battle. Group members who were not aligned with the collective goals of the group posed serious threats to the welfare of all group members.

To guard against costly deviations from group goals, societies developed intricate social expectations for daily interactions that provided a way for members to constantly assess the loyalty of each person. When individuals adhered to expectations, such as a friendly greeting, a heartfelt apology, or turn taking, they demonstrated in small ways that they wanted to adhere to the broader goals of the group. Alternatively, when group members observed someone deviating from expectations, they were alerted to the possibility that this member might be veering away from the good of the group. Like an overly sensitive smoke detector that goes off with the tiniest hint of smoke, group members perceived small deviations from routine social expectations as reason for alarm.

In modern societies, people still use small social expectations as an important mechanism for evaluating people's social worth. In fact, minor social expectations may be more important than ever because people have to consistently interact with people they do not know well. In countries like the United States, where over 80 percent of citizens live in urban areas with thousands or millions of people, it's impossible to know the reputation of each person. The modern urbanite is constantly required to evaluate the trustworthiness of people he or she does not know well, whether it's at work, on public transportation, or on a dating app.

TOP THREE EXPECTATIONS IN TWO HIGH-EVALUATION SITUATIONS

ONLINE DATERS ARE ATTRACTED TO PEOPLE WHO HAVE:

1. Good teeth (65%)
2. Good grammar (62%)
3. Nice clothing (52%)

EMPLOYERS ARE ATTRACTED TO PEOPLE WHO HAVE:

1. A positive attitude (84%)
2. Communication skills (83%)
3. Teamwork skills (74%)

Dating results based on a Match.com/USA *Today* survey of more than 5,000 singles, and employer results from "The Multi-Generational Job Search" survey of 3,000 human resources employees.

We now know from thousands of social psychology studies that people use split-second observations about others' style of dress, hygiene, eye contact, and countless other cues to form judgments about whether they would like to include or exclude them from their social groups.

All of these expectations and the associated ramifications can sound overwhelming, but most people meet the majority of social expectations they face. For example, if you showered within the past two days, brushed your teeth today, and put on a shirt without an offensive odor, then you went three for three on three key expectations for personal hygiene. Even awkward people meet the majority of social expectations during the course of a day, but the hundreds of expectations we meet receive far less attention than the one or two expectations we do not meet. When we do veer from social expectations or suspect that we are about to veer from expectations, we feel that unmistakable feeling of being awkward.

Although most people have a sense that first impressions are important, social and personality psychologists have shown through hundreds of studies just how critical the first five minutes of an interaction are. Some judgments about a person's likability are made within the first ten seconds of an interaction based on things like hygiene, posture, eye contact, and tone of voice. Although people revise their judgments, first impressions establish a bias about people as likable versus unlikable or trustworthy versus untrustworthy.

So deviations from small social expectations inherent in day-to-day interactions have broader implications for one's belonging. Awkward acts are usually innocuous—poor fashion choices or undone zippers are not going to kill anyone—but small deviations from expectations stir a primal alarm that the awkward act may be a sign that someone is not "one of us." Judgments based on a few minutes of interaction might sound unfair or irrational, but for thousands of years, humans have relied on these early signals to navigate social life and this tendency will not go away anytime soon.

All of this can sound discouraging for those of us who are awkward, but it does not have to be that way. The trick for awkward people is not to ask the broad question, "Why am I awkward?" The better question, one that fits with most awkward people's ability to dissect complex problems, is to ask, "Why do I have awkward moments?"

We All Have Awkward Moments

AS A CHILD I had a bad habit of stopping in entryways. I looked like a puppy that had wandered into the middle of a busy intersection and was incapacitated by indecision. The moment I walked through a doorway was the moment I thought about the social interactions I would encounter inside. My uncertainty about how to navigate those pending interactions sparked my instinct to leave, but I knew that I needed to push past my trepidation. As often happens to awkward people, my anxiety about the pending social situation neither led me to flee nor made me fight through my fears, but instead produced immobilization.

Most kids have an intuitive sense about how to manage routine expectations during a birthday party or a sleepover, but my parents had to repeatedly coach me about basic elements of most social interactions. Well into my teens, they had to remind me to make eye contact when I spoke to people, to shake hands when greeting someone, or to say good-bye when I left. Given that I did not have an intuitive understanding about how to navigate social situations, I had to study interactions like an academic subject, which included a rote memory approach. Before each social event, my parents would engage me in a Socratic dialogue as a way to quiz me about what would be expected of me, but once I entered a building a form of test anxiety overcame me that blocked my access to the social expectations I had memorized.

My parents realized a new strategy was needed and decided to simplify with a strategy they branded as the "first-three." Instead of reviewing all of the social expectations I would need to remember during an upcoming social situation, they would review the three expectations I would encounter first. The goal was to make me an expert at the first two minutes of interactions. If I could execute the early niceties that are commonly expected in social interactions, then I would feel less anxious and hopefully pick up the social rhythm of the interaction.

For example, before I walked into a birthday party, my parents would review the first-three for greeting my friend's parents: (1) look them in the eye instead of at my shoes, (2) deliver a firm handshake, and (3) confidently say, "Hello, nice to meet you." Eventually, these clusters of three expectations would become automated, such that simply thinking about the first-three for greetings triggered the triad of behaviors. Once I mastered the first-three, I could move on to another set of three expectations to be met, such as break eye contact every eight to twelve seconds, ask how someone's week has been, and follow up that response by asking what made it a good or bad week.

We can visualize the first-three as an equilateral triangle with each corner representing a social expectation. My goal was to try to make my social behavior meet each of the three expectations in the triangle. Let's consider the first few seconds of an interaction, which usually involves someone making visual contact with you, followed by a greeting, such as a hello, handshake, or hug. Personality psychologists have found that unacquainted people use behaviors like these to form sweeping judgments about each other within seconds of interaction.

For example, Laura Naumann at the University of California, Berkeley, and colleagues investigated which nonverbal cues research participants might use to judge someone's likability based solely on a full-length photo. They found that participants based their judgments upon such common social cues as an energetic stance or whether the person was smiling in the photo. In another study, Mitja Back at Johannes Gutenberg University and his colleagues simply asked participants in a classroom to stand up and introduce themselves, then had participants privately rate each other on variables such as likability. Back found participants consistently drew on cues such as a friendly vocal tone and confident nonverbal gestures to form sweeping judgments about whether they might like the other people in the room. These studies and dozens of others suggest that people have strong expectations for how likable people look and behave during the first few seconds of an interaction.

Awkward moments actually occur when we meet the majority of social expectations, but deviate from one or two small expectations. For example, you might greet someone with a pleasant hello, smile, and confidently extend your hand for a shake, but realize that your hand is still damp from washing it in the restroom, and this slight deviation makes the moment feel awkward. When people meet none of the expectations—say something unpleasant, make no facial expression, and stand with their eyes cast downward—then others do not see them as awkward, but rather as arrogant or with significant psychological issues.

Awkward moments are simply deviations from minor social expectations and even the most socially skilled among us know the feeling of an awkward moment. Damp hands or spinach lodged

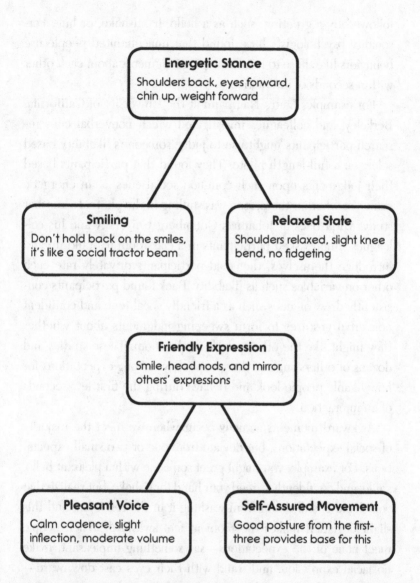

Figure 1.1 The first-three and second-three to consider during first impressions. The top triangle represents visual cues people use to judge someone's likability (top triangle) and the bottom triangle shows the cues people use to judge someone's likability when unacquainted people exchanged introductions.

in your teeth do not pose any kind of real threat to you or anyone else, but they are small signals of deviance from social norms. We know that other people use these small deviations to make inferences about our social value and that's why awkward moments incite such strong emotional reactions. For socially skilled people, the majority of their awkward moments do not pose a serious threat to their belonging, but chronically awkward people have an ominous feeling that too many awkward moments could eventually carry serious social consequences for their social inclusion.

Although everyone can feel awkward, there is a difference between *awkward moments* and being an *awkward person*. When someone is chronically awkward, then the accumulation of their awkward moments can threaten their social inclusion.

Squares, Geeks, and Nerds

AS I ENTERED adolescence, my peers who intuitively grasped 1980s pop culture fell into cool categories. Kids who really loved heavy metal music were stoners, kids who popped the collars of polo shirts were preppies, and those who were good at football were jocks. These social labels were all far more desirable than the category that was the 1980s kiss of social death: nerd.

The nerd was extremely enthusiastic about esoteric interests like mathematics, Dungeons & Dragons, or clarinet. It didn't take long for nerds to realize that their tremendous enthusiasm for their unusual interests would not punch their tickets to popularity. Nerds' esoteric interests also distracted them from attending to things like trending fashions and social graces. Being a nerd meant that you were different. Other kids could feel suspicious about this nonconformity, and suspicion is a powerful anticatalyst to making new friends.

Some etymological explanations for "nerd" suggest that its origins were not in teenage slang, but rather from a 1950 Dr. Seuss book titled *If I Ran the Zoo,* which described a comically unpleasant creature called a nerd. "Geek" was originally a term for carnival sideshow freaks known for their behavioral oddities. The John Hughes' 1985 movie *The Breakfast Club* included a wider-ranging terminology, such as "weirdos," "brains," and "basket cases." The 2004 movie *Mean Girls* updated the terminology for fringe groups, with "burnouts," "desperate wannabes," and "mathletes." Although "geek" and "nerd" were terms that originated as insults, they have increasingly assumed positive connotations. It's as if the nerds and geeks have reclaimed these terms as their own, proudly embracing their atypical identity in the social world.

In 2011, "awkward" became the term du jour for the socially clumsy. Google tracks search trends from their users and when I looked at the number of people who Googled the question "Why am I so awkward?" I saw a spike in 2011 that remained consistent for the past five years. The sharp rise in people's interest in awkwardness may partly reflect the trendiness of the word, but may also reflect that more people are feeling socially awkward and wonder why that might be the case.

Today, it's kind of cool to be a nerd. For some reason we can't get enough of awkward physicists on television shows like *The Big Bang Theory* or awkward millennial sex scenes on *Girls.* When the *Star Wars: The Force Awakens* movie opened in December of 2015, fans proudly posted their cosplay photos on social media with self-aware hashtags like #awkward or #cantstop #wontstop.

Although I am encouraged by the growing freedom awkward people have to embrace their unique interests and identity as such, there remain significant challenges that come along with being awkward. While awkward moments are sometimes uproariously funny, chronic awkwardness can threaten one's social inclusion and there are few things more troubling than feeling that one is on the outside looking in.

The *American Heritage Dictionary* defines "awkward" as a lack of skill or grace, which is a simple and accurate definition of *what* it means to be an awkward person. The roots of the word come from the Old Norse *afgr*, which means "facing the wrong way." Unlike the definition of "awkward" that has to do with what someone is, *afgr* is more about *how* someone sees and moves through their social world.

"Awkward" is a useful and relatively benign term compared to some of the other names kids call each other, but awkward people already know that they see the world differently from most people. What awkward people need is guidance about how to navigate the social world with their unique perspective, and the burgeoning science of relationships that we will review in the chapters to come reveals important social expectations and behaviors that are critical to maintaining gratifying social relationships.

The imagery inspired by *afgr* gives us a useful clue for developing a more functional definition of awkward people. *Afgr* suggests that these people are facing the wrong way, but I like a slightly different view. I like to think that awkward people are simply looking elsewhere.

But if the awkward are gazing elsewhere, what do they see?

Seeing the World Through Awkward Eyes

IMAGINE A BROADWAY theater full of people who have come to see *The Lion King*. The houselights go down, drumbeats begin to pulse, and a soft red light evenly illuminates the entire stage like an amber sunrise. Dozens of actors operate life-size animal costumes, one actor per lion, four per elephant, and three actors center stage who introduce the play's protagonist, Simba. The opening procession of *The Lion King* creates a spectacular effect with dozens of animals weaving effortlessly around center stage, where the Lion King eventually appears. This synchronous choreography creates a whole that is more than the sum of its parts.

Cut. Take two.

In a second rendition, the houselights go down, drumbeats begin to pulse, but a spotlight cast to the left replaces the broad, amber light of the first rendition. It's a brilliant white light and anything that moves into it appears crisp and vivid. It's the same production, same song, same synchronous choreography, but this is a very different experience. This audience sees a giraffe meander into the spotlight, then disappear into the middle of the stage. An elephant's backside is seen in the spotlight while her front side is in the dim light beyond the spotlight.

People know that the action spans the width of the stage, but the sharp contrast between the spotlighted and dim areas of the stage makes it hard for them to pick up on all of the action. If you see a spotlighted version of the story, then you are most likely to look wherever the spotlight shines, and that means that you are more likely to miss key moments that tend to take place at center stage. But what you see is crisply illuminated by the spotlight, which means that you can notice beautiful detailing in the costumes, a bead of sweat running down the left side of an actress's forehead, or a subtle upturn of her mouth as the audience applauds. You could try to shift your attention to the poorly lit parts of the stage, but it's a struggle to see the action in these dim areas, and after a while you could tire of straining to make sense of them.

Imagine how someone seeing a spotlighted version of the play might explain the plot of *The Lion King*. They would probably have a general sense of the plot, but their summary would be atypical because their perception of the experience is different from that of people who saw the first production with the stage broadly illuminated. While the group who saw the broadly illuminated stage would have a holistic view of the plot, the people who saw the spotlighted version would have a deeper understanding of everything that took place stage left, but they would have missed key information that took place outside of the spotlight.

In much the same way, awkward people see the vast world before them with a spotlighted view. Awkward people are naturally drawn to the part of their world where their spotlighted attention shines brightest and this creates a narrow, intense focus. It's similar to what researchers Francesca Happe at King's College and Uta Frith at University College London call a "localized processing" style, which describes people who tend to narrowly focus on some of the trees rather than the entire forest. When people are disposed to a localized processing style, they tend to create social narratives that feel fragmented and incomplete. Happe, Frith, and others have found that awkward people are more likely than non-awkward people to process information in a detail-oriented way, which means that they sometimes have trouble seeing the bigger picture.

Awkward people's narrow and intense focus tends to fall on parts of the stage other than where other people intuitively look. For example, directors traditionally have critical interactions take place center stage or may begin a scene center stage. Alternatively, directors might start a scene to the audiences' left because they know that people who read left to right expect that action will begin left and move right. Most people naturally know to look center stage or to their left when a scene is about to start, but by analogy, awkward people are looking elsewhere because their spotlighted attention falls on unusual parts of the stage.

While the rest of the audience is watching the Lion King's protagonist Simba being introduced center stage, awkward people are marveling at the mechanics of the giraffe costume on the left side of the stage or enjoy observing the unusually enthusiastic cellist in the orchestra pit. Although awkward people are missing important social information that falls outside of their narrow aperture, what they do see is brilliantly illuminated and this gives them a deep, nuanced perspective about things that no one else takes the time to notice. The parts of the world that they can see are seen with remarkable clarity. They become experts in all things stage left and their clear, focused view on their specialized interests give them a unique view of that part of the world.

Sometimes awkward individuals' unusual perspective can be funny or creative. There is some evidence that awkward people are more likely to see social outcomes as magical instead of predictable. Because they are not immediately drawn to social information, they pick up on the flow of social events midstream. This is why people sometimes describe the awkward as having a childlike wonder, a naive view of cause and effect in social situations that most adults find predictable.

While socially skilled people have an intuitive sense of social situations, awkward people have to be deliberate to understand other people's intentions and figure out the appropriate social response. During my graduate training, this distinction between intuitive versus deliberate, labored understanding was clearly impressed upon me by one of my counseling clients. The client was a brilliant doctoral student in chemical engineering who was very socially awkward. He told me about his mishandling of an encounter with a romantic interest and I followed up with a naive and poorly framed question: "Why do you think you have these lapses in your attention to social expectations?" He retorted, "Why do you think you have lapses in your attention to advanced organic chemistry?" It was an incisive and fair point.

When I was twelve years old, my milk-pouring accidents dramatically decreased as the result of an observation from one of my aunts. She noticed that I never looked at my glass. While my mother's gaze and everyone else's attention were intently focused on the glass, as if trying to telepathically will the glass not to topple over, my spotlighted attention were fixated off center, on the carton of milk I held in my hands.

All I could think about was my narrow goal of getting the milk out of the carton and into the glass as soon as possible. I did not understand the relationship between the carton and the glass because I was so fixated on the carton and the *outcome* while not considering the *process*. Just like I could become so narrowly fixated on eating dinner or playing baseball that I lost sight of the fact that dinner is a social time or that the point of playing games as a kid is to enjoy the company of others.

We will see from behavioral genetic and brain-imaging research that awkward individuals' narrow aperture of attention is dispositional, powered by neurological hardware that is as heritable as one's body weight or running speed. The trade-off for awkward people is this: their spotlighted attention makes it harder for them to see social expectations that most people easily recognize, but awkward people also get to see whatever falls into their spotlight with brilliant detail. It's easy for awkward people to become fully absorbed in their spotlighted area of interest and to feel deeply gratified by seeing things in these areas with unique clarity. There is a tremendous upside that can come from a spotlighted view of the world.

The trick for awkward people is learning how to adjust their aperture and shift their focus to areas of life that fall outside the natural set point for their spotlighted attention. Solving the mystery of how to be socially effective and find the belonging they need takes deliberate effort and a willingness to shift their spotlighted focus to social considerations. The good news is that people can experience significant improvements socially when they turn their obsessive focus on dissecting the components of social interaction and then integrating those components into a methodically

constructed understanding of and approach to social life, even if
that means that they have to move their spotlight to methodically
master three social expectations at a time.

In the chapters to come, the stories of social awkwardness are
sometimes amusing, at other times heartbreaking, but ultimately
they are uplifting tales and insights about how to embrace your
quirks and harness your remarkable potential.

2

IS THERE ANYTHING WRONG
WITH BEING AWKWARD?

The summer before seventh grade, I began to formulate a strategy for social success in junior high school. I knew that the complexity of the seventh-grade social scene was going to challenge my social skills and this kicked my mind into a proactive contemplation about how to deal with the forthcoming challenges. Like most kids, I worried about what to wear, who I would sit with at lunch, and what it would be like to go to my first dance. Although these were normal social concerns, the way I thought about preparing for these situations was unusual and my private deliberations resulted in the conclusion that my social success would rely upon my ability to convey a more mature and professional Ty Tashiro.

I am not sure why I believed that the road to junior high social success would be paved with maturity and professionalism. I think there may have been two factors that led to this conclusion. I probably overgeneralized my parents' forewarnings about the need to make mature decisions about saying no to drugs, alcohol, and other vices, and my favorite television character was Alex P. Keaton from *Family Ties*, who was a teenage boy who dressed and acted like a forty-year-old stockbroker.

My blanket philosophy that an adultlike approach would be my best bet led to a number of misguided tactical decisions. When the first day of school arrived, I chose an outfit that included a starched baby-blue oxford, a crisp pair of pleated khaki pants, and a pair of extra-large, square silver glasses that looked like the bifocals my grandparents' friends wore. If I were a sixty-year-old accountant, I would have looked dashing.

Like many awkward kids, I was private, even aloof, and that usually meant I shared little about my thought processes with my parents or anyone else, for that matter. I suspect that when my parents saw my outfit, their minds raced to figure out whether to fight this battle over my stylistic choices. Parents have to be careful about micromanaging their kids, and awkward kids can be particularly stubborn about being micromanaged. There was technically nothing scandalous about my outfit and I was so close to falling in line with the preppy fashion expectations of the early eighties. If I had left my shirt unstarched and untucked I might have been all right, but these small stylistic deviations along with my bifocal-like glasses made things awkward.

In her brown Oldsmobile station wagon, my mom drove me to Longs Peak Junior High for my first day of school. As we crept through the circular driveway at school, the discrepancy between my fashion choices for the day and those of my new classmates became clear. My peers wore tattered black jeans that were rolled into a pleated cuff above their ankles, and black T-shirts advertising badass bands who sang about Satan and drinking the blood of bats. They wore gold-framed aviator sunglasses that Tom Cruise wore playing with his boys in *Top Gun*. As my mother and I pulled up to the entrance of the building and took in the edgy styles, animated discussions, and large scale of this bustling social scene, there was a collective gasp in the station wagon.

As I opened the car door, I suddenly wanted the superpower of invisibility. I tried to minimize my lanky five-nine frame as I stood up and privately asked some important questions for the first time. Who would I talk to? Why were my glasses so large? Why had none of the other students worn starched oxfords? My ruminations were interrupted when I heard my name called by a group of boys I had known in elementary school. Ed Seemers, Will Hartford, and Sam Hassan were polite, studious, salt-of-the-earth boys who were huddled by the flagpole. I was relieved to join their huddle. We were not cool by any stretch of the

Figure 2.1 My seventh-grade school photo

imagination, but we were all relieved not to appear as lone wolves.

After a few days, our band of misfits realized that there was no recess-like activity in junior high. No one engaged in tag, king of the mountain, or other games that had been popular in the sixth grade. After discussing this odd turn of events, we reached consensus that junior high culture sucked. People stood around and talked about trends like a new cable channel called MTV or the artistry of Michael Jackson's *Thriller* album, which was no way to spend recess-like time. Will Hartford, who was the alpha male of our group by virtue of his lumberjack size, declared that we would play even if everyone else thought they were too cool to play at school. After some deliberation, we decided to go with one of our playtime activities from sixth grade, reenactments of wrestling matches from the World Wide Wrestling Federation.

A patch of grass on the south end of the soccer field would make the perfect wrestling ring. The goalie box could be the boundary and the chain-link fence that bordered the south side of the box could be used like the ropes of a boxing ring. Hartford declared that he would play Hulk Hogan, Seemers chose Randy "Macho Man" Savage, and Hassan selected the Iron Sheik. In keeping with the theme of semi-offensive racial stereotypes, I chose to portray Mr. Fuji, the lone Japanese wrestler in the federation.

There was an improv-like quality to the wrestling that Friday, an unspoken understanding that each wrestler's turn needed to propel the action toward a larger narrative. For example, it was an unspoken expectation that you should let your opponent keep you in a choke hold for about eight seconds, before raking their face with your fingertips, which was usually followed by a body slam. When the improv became a bit stale, one could always rely upon the instant drama created by swinging an opponent into the fence. The fence bounce was great theater because there was something pleasing about the rhythm of swinging an opponent into the middle of the fence, watching him bounce back in double time, and then giving him a punctuated stop as you pretended to clothesline him with your outstretched arm.

At some point during this raucous theater, I paused for a moment to wipe the sweat from my brow and I pushed my silver eyeglasses up my slight nose. Then I had a sharp revelation. None of the other seventh graders was joining us, which I guess was to be expected. In fact, everyone else stood a safe distance from our wrestling debacle, apparently busy making better social decisions. A few of them watched us with a mixture of fascination and horror. As this realization dawned on me, I felt my stomach sink and a panic gripped my chest. I realized that role-playing the WWWF was so sixth grade.

Precisely at this moment of insight, Hulk Hogan placed his tight grip onto Mr. Fuji's forearm. He began to swing me around like an Olympian getting ready to do the hammer throw. He was building momentum to bounce me off the chain-link fence and then deliver a flying body slam. As Hogan spun Fuji around with increasing speed, the centripetal force concentrated my anticipatory dread about the social ramifications from the hundreds of students who were not behaving like they were still in elementary school. I did not have to suffer this for long. When Hogan released Fuji from his orbit, he made a slight miscalculation while plotting the trajectory, a small error that sent Fuji forehead first into one of the steel fence posts.

When I regained consciousness I saw a blurry image of people gathering around me. I began to feel around the grass for my dislodged glasses, and when I could not locate them, my hands began to move with a frenetic urgency. Then, a large man who looked like an elderly, cardigan-wearing version of the WWWF's Andre the Giant burst through the circle forming around me. Coach Stenson stutter-stepped to a halt beside me and his arthritic legs creaked as he knelt down. He looked at me for a moment through the bottom of his large, silver bifocals. Then, he picked up my own large silver glasses, and gently set them back on my face.

Coach Stenson was the varsity football coach and a venerated patriarch around school. We had never spoken before my WWWF mishap, but he knew my father and had probably been keeping an eye on me from afar. Coach Stenson barked at the crowd around me, "Nothing to see here!" Once the crowd had dispersed and I managed to sit up, he firmly gripped my shoulder, looked me in the eye, and in a measured tone said, "Son, you have got to slow down. You have got to look around. And you need to figure this thing out before you dig yourself into a hole. Now go to the nurse. You're probably concussed."

In the nurse's office, I sat on the green vinyl couch with an ice pack over the contusion on my forehead. While the nurse asked me my name, where I lived, and a few other concussion-protocol questions, my mind furiously searched for the answer to another question: How could I not see that wrestling reenactments were a bad idea?

Strange and Intense

HANS ASPERGER WAS a quiet boy. Peers described him as "remote" and biographers note that he was generally aloof. He was a boy who enjoyed the solitary time spent delving into his nonsocial interests rather than the messy business of social interactions. Although he was a clumsy child, Hans frequently enjoyed long hikes by himself in the Austrian mountains. He possessed precocious linguistic abilities and as a child was obsessed with the writings of Franz Grillparzer, an Austrian poet known for his nihilistic poems about political oppression and death. One of the few instances when Hans shared his unusual interests was when he enthusiastically recited Grillparzer's morbid poetry to his bewildered grade-school classmates.

Hans Asperger's unusual social demeanor and unusual obsession with language made it hard for him to make friends as a child and he would continue to have trouble connecting with others throughout adulthood. Although he must have read voraciously as a prolific psychiatric researcher, Asperger spent much of his leisure time reading classic literature and books about the humanities. One of his daughters described him as removed from family life and his obsession with reciting long quotes to his family as "strange and intense."

In 1944, Asperger published his most notable psychiatric paper, a case study about four boys whose symptoms included low empathy, difficulty maintaining eye contact, and an obsessive, narrow focus on peculiar interests. Asperger coined the term "autistic psychopaths" to describe these boys. Meanwhile, Leon Kanner from Johns Hopkins University had made similar observations he published in a 1943 case study of eleven boys Kanner described as abnormally withdrawn and characterized by unusually repetitive behavioral rituals.

"Autism" is a stark term, derived from the Greek word *autos*, which means "self." It's an image of the self that is disembodied from other people who are engaged in social activity. Asperger and Kanner described autistic psychopaths with the same triad of symptoms: (1) a lack of interest in social activity, (2) a lack of empathy, and (3) a rigid insistence on sameness. In 1980, this triad of symptoms would be the foundation for the American Psychiatric Association's introduction of a formal autism diagnosis in the third edition of the *Diagnostic and Statistical Manual of Mental Disorders* (*DSM-III*) and the next edition of the manual (*DSM-IV*) added Asperger's syndrome.

Both autism and Asperger's syndrome were characterized by social skill and communication deficits that included symptoms such as trouble with back-and-forth interactions, problems comprehending nonverbal behavior, and difficulty understanding and forming relationships. Repetitive behaviors included things like inflexible routines, under- or over reactivity to sight, sounds, or touch, and extremely narrow and intense interests.

The advent of autism as a formal diagnosis likely influenced a number of important breakthroughs in how we diagnose and treat autism. A formal autism diagnosis also opens access to school accommodations, social services, and insurance reimbursements for mental health services that are important for autistic individuals dealing with a serious and potentially debilitating condition. But it's important to be careful about diagnoses.

One way that clinicians exert caution while trying to make a diagnosis is through use of something called the *rule of five*. Clinicians usually ask patients about what seems to be troubling them. As they describe their symptoms, clinicians are taught to begin generating a list of the five most probable diagnoses based on their symptoms. The imperative to generate an overly inclusive list of possible explanations is a shortcut that helps clinicians avoid selecting the first explanation that pops into their heads. It reminds them to consider both diagnostic and non-diagnosable explanations for symptoms. Some symptoms may indicate a serious condition or just that someone has a few unusual quirks.

It's hard not to speculate about whether Hans Asperger would have qualified for his namesake diagnosis. I also wonder whether Asperger recognized parts of himself in the four boys from his original case study. Their abnormal social behaviors, difficulty communicating with others, and obsessive interests could have easily been used to describe Asperger.

Although Asperger had symptoms that point to an Asperger's syndrome diagnosis, there was also evidence that would argue against an autism diagnosis. Most descriptions of *DSM* disorders, including autism, require that the symptoms have a significant and adverse impact on patients' lives. Clients need to experience significant career, interpersonal, or legal troubles as a result of their symptoms to receive a formal diagnosis. Asperger achieved an illustrious academic career, stayed out of jail, married, and formed relationships with some of his colleagues. So it's questionable whether he would have qualified for the diagnosis that bore his name or if he would be better described as something else.

Is Awkwardness on the Spectrum?

I WAS AWARE from the pamphlets at the pediatrician's office and my Judy Blume books that junior high is an awkward time for everyone, but I had a sense I was definitely at the high end of the junior high awkwardness continuum. I knew that Coach Stenson was right and I appreciated that he put me straight. If he followed the conventional wisdom at the time, then his primary objective would have been to make sure I left the situation feeling good about myself. The 1980s self-esteem movement, popularized through a wave of self-help books and talk show gurus, spread the belief that raising self-esteem would cause kids to get better grades, stay drug free, or feel less lonely. However, if he and other influential adults had simply placed a psychological Band-Aid over my injured self-esteem, they would have masked a more fundamental problem. Even before my visit to the nurse's office, I had a sense that I did not need to work on my self-esteem, I needed to develop social skills and learn how to channel my unusual interests.

After the WWWF debacle, I began to wonder whether there was something fundamentally wrong with me and if there was an explanation for kids like me who had trouble figuring out how to manage social life. I didn't know anything about psychological diagnoses at the time, but we can speculate about how I would have been described by looking at my presenting problems. If a psychologist had written a clinical summary to describe what seventh-grade Ty Tashiro was like, it may have looked like this:

Client appears uncomfortable looking people in the eye. Poor posture. Wore a starched oxford with pleated khakis pulled high on his waist. He reports being shy and rarely initiating conversations with peers, but he does identify three friends carried over from elementary school. Reports that he is often worried about saying the wrong thing in social situations. Client makes an unusual number of lists in his Trapper Keeper, which include a top-ten list of baseball pitchers based on an equation accounting for their earned-run-average and win-loss record. Patient is unusually rigid about his adherence to daily routines. Tuesday mornings he wakes at 6:45 A.M. to watch the sanitation workers take away the trash, Monday through Friday he reserves 3:30 to 5:30 P.M. for a series of structured basketball drills that are listed in his notebook with the amount of time to be spent on each drill. Sundays after dinner he plots the trajectory of a handful of stocks with hand-drawn line graphs from the Sunday paper. Disruption of any of these routines causes significant psychological distress.

My behavior was definitely not normal, but would you have called me unique or was I better described with a diagnosis? If we apply the rule of five to my case, then clinicians would probably consider five possibilities: high-functioning autism, social anxiety, introversion, a personality disorder, or social awkwardness.

Part of the confusion around these kinds of diagnostic distinctions is that diagnoses like major depressive disorder, substance abuse, social phobia, autism, and hundreds of other *DSM* diagnoses are categorical, which implies that people have a disorder or they do not have a disorder. But what if I told you that autism characteristics are not confined to the 1 percent of people who are autistic and instead spill generously toward the middle of a bell curve where normality resides?

Simon Baron-Cohen heads the Autism Research Centre at the University of Cambridge and he is one of the leading experts in the study of autism. In a 2001 paper published in the *Journal of Autism and Developmental Disorders*, Baron-Cohen and his colleagues reported the results of a series of studies intended to validate a measure of autism characteristics called the Autism Quotient. The Autism Quotient includes fifty items that assess five characteristics commonly exhibited by people with autism: social skill deficits, communication problems, detail focused, trouble switching attention, and an active imagination. Scores on the Autism Quotient can range from zero (no autism characteristics) to fifty (all characteristics present).

Baron-Cohen and his colleagues administered the Autism Quotient to two groups, an autism group that included individuals with Asperger's syndrome and high-functioning autism and a control group that included 174 adults recruited from the general population. The first finding of interest was that the average score in the control group was not zero. The control group's average Autism Quotient score was sixteen, which suggests the average person feels challenged by a few aspects of social life. By comparison, the average score in the autism group was thirty-five, which was more than double the average of the control group. Baron-Cohen found that the optimal cutoff to distinguish people with autism and without autism was thirty-two.

Also notice that the distribution of autism characteristics in the general population falls along a bell curve, which means that some people have scores that are well above average. People in the above-average range of autism characteristics, those who scored

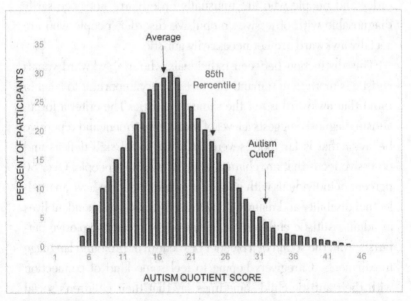

Figure 2.2 The distribution of autism characteristics in the general population. The number of autism characteristics are plotted on the horizontal axis and the percent of participants with each score are plotted on the vertical axis. Based on a study by Baron-Cohen et al. (2001) in the *Journal of Autism and Developmental Disorders.*

between twenty-four and thirty-one on the Autism Quotient, would fall roughly between the eighty-fifth and ninety-eighth percentile. They are somewhere between the average score of sixteen autistic characteristics and a diagnosable score of thirty-two autistic characteristics. So what do you call someone who is not autistic, but has considerable difficulty with social skills, communication, and an unusually obsessive focus? I would call that awkward.

The relationship between autism and awkwardness illustrates a broader concept in clinical psychology and psychiatry, which is that people who are considered in psychological terms to be "normal" can have milder forms of characteristics that are associated with serious conditions. Just as people with melancholy characteristics are not necessarily diagnosable with major depressive disorder and people who are unusually orderly are not necessarily diagnosable with obsessive-compulsive disorder, people who are socially awkward are not necessarily autistic.

This distinction between individuals who are awkward versus autistic is more than semantic; in fact it's very important to keep in mind that awkward is *not* the same as autistic. The criteria for an autism diagnosis suggests a level of social impairment and repetitive behavior that is far more severe than the social skill deficits and obsessive focus that are characteristic of awkward people. Over 50 percent of individuals with moderate to severe autism have an intellectual disability and many will be unlikely to live independent lives as adults. Autistic children's behavior might include explosive outbursts from the sound of a blender or vacuum or profound language impairments. Caregivers hoping to feel some kind of connection with their autistic child sometimes say that their children's social and communication deficits make the children feel "unreachable."

At a societal level, careless or overzealous diagnoses of autism dilute the resources available for autistic people given the limited mental health budgets in schools and communities. There are also negative consequences when clinicians try to squeeze awkward people into autism diagnoses, because a misdiagnosis can result in psychological or educational interventions that do more harm than good. It's important not to refer to awkward people as autistic or "on the spectrum" for pragmatic purposes, but also because doing so disrespects the significant struggles people with autism and their families face.

As I look back on my childhood social struggles, a diagnosis of high-functioning autism or Asperger's syndrome did not seem like an apt description of my social struggles. As an informal assessment, I took the Autism Quotient and asked a couple of family members to rate me on the Autism Quotient in reference to how they remembered me as a seventh grader. My scores fell short of the cutoff for high-functioning autism or Asperger's syndrome, but let's say that my scores were clearly above average.

A MEASURE OF AWKWARDNESS					
Compared to most people, are these items characteristic of how you typically are?					
10th	20th	50th	80th	90th	
VERY RARELY	NOT OFTEN	AVERAGE	FREQUENTLY	ALMOST ALWAYS	
					PERCENTILE
1. I have trouble with social skills.					
2. I lack common sense with everyday tasks.					
3. I am uncertain about how to behave in new social situations.					
4. I have a hard time understanding what other people are thinking.					

5. I am prone to saying the wrong thing.	
6. I have a hard time understanding the point people are trying to make.	
7. I have a hard time communicating with others.	
8. I lecture people instead of having a back-and-forth conversation.	
9. I have trouble reading others' emotions.	
10. I am uncomfortable dealing with emotions.	
11. I find it difficult to express how I feel.	
12. I struggle with showing empathy for other people's situations.	
13. I become obsessed with one thing for months at a time.	
14. I choose to work on solitary tasks versus socializing with others.	
15. I tend to see details instead of the big picture.	
16. I need to have a system or method for how I do things.	
This is an informal measure I constructed to provide a qualitative sense of awkward characteristics. Add together your percentile scores and divide by sixteen to get your average percentile score. If you want to break it down by category, then the items are chunked as follows: social skills (1–4), communication (5–8), emotions (9–12), obsessive interests (13–16). For more information about your score and additional resources, go to tytashiro.com.	TOTAL

Extroverted, Confident, and Totally Awkward

WITH A HIGH-FUNCTIONING autism diagnosis ruled out as a cause of my social difficulties, there are three explanations besides awkwardness to consider as possible explanations: social anxiety, a personality disorder, and introversion. We will see that all of these traits can be related to awkwardness, but they are not synonymous with awkwardness.

As a seventh grader I usually felt intense anxiety about my ability to navigate upcoming social situations such as my daily bus ride to school and going to birthday parties, which suggests that social anxiety, also called social phobia, could be a plausible explanation for my struggles. Social anxiety is a diagnosis for people who feel an excessive fear of social interaction and an unreasonable concern that they will embarrass themselves or be negatively judged. The difference between social anxiety and awkwardness is that social anxiety is primarily an *unreasonable fear* about being inappropriate whereas awkwardness refers to one's actual *ability* to be appropriate. Awkward people are often anxious about how they will navigate upcoming interactions, but their worry is not necessarily excessive or unreasonable. It was actually reasonable for me to have some worry about doing something inappropriate, which rules out social anxiety as a primary explanation. Based on my past attempts at navigating interpersonal situations, my concerns about making a less-than-stellar impression were reasonable.

I could appear insensitive because of my aloof nature and inattention to social expectations, like failing to follow the social rules of people waiting in line at a store or failing to respond empathically to someone's difficult situation. Personality disorders, such as being a sociopath or a narcissist, are characterized by pervasive insensitivity to others' needs that is driven by their cloying selfishness. Awkward people can also appear insensitive, but unlike sociopaths or narcissists, their insensitive behavior is often unintentional and caused by their lack of understanding about how to handle a delicate situation. Sociopaths and narcissists have an astute understanding of social expectations and they can appear charming, but they use their social savvy to manipulate others. Although there is no excuse for the instances when I inadvertently hurt other people's feelings or my other insensitive moments, they were better explained by my social clumsiness rather than malice.

Compared to most kids, I preferred to spend more time alone, liked one-on-one interactions instead of groups, and I appeared shy during new social interactions. Introversion is distinguishable from awkwardness because most introverted people can readily understand social expectations and effectively meet those expectations, it's just that they prefer not to interact as often as people who are extroverted. Introversion is about *preferences* for social interaction, whereas awkwardness is about the *ability* to effectively interact. As Susan Cain explains in her book *Quiet*, introverted people might have social troubles because their preferences for social interaction do not match the cult of extroversion that predominates in countries like the United States. Although introverted kids may look apprehensive when they walk into a social situation, they do not become immobilized by uncertainty about what to do when they walk in the door. Although I was introverted, introversion was not the best explanation for my social struggles.

Among the five explanations we considered for my social struggles—awkwardness, autism, social anxiety, personality disorder, and introversion—awkwardness appeared to be the best way to describe my social behavior. Being a socially awkward person is not best explained by an emotional disposition, a motivation, or a preference; rather it's a lack of intuition about how to navigate social life. This conclusion brings us back to our original question, Is there a problem with being awkward? In the world of clinical psychiatry and psychology, the answer would be no, but we have also seen that awkward individuals have significant deficits in social skills and communication that make it difficult for them to effectively engage in the complexities of social life. Awkward individuals find themselves at a complicated intersection, caught in the gray area where society tries to draw clear lines between normality and abnormality. It's hard for awkward people to navigate simple social situations like going to the store or asking a teacher for assistance, and these struggles with routine social interactions can keep others from discovering what awkward people are really like. We usually need to give them some time to understand their unique views, appreciate their sharp wit, or benefit from their kindhearted gestures. Sometimes awkward people think to themselves, "If only other people could get to know me, then I think they would like me."

I have repeatedly found that a little patience with awkward individuals' clumsy handling of minor social expectations is well worth the wait. Someone's social grace has little to do with their sense of fairness, kindness, or loyalty. In fact, awkward people sometimes have a heightened sense of fairness or compassion because they know what it's like to be on the receiving end of unfair or unkind acts. A good example of this comes from our aloof, isolated, and clumsy Hans Asperger.

Asperger published his seminal paper about autism in 1944, but his work with the boys featured in this case study began years earlier in his laboratory at the University of Vienna. In his book *NeuroTribes*, Steve Silberman provides a detailed account of how Asperger's research was complicated by the rise of fascism in Nazi Germany and its spread to Austria. Many of Asperger's medical school colleagues at the University of Vienna fled to other countries or were sent to death camps for their Jewish heritage. The Nazi doctrine included beliefs about eugenics and Asperger's autistic children were exactly the kinds of kids who were at risk of being shipped off by the Nazis to death camps for being "genetically inferior."

I imagine Asperger in the midst of this turmoil trying to make sense of the illogical and hateful ideologies spreading like a disease through Austrian culture. Here was a man who had trouble understanding how to navigate the smallest social expectations and who seemed less than fully capable of forming emotional ties even to those closest to him. But Asperger clearly understood that decent societies need to adhere to larger social expectations, such as respecting diversity, holding life dear, and helping those in need.

Asperger risked his personal safety by continuing to research and talk about his autistic patients, and he somehow mustered enough social acumen to deftly advocate for his patients in the face of grave danger. During a pair of raids on his lab, when the Nazis came to arrest him and presumably send his patients off to extermination camps, he managed to talk his way out of danger along with the help of his more socially skilled colleagues. While he delivered lectures about his research he intentionally called his patients "little professors" rather than "autistic psychopaths," which was a deft political move to communicate their social value and a way to protect these children he had grown to love and care for.

Dreaming of Social Fluency

AFTER MY WWWF debacle, I became fixated on Coach Stenson's charge to figure out the "social thing," but I discovered that trying to become less awkward when you have an awkward mind is like trying to find your misplaced prescription eyeglasses. You need to find your glasses so that you can see more clearly, but you cannot find your glasses because you cannot see clearly. It's a cruel irony, but you have no choice but to keep looking for what you need. The task for awkward people is to find a way to systematically search for what they need and, when they find it, they see the social world in a new way.

My social life would get much better and ultimately ended up exceeding anything I imagined as a seventh grader. I have also seen a number of my awkward friends, students, and clients improve their social skills and enjoy social lives that are immensely gratifying to them. What is common across the awkward people I have seen improve their social lives is that they had a plan, were open to changing their habits, and were willing to engage in the systematic practice necessary to improve their social understanding and skills.

When some of my sociable friends heard that I was writing a book about awkwardness, they frequently posed a fair question: If awkward people know they are awkward, then why don't they just stop being awkward? It's a fair question, but it shows the disconnect between how socially skilled and awkward people see the world. Sociable people see life broadly illuminated while awkward people see it with a narrow spotlight, which makes sociable people wonder how an awkward person does not recognize the interactions that are taking place center stage, while awkward people wonder why socially fluent people are not as compelled by what they are seeing with their spotlighted view.

Awkward people usually would love to be less awkward and dearly wish that they found it easier to navigate social life. But they need specific insights into the rules of social interactions that feel like proprietary information no one will tell them in plain terms.

A moment of valuable insight about how I could improve my social skills occurred during my middle-school Spanish class. Señorita Montgomery told us that we would know that we were becoming proficient or even fluent in Spanish when we began to think or dream in Spanish. She said that once the meanings of words and the grammar rules became automatic, we would be able to focus more on understanding abstract things like what people were feeling and pick up on cultural nuances. I realized that being socially skilled is like becoming fluent in a language and that most people are *socially fluent*. Just as most children cannot help but become linguistically fluent in their native language by grade school, most children immersed in a social world become socially fluent by grade school.

The idea of social fluency was further reinforced when I asked my mom why some of the kids at her clinic saw speech and language pathologists. She told me that these kids were no different from anyone else, but some of them had difficulties such as stuttering because their mouths would not cooperate with what their minds intended. She said that stuttering could be embarrassing and when kids became self-conscious the anxiety they felt could make a stutter worse.

I realized that learning a language or learning to overcome a stutter requires a bottom-up approach that begins with mastering a set of fundamentals. To learn Spanish I had to memorize vocabulary words, practice properly rolling my double *r*, and learn grammatical rules about how to order words. Kids with a stutter had to spend hours practicing *th* sounds from hitting the back of their teeth, or the articulation of an *l* sound by lifting their tongues to the top of their mouths and then exhaling as they let their tongues lower.

I realized that at some point, second-language speakers no longer have to listen carefully for the noun in a sentence or work hard to think about whether the verb was used in the past, present, or future tense. Eventually with enough practice, people learning a second language shift from a mechanical understanding of vocabulary and basic grammar to a fluency that allows them to speak without having to consciously think about vocabulary and grammatical rules. Once people start to experience proficiency or fluency, they are able to enjoy the person and the situation, which allows them to reach a depth of connection that is far more gratifying.

I knew that my best bet to figure out social life was to turn the strength of my methodical nature on my social struggles. So I began my quest for social proficiency by establishing a routine and making lists. I set aside a half hour every school night before bedtime to think through my social interactions from the day and to make a list of the skills I needed to work on the following day. It was a humbling and contrived attempt to figure out social life, but eventually I began to see some progress. I also resolved to aspire to something more than just being less awkward, I wanted to become socially fluent, and I knew that I would be on my way when I started to dream about things besides baseball statistics and all-star wrestling.

3

LOOKING FOR SOME SWEET SKILLS

I pressed the button to illuminate the face of my calculator watch. The time read 20:30:01. We were now more than halfway through the Winter Wonderland dance at Longs Peak Junior High and not a single soul had traversed the vast sea of linoleum floor that separated the girls on one side of the cafeteria and the boys on the other. Weeks ahead of the Winter Wonderland, students had been abuzz about who they would approach for a slow dance, but for the past ninety minutes the girls had stood in tight huddles on the north side of the cafeteria and the boys stood with their backs against the lime-green bricks of the south wall while trying their best to look aloof. Despite all of the hopeful energy leading up to the dance, we stood trapped on our gender-segregated sides, inhibited by an invisible force field of fear.

All of that changed when the DJ laid down the first slow song of the night, Journey's meandering ballad "Open Arms." He turned down the lights, turned up the spotlight on the disco ball, and let loose a large plume of smoke into the middle of the dance floor. Those first few delicate notes of "Open Arms" triggered something in the mind of Kellie Kimpton, who was a consensus top-five hot girl at Longs Peak. She was the kind of girl most boys dreamed of dating and most girls wanted to be like. So everyone noticed when Kellie abruptly pivoted away from her huddle of girls on the north side and turned her bright green eyes south.

Kellie's squad of hot girls broke their huddle, fanned out into a wedge with military-like precision, and began their march south. Boys who had previously puffed their chests about their audacious plans for wooing girls onto the dance floor now stood with their backbones pressed tightly against the green brick wall. As Kellie's crew broke through the cloud of smoke in the middle of the dance floor, an acute panic spread among the boys around me when they realized that the formation was headed right at them. I failed to use the girls' trajectory to anticipate the impending social interaction and I was immune to the emotional contagion spreading like wildfire among the other boys. So I was particularly alarmed when Kellie grabbed my hand and pulled me onto the dance floor.

As a socially awkward eighth-grade boy, my mind was ill equipped to detect flirtatious cues, much less understand that someone might be romantically interested in me. As a socially fluent girl, Kellie had deduced weeks ago that she would need to ask me to dance because her flirtations had lost all subtlety and I had shown no signs of having a clue. Kellie and I knew each other from Spanish II, where we were randomly assigned to sit together at a double desk. I found it easy to interact with her while we worked collaboratively on structured activities like dialogues about ordering at a restaurant or buying a train ticket.

She was so far out of my league in the junior high social hierarchy that I had never considered that she would be interested in anything besides being amigos. During the weeks leading up to the Winter Wonderland dance, Kellie began calling me almost nightly on my parents' landline under the pretense of needing help with her Spanish. As our study sessions veered from Spanish-related content, I never thought much about what she meant when she said, "I really hope I can date a guy as nice as *you*," or "*Some* girl would be really lucky to have *you* as her boyfriend."

The problem with decoding mutual romantic interest is that the messages are intentionally encrypted. When mutual interest is unclear, people float the occasional compliment about someone's appearance or brush someone's knee with their hand, but these forays into flirtatious territory are often followed by retreats to more platonic behaviors. This erratic push-pull method of flirtation can be exhilarating for many people, but this approach dilutes the social signals to a point of imperceptibility for awkward people. The awkward have significant difficulty detecting obvious social cues, much less the kinds of subtle cues that are supposed to convey romantic interest.

I was predictably disoriented by my first slow dance. Kellie rested her hands on my shoulders, and for two seconds that felt like an awkward eternity, I stood with my hands immobilized by my sides before I remembered that they went on her hips. For someone with social-processing limitations, dancing with Kellie Kimpton was a lot to handle. Journey was crooning about two people on the precipice of falling in love, the bright blue sparkles from the disco ball looked like glitter spinning around us, and the DJ had found new life now that people were dancing, and he kept unleashing clouds of smoke that irritated my overly sensitive tear ducts.

Kellie moved closer. Her face was two inches from my face and she was now egregiously violating the conventional eighteen inches of distance. She smelled like a field of strawberries. We were the same height, which resulted in my realization that my eyeballs had never been this close to a girl's eyeballs. I noticed through the periphery of my large square glasses that Kellie and her crew had broken the force fields of trepidation on both sides of the cafeteria. Liberated students nervously waddled around in pairs, their arms fully extended with their hands lightly resting on shoulders and hips. Most of them hoped to avoid too much eye contact and so they occasionally shifted their attention to my underdog story that was unfolding in real time.

As Kellie and I slowly waddled in the blue spotlights on the dance floor, I noticed that some of the other boys and girls were making rapid circular motions with their hands. After a moment of confusion, I realized that they were trying to tell me that I should hurry up and go for the kiss. I knew they were right, but if I had inaccurately read Kellie's social cues I would certainly look foolish, and even worse, I risked the emotional cataclysm that befalls twelve-year-old boys who get their hearts broken.

As I heard "Open Arms" arch into the triumphant third verse, Kellie moved her hands from my shoulders to the middle of my back and leaned the top of her forehead on the middle of my forehead. I felt like Steve Perry was singing *to* me, crooning that he knew what it's like to long for a girl. All I had to do for this to become "totally awesome" was broach the remaining 1.5 inches between our lips.

Then, precisely as my courage peaked, Kellie pulled closer to my left ear and softly whispered something that sent my mind scrambling to figure out what she meant: "I've never felt this way about a friend before . . ."

This Is Your Brain on Awkwardness

AWKWARD PEOPLE SOMETIMES feel like the social features of their brain are like the light-speed function on the *Millennium Falcon*. In the original *Star Wars* trilogy, most scenes with the *Millennium Falcon* involve the co-pilots Han Solo and Chewbacca under attack by enemy spacecraft. They are always outnumbered and eventually escape becomes a necessary course of action. Solo orders Chewbacca to prepare for light speed, which causes audiences to hold their breath because they know there is a fifty-fifty chance the light speed will malfunction. When the light speed fails to engage, there is an anticlimactic sound as the engines sputter and their desperate circumstance is punctuated by Chewbacca's exasperated roar.

After socially fluent people commit an awkward act, it's natural for them to wonder why they didn't make better decisions in a situation they usually handle with grace. But for chronically awkward people, their string of ongoing awkward acts can lead them to wonder whether there is something fundamentally different about how their minds handle social situations. There is now an emerging area of neuroscience research that provides some clues about how the awkward brain works.

Matthew Lieberman is a professor of neuroscience at UCLA who provides a fascinating overview of how our brains handle social information in his book *Social: Why Our Brains Are Wired to Connect*. Lieberman's lab and others have found that people have two separate brain networks, one for nonsocial problems and another for social problems. When people recruit their Vulcan-like reason or logic to solve a nonsocial problem such as reading a passage about neuroscience, a network of brain regions become active that I'll colloquially refer to as your *book smarts*. Conversely, when people solve social problems such as trying to empathize with a friend's situation or figure out whether someone is romantically interested in him or her, they activate a different network of brain regions neuroscientists call the *social brain*. Here's the catch. When our book smarts activate, our social brain becomes less active and conversely, when our social brain activates, our book smarts become less active.

This distinction that Lieberman makes between social and nonsocial problem solving is important because new brain-imaging studies have shown that awkward people show irregular patterns of brain activity when they process social information. Whether it's making sense of another person's intent or deciphering someone else's emotional state, awkward people tend to show less activity in social brain networks and they sometimes show hyperactivity in networks that are typically associated with book smarts.

These findings suggest that awkward people may not intuitively see social patterns or infer broad meaning, but instead have to assemble social information as if they are solving an equation or piecing together a puzzle. For example, when you read "Kellie" in the preceding pages you probably did not have to sound out the individual letters like they would on *Sesame Street*. Being a fluent reader, you intuitively processed "Kellie" not as six individual letters, but as a single word, and you did it in a split second without conscious awareness.

But what if the word looked like this: Kel$li@e?

All of the essential information is included for you to read the word, but the two extraneous symbols likely stopped you from automatically recognizing it, which made your processing slower and more deliberate. That's similar to what it feels like for awkward people, who do not intuitively recognize the general meaning from social cues, but instead see social situations as fragments and brain scans suggest that they are scrambling to assemble those fragments into a coherent whole.

Instead of an awkward boy understanding a situation as a "slow dance," he sees the situation in the component parts, "a song, hands on hips, left foot, then right foot, eye contact . . ." For awkward people, relatively straightforward situations can grow exponentially complex in their minds.

Fortunately, there is also evidence to suggest that these difficulties can be overcome with some tweaks. We will see that awkward people can decipher the components of social situations as well as socially fluent people when they are reminded to be deliberate about looking for essential cues and have a little more time to process what those cues mean. The skills needed to make sense of social situations are not only about understanding what other people say, but also grasping the nuances about how they said something. I'll review three important cues that tend to give awkward individuals trouble: nonverbal behaviors, facial expressions, and decoding language used during social conversations.

Get a Cue

THE GUYS STANDING next to me at the Winter Wonderland dance had anticipated the likely social interaction with Kellie and her crew. While the boys around me were mentally preparing for a potential social interaction, my mind was still calculating the proportion of time elapsed to time remaining at the dance. It's as if my mind wandered far from the common sense I would need to navigate the impending social situation.

When Kellie grabbed my hand to pull me onto the dance floor, my mind rushed to reallocate my mental resources to this unexpected social opportunity.

There were a number of nonverbal cues the other boys intuitively picked up as the DJ started the first slow song of the night. Kellie's decisive turn toward the south wall, her group's coordinated trajectory across the dance floor, and their unbroken eye contact were all obvious signs that interaction was imminent. As with many social situations, I noticed some of the same cues other people saw, but my mind did not intuitively convert the cues into a useful conclusion. There are now a number of psychological studies that can help us understand which cues are essential to decoding social interactions and why awkward people might miss some of these cues.

Judith Hall at Northeastern University and Marianne Schmid Mast at the University of Neuchatel investigated how nonverbal behaviors affect people's ability to accurately identify what someone else might think or feel, which is what psychologists call empathic accuracy. They asked research participants to watch a video of two people interacting and then asked observers to identify what each person in the video was thinking or feeling at sixteen different points in the video. Hall and Mast then compared the observers' guesses to what the two people conversing in the video reported actually thinking and feeling at those points.

The twist was that Hall and Mast varied how much information each observer would have by randomly assigning them to one of four conditions: audio only, reading a transcript of the audio, video only, or audio and video combined. As expected, observers in the audio plus video condition achieved the highest rate of empathic accuracy (56 percent). Observers in the audio condition were more accurate (50 percent) than participants in the transcript condition (40 percent). What is somewhat surprising is that viewers in the silent video condition, who had to rely on nonverbal cues, were able to guess the discussants' emotions at a rate far better than chance (34 percent).

Brooke Ingersol at Michigan State University investigated whether participants who scored high on a measure of awkward characteristics would have more trouble interpreting nonverbal cues compared to non-awkward individuals. For example, awkward individuals were less likely to see rapid head nods as a signal that they should finish speaking. They were also more likely to think that it's all right to gaze more at strangers while physically close to them. Although awkward people do not intend to talk longer than others prefer and hope to avoid making others uncomfortable on a crowded elevator, their misinterpretation of nonverbal cues not only inhibits their ability to accurately read social situations, but can also send the wrong message.

Whether it's a gaze averted, a twinkle in someone's eye, or a head nod, we rely heavily on nonverbal cues to effectively interpret what others are telling us and to communicate our own intentions or feelings. What we will see next is that awkward people miss nonverbal cues that are obvious to others because they are prone to directing their attention away from the nonverbal cues that sit center stage.

NONVERBAL BEHAVIORS DURING CONVERSATIONS

In an ongoing conversation, the cues people use to evaluate others' likability are not so much about what you say, but rather how much they feel that you are genuinely interested in what *they* have to say. The following list comes from a meta-analysis that looked at which nonverbal cues during conversations were most strongly related to making a positive impression.

1. Body squared to partner and a forward lean
2. Smiling
3. Head nodding

Can You Really "See It in Their Eyes"?

WHEN KELLIE AND I first stepped onto the dance floor, I awkwardly set my hands on her waist while she firmly gripped my shoulders with both hands. Her eyes looked straight ahead toward mine, and I felt as if they were radiating invisible rays that quickly began to overheat my social brain. I was not used to looking people directly in the eye.

Kellie appeared straight-faced. Her mouth was neither up-turned nor downturned, her brow neither rose nor fell, which only left her eyes as a cue. They were wide and her pupils dilated, which gave me a sense that she was either surprised or scared or some combination of both. After a few seconds of this intense eye contact, I felt overwhelmed by the intensity. Like a spring-loaded mechanism returning something to its resting position, my gaze rotated slightly to the left, where it settled on the sparkles from Kellie's earrings. I felt like I had come up for air.

If you have to pick one place to look for important social cues, then look at someone's face. Legendary anthropologist Margaret

Mead observed that facial expressions are one of the human traits that is universal. Cultural differences can shift the meaning of some facial expressions, but in general a smile means good things and a scowl means bad things across cultures. We rely heavily on the rich cues from facial expressions to recognize if someone is a friend rather than a foe and to decipher other people's emotional state and intent.

Paul Ekman is a professor emeritus from the University of California at San Francisco who has found that facial expressions are reliable signals of one's true emotional state. He has found that micro-expressions made by the eyes, lips, and other parts of the face can be reliably integrated into signals for various facial expressions. For example, a smile with accompanied creases along the sides of the eyes is a true smile whereas a smile with no crease along the sides of the eyes is a dead giveaway for a fake smile. Conversely, a furrowed brow, intense gaze, and narrowed lips are indicative of someone who feels angry.

Of course, people do not go through life freezing their facial expressions for micro-expression analysis. When socially fluent people enter a social situation, their instinct is to look first at people's faces. From a quick glance, socially fluent people recognize whether the mood of the other people in the room is somber, elated, or nervous.

There are at least two explanations for why awkward people have a harder time using facial cues to detect emotions. Ralph Adolphs and his colleagues at the California Institute of Technology conducted a clever study comparing which facial features awkward versus non-awkward study participants would use to judge emotions. As in most studies of emotion recognition, they found that non-awkward participants relied heavily on the eye region of the face to detect emotion. By comparison, awkward participants devoted far less attention to the eye region and instead looked more to the mouth region.

In another study of emotion processing, researchers at the University of North Carolina used fMRI to image the brains of awkward versus non-awkward participants while they were asked to identify emotions from photos of faces. They found that awkward participants performed just as well as non-awkward participants on the emotion recognition task, but imaging results showed that during these tasks, awkward participants had reduced activity in areas typically recruited for emotion recognition and they showed hyperactivity in regions usually associated with nonsocial problem solving. It's a remarkable pattern of findings that is evident in other imaging studies and suggests that while awkward individuals may not intuitively process social information the same way as most people, they find work-arounds to solve social puzzles.

When awkward people do look at someone's face, they tend to use a bottom-up style of processing, which means that they initially gravitate toward individual facial features rather than seeing the face as an integrated whole. Socially fluent people see a face and instantly know that someone is happy ☺. But awkward people see a mouth—)—and then eyes—:—before they put those two pieces together to reach a conclusion that someone is happy—:)

In this example, the awkward person reaches the same conclusion as non-awkward people, which is that the person's facial expression is indicative of happiness, but the process for awkward people is more laborious and the conclusion they reach is qualitatively different—:)—than the one reached by non-awkward people who process faces holistically: ☺ This provides a good example of how awkward people process social information as pieces of a puzzle to be solved versus a scenario naturally processed all at once by their social brain.

However, when awkward individuals are reminded to look at faces for emotional cues, they direct their attention to faces far more quickly and their empathic accuracy improves. This suggests one of the key footholds for how awkward people might cope with their awkward tendencies is to find ways to focus their attention on the right things. Studies that look at what happens when people have nothing to think about or let their minds wander show that non-awkward people tend to keep their social brain running at all times, even when there is no social activity. By comparison, awkward people do not seem to keep their social brain running at all times and might need to be reminded to turn the ignition on for their social brain.

How Did My Foot Get in My Mouth?

WHILE I TRIED to decipher Kellie's nonverbal cues and read the intent in her eyes, I was also trying to come up with something clever to say. Never before had I been in a position to say something romantic and I quickly learned how hard it is to strike the right tone while delivering such a delicate message. Once she whispered her ambiguous statement, "I've never felt this way about a friend before . . . ," I was completely at a loss for what would be an appropriate way to respond.

Awkward individuals have difficulties with both comprehension and articulation. We know from awkward participants' responses to measures like the Autism Quotient that they are more likely than socially fluent people to have difficulty with pragmatic language, which refers to the ability to communicate effectively during social conversations. Let's take a look at four areas of research that can help us understand these difficulties with pragmatic language: extracting meaning from what others say, saying too much, not knowing what to say, and inadvertently being too blunt.

When it comes to comprehension, awkward people have trouble with things like extracting the unspoken meanings conveyed during social conversations, and comprehending sarcasm and some jokes. But even when awkward participants' verbal IQ scores

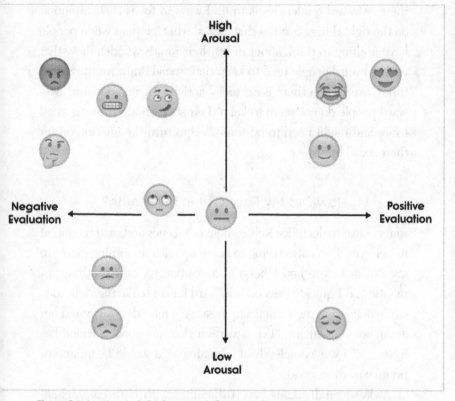

Figure 3.1 Another helpful framework for decoding emotions is thinking about how they are organized. Researchers find that emotions can be organized around two axes. The horizontal axis represents whether someone evaluates his or her current feelings as negative or positive. The vertical axis represents how physiologically aroused people become.

are average or above average, they still show difficulties extracting the intended meaning from social conversations. However, awkward adults also show comparable performance to socially fluent people on reading comprehension tasks that require them to infer the thoughts and feelings of characters in stories, which suggests that they extract deeper meanings from written communication.

Although researchers have yet to figure out the precise reasons for awkward individuals' language comprehension problems, there are many plausible hypotheses. Perhaps awkward individuals' difficulties picking up nonverbal cues and facial cues account for their social comprehension deficits. Alternatively, they might have trouble making use of information from vocal cues such as cadence or vocal tone. Regardless of the mechanism, it's helpful to know that awkward people have difficulty understanding the true meaning or intent from some social conversations, which certainly makes it harder for them to know what to say or how to say it.

Awkward individuals report that they are unsure about what they should say in social situations. They struggle with things that come naturally to others, such as what to say while initiating a casual social interaction or engaging in small talk. Awkward people have many interesting things to say, but it's like they are a book missing the preface and first chapter, those early sections where the author and reader get acquainted with each other before diving into deeper material.

If awkward people want to become more comfortable about what to say, then they can benefit from knowing what most people like to talk about. There is unequivocal evidence from hundreds of studies that people most often talk about topics that are social in nature. People love to talk about relationships, whether it's strategizing about how to resolve a conflict with a coworker or the latest drama from the Kardashians. When people talk about relationships they are able to further process their social conundrums and garner valuable feedback from friends. Most people also enjoy gossip, which usually carries a negative connotation, but gossip can be positive or negative conversations. For example, both of these statements would be considered gossip: "Ellen is really smart, you should talk to her" and "Barbara should not be trusted."

When some awkward individuals do speak, they have trouble knowing when to stop talking. Awkward people are prone to lecturing instead of having a conversation and no one likes to be lectured. When they fall into lecture mode, it tends to be about their nonsocial interests, and some awkward individuals speak with an intonation that sounds condescending even if they do not intend for their voice to carry that tone. It's easy to imagine how a conversation partner could leave an interaction feeling as if he had just been a passive bystander to a lengthy diatribe.

A LIST OF FIVE THINGS TO SAY

Good conversations are triggered by your ability to get the other people to talk about their interests. Here's a list of standard small talk questions and alternative questions that can produce more engaged dialogue.

1. "What do you do?" → "Tell me about what interests you right now?"
2. "How did you meet Andie?" → "Will you tell me the story of how you and Andie met?"
3. "How are you?" → "What are you looking forward to this week/weekend?"
4. "Where are you from?" → "What do you enjoy about living in New York?"
5. "How's work?" → "What do you hope will have happened at work one year from now?"

In most instances, awkward people do not intend to bore others or come across as condescending, which raises the question of why they would elect to lecture instead of have a back-and-forth conversation. Recall that awkward people's minds are not mulling through social information during times of inactivity, which means that they would have spent less time mulling over social information and have less to say about social topics. But awkward people may think a lot about things like *World of Warcraft*, deforestation, or whether winter is really coming on *Game of Thrones*. It's understandable that if these are the topics people know, then they would talk about what they know and what interests them. If they are talking with someone who is also obsessed with *World of Warcraft* or global warming, then there's no problem because both sides have the knowledge to participate in the conversation. But when awkward people speak with people who are not obsessed with their nonsocial interests and instead want to take a deep dive into a social topic, then the awkward person may subconsciously prevent a back-and-forth discussion about unfamiliar topics by lecturing in a sort of social filibuster.

When awkward people fall into lecture mode, one of the risks they run is turning an offensive comment into an offensive monologue. To consider why awkward people are more prone to inadvertently offending others or putting their foot in their mouth, it's helpful to think about the distinction between being right versus being socially correct. Being right is about whether what you say is objectively true, but saying something socially correct is about whether you say something to propel an interesting or useful conversation.

As I danced with Kellie and my mind searched for something clever to say, some of the first thoughts about sweet nothings to whisper in her ear included, "You smell like a field of strawberries" or "Our eyeballs are almost touching." Fortunately, I managed to keep these accurate but socially incorrect statements from escaping my mouth. I have certainly heard worse. Like an instance when my friend Elias was telling a group of new acquaintances at a party that "things just didn't work out" with his ex-girlfriend. It was his way of saying, "Can we brush over that topic for now?"

Another friend, Steve, who was pretty awkward and who was already privy to the full story of Elias's breakup, did not get the deeper meaning from Elias's statement. Steve blurted out a rhetorical question for editorial clarification: "Elias, didn't you break up because she cheated on you?" This was technically right, but far from socially correct. Other people understandably perceive these kinds of true but socially incorrect statements as offensive or malicious. But awkward people are mortified once they understand just how socially incorrect their statements sound.

Awkward people begin to realize they have a way of putting their foot in their mouth because they misunderstand what others are trying to tell them. Because of this, awkward people can become hesitant to say anything at all because they do not want to risk saying something offensive and feel self-conscious about sharing their unusual interests with others.

The key to your conversation partner enjoying her interaction with you relies more upon how you respond to what she is saying than your ability to say something clever or demonstrating how much you know. Becoming a better communicator and building rapport with others is about encouraging them to talk about things that interest them and conveying empathy for what they are trying to tell you. When you show your genuine interest in what others have to say, the deeper message you send is that you are invested in their well-being. Showing you are invested in what others have to say taps into their evolved need to find people who are likely to be interested in their welfare.

When Minds Meander

WHEN I HEARD the delicate melody of "Open Arms" swell into the final chorus, I felt my heart rate speed up and my thoughts began to race. There were so many intense cues: Kellie holding me tightly against her, her lips hinting at a pucker, and the soft whisper of the vexing "friend" comment. It was too much for my social mind to handle. So I guess that's why something more primal than my book smarts region or social brain took over, and I made a decisive move to bridge the remaining 1.5 inches between my lips and hers.

However, there was a less than intuitive combination of social cues that I had not considered and it was my oversight of these that left me with a mouthful of Kellie's luxurious blond hair. When you are twelve years old, this sort of rejection can sting for quite some time. Later, the logical part of my mind realized that I was going through the kind of classic teenage angst that I had read about in my Judy Blume books. The kind of minor problem that was small in the continuum of problems in the world. Yet the emotional part of my mind recalled that fateful night with sadness, at other times disappointment, and sometimes the memory felt so real that my face flushed with embarrassment or my heart sank with disappointment.

Yet the Kellie Kimpton moment was a boost of encouragement in other ways. It was a sign that my efforts to build social skills might be paying off. I was noticing a broader range of social cues and slowly beginning to improve my accuracy with interpreting those cues. It was a methodical, plodding effort to inch forward a little bit with each passing day, but I began to see that I was finding a social rhythm.

My efforts to figure out the nuances of social life felt like those times in music class when our teacher asked all of us to clap along to the beat. As someone with a poor sense of rhythm, I found this simple task to be remarkably difficult. Technically, I would clap my hands together, it's just that I was not clapping them to the beat. I heard the beat and could watch others clapping to the beat, but the more I concentrated on putting my hands together in step with everyone else, the more I became off the beat. Popular wisdom tells us to "move to the beat of your own drum," but we all know that navigating social life is never that simple. You have to admire the chutzpah of the awkward because they try to find the beat despite their self-awareness that other people are noticing that they are not quite getting it. For the awkward person who is trying to get the social beat through trial and error, there's a persistent anxiety because social errors take place in the public domain for all to see, and when we consistently fall short of social expectations we risk one of the worst possible human outcomes: being ostracized.

Alternatively, few things in life feel better than the sense that we are in synchrony with those around us. Something as simple as clapping in unison with strangers who like the same brand of hip-hop can give us the sense that we are part of something larger than ourselves. Although there are valuable scientific findings regarding how nonverbal behaviors, facial expressions, and pragmatic language are interpreted and expressed, the moment-to-moment detection, interpretation, and use of these social gestures is an art form. They are not silly embellishments or luxuries, but rather essential ingredients to understanding what people are trying to tell you and they are necessary for clearly communicating one's good intent.

Later that spring at a track meet, Kellie and I sat side by side on the infield while her boyfriend prepared to run the 4 x 200 relay. Since the Winter Wonderland dance we had maintained our collegial relationship in Spanish II, and even though there was a shared awkward memory between us, a comfortable fondness remained as well, which continued to grow.

It took me a long time, well into adulthood, to learn that moving toward a deeper level of emotional connection with someone can be like a game of chicken. When two people first begin to gather emotional momentum, it's an intense feeling that is so good, they fear the feeling could burst. They feel the rush of speeding toward something unknown and as they near the point of contact, their feelings can grow so intense that a protective mechanism switches on at the last second. A mechanism that leads one or both of them to turn away.

From the corner of my prescription-lens–covered peripheral vision, I saw that Kellie's attention was not directed toward the track, but focused instead somewhere just in front of my left ear. I pretended not to notice. Eventually, her intense gaze overpowered my willful ignorance and like a tractor beam she pulled me into eye contact. Then, Kellie said something very thoughtful, something of precocious maturity:

Kellie: Ty, do you ever think about that time we danced together?

Me: To "Open Arms"? Did you know after that song Journey went on to—

Kellie: Hey, I know that was probably kind of confusing for you.

Me: Oh, I don't know, I guess that's—

Kellie: I totally liked you. But I got nervous. I'm so sorry if I hurt your feelings.

Me: Thanks. It's okay, Kellie. Feelings can be pretty confusing sometimes.

4

EMOTIONS MAKE ME FEEL FUNNY

Ellie and her parents sat evenly spaced on the leather couch in my therapy office, their hands neatly folded on their laps. Ellie's father wore a navy sport coat with a polka-dot bow tie and her mother wore a crisp navy blue linen dress with pearls lying neatly across her neckline. Ellie had chosen a pink-and-white-striped seersucker dress and her mother had methodically woven Ellie's brunette hair into a neat braid. They looked like a living J.Crew catalog and this snapshot made it difficult for me to imagine Ellie as a five-year-old capable of wielding emotional upheaval upon a household.

I began counseling Ellie during my second year of graduate school. At that point in my training, the senior clinicians who had been supervising my counseling work were pushing me to explore my clients' emotional lives, but I had a hard time understanding why delving deeper into a client's negative emotions would alleviate his depression, anxiety, or anger. I saw emotions as an impediment to well-reasoned insights. So I always felt uneasy when I tried to ask a client the clichéd therapist question, "So, how does that make you feel?" Until I saw Ellie, I never understood why emotions are integral to understanding what makes people tick and how they bring together disparate social cues into a coherent whole.

Ellie's parents were physicians who spoke in fluent *DSM-IV* terminology while they described her temper tantrums as ". . . acute, chronic, and severe." Her outbursts included sudden bursts of intense screaming in public and hitting or biting her parents. The tantrums sometimes lasted for hours. At times Ellie became so enraged in restaurants or stores that her parents had to physically restrain her with a bear hug while rushing her outside. Lately, Ellie responded to these "carry outs" by repeatedly screaming, "Help me!" which created more than an awkward situation for everyone involved.

While her parents described the scope of their child's presenting problem, Ellie looked as if they were discussing something that she had never heard about, the look kids have at the dinner table while grown-ups discuss politics or granite countertops. I asked Ellie if she would like to explore the toy bin in the corner of my office while her parents went to the waiting room for a few minutes. She nodded her approval and after her parents left, Ellie and I sat down on the beige carpet by a bin of toys. When adults go to therapy for the first time they can feel fairly unnerved by the situation and kids are no different. I wanted Ellie to feel a sense of control and as a small gesture to show her this, I told her that she could choose the toys for us. She looked simultaneously eager and immobilized, like a kid already afraid of what she could do.

Ellie chose the colored pencils and large sketch pad. I asked her to draw a picture of her family and she readily obliged. She was a precocious artist. She drew with dimensionality and detail that was very unusual for her age. She depicted herself wearing a pink-striped dress with her parents on either side of her. All three of them were smiling and holding hands. But then Ellie began drawing someone else to the left of her parents, which was unusual because she was an only child. The fourth person she drew looked just like another Ellie, except that she was wearing a deep purple dress and looked mad as hell. I asked her:

Ellie, that's a great picture, can you tell me about it?
Um, this is my mom. This is my dad.
They look happy. How about the two girls in the picture?
This girl in the pink dress is Ellie.
She looks happy too. And who is the other girl in the purple?
That's the Ellie no one likes.

You don't have to be a psychologist to see what was going on in this picture. Ellie was aware that her behavior could turn into something she hardly recognized, but my hunch was that her parents might be explaining the reasons for their displeasure in terms that Ellie did not understand. The trick was to find a way to help Ellie understand why no one seemed to like that version of Ellie.

Do you know why no one likes the purple-dress Ellie?
No.
Do your parents ever say why they don't like the purple-dress Ellie?
They don't like temper tantrums.
What happens when someone has a temper tantrum?
I don't know.

This confirmed my first hypothesis. Ellie's parents scolded her for temper tantrums, but Ellie didn't know the true meaning of temper tantrums. Her lack of comprehension was understandable when you look at the situation through the eyes of a child. Emotions are an abstract concept, a mixture of physical reactions and thoughts that we label with words like "joy," "contentment," or "anger." This abstract quality can make emotions confusing for young children, who have concrete mental abilities, which is to say that they generally understand the world in terms of what they can see and touch. So how do you help someone with concrete mental abilities understand abstract concepts like emotions?

I knew from my initial discussion with her parents that when Ellie had a temper tantrum her parents sometimes took away her television privileges as a punishment. This concrete act gave me a foothold for a line of questioning:

Ellie, when was the last time you lost your television time?
Last night.
Do you remember what you were doing right before it was taken away?
Eating ice cream.
You get in trouble for eating ice cream?!
(Laughing) No! I got in trouble after that. (Stops laughing) I wanted more.
So you asked for more ice cream and then what happened?
My mom said no.
And then what did you do?
I screamed.
Can you show me the face you were making while you screamed?

Ellie paused for a moment to set up the scene while she looked down to gather herself. When she kicked her head up she was in full character, with her brow furrowed, eyes narrowed, lips tightly pursed, and hands clenched. After I paused for a moment to appreciate this theatrical display I said, "Ellie, your face, your shaking fists . . . that's what happens when you have a temper tantrum."

I felt like we had done some good work for a first session and I told her we would get to talk some more later that week. As we stood up to leave, I felt a tug on my pants leg:

Um . . . Ty. What does your angry face look like?

Well, Ellie . . . I guess I don't know.

Why not?

That's a good question. But I'll be sure to find out and tell you next time . . .

Can We Just Skip the Emotional Parts?

EMOTIONS ARE AT once delicate and full of explosive potential. For awkward people who are prone to social clumsiness, navigating the world of emotions can feel like walking through the glassware section of a store with a large backpack. Other people can be confused by awkward people's unemotional reactions to exciting or perilous circumstances, just as they can be, at other times, when awkward people become surprisingly emotional about seemingly minor inconveniences. Any confusion about awkward people's emotional lives is understandable because we will see that awkward people have emotional hardware that is calibrated differently from other people's and over time this can erode their confidence that they can appropriately handle emotional situations.

It's human nature to form rationalizations for why we are not good at something and one way of doing this is to convince ourselves that the thing we are not good at is unimportant. For some awkward individuals who struggle with reading and expressing emotions, it's tempting to rationalize emotions as superfluous psychological glitter that threatens one's ability to be a reasonable person. Ellie had a striking aloofness to her for a girl of her age, which was probably partly dispositional, but it was possible that her aloofness also became entrenched because she learned that it served a function of keeping circumstances around her low in emotional intensity.

One intuitive approach to decreasing temper tantrums is to give the person a way to cope with reducing his or her anger, but another less intuitive approach is to think about being proactive about releasing the energy that fuels the tantrums in smaller doses. Ellie rarely looked anyone in the eye, tried her best to stifle her smiles when I said something amusing, and she spoke in a monotone voice about highly emotional events like her temper tantrums. Although Ellie's aloofness did minimize the chances of other people becoming emotionally reactive, it did not fully prevent a buildup of emotions within her. Like anyone Ellie experienced daily inconveniences, hurts, and frustrations, but without even the slightest display of an emotional reaction, those negative emotions began to build exponentially in her mind like a nuclear chain reaction until they exploded in her tantrums.

Empathy is defined as the ability to understand another person's emotional state and to deliver an appropriate response. Emotions are critical to becoming socially fluent because they carry an extra layer of meaning that is inextricably woven into the fabric of verbal and nonverbal communication. Attempts to remove emotion from daily interactions does not minimize its effects, but rather amplifies consequences because other people expect certain emotional responses. The absence of expected emotional responses tends to trigger uncertainty, and when people feel uncertain their emotions can run wild.

Numerous studies have shown that awkward individuals have more trouble empathizing with others' emotions. Simon Baron-Cohen and Sally Wheelwright from Oxford University found in two studies that the ability to empathize with others' emotional states was normally distributed in the general population, and that most people can read others' emotions to tell if they are bored with a conversation, if someone means something different from what their words alone would indicate, and that they can avoid being overly blunt when they want to. They found that as participants' levels of social awkwardness increased, their levels of empathy decreased, which means that awkward people have trouble with ensuring that others are engaged in a conversation, they are susceptible to taking statements too literally, and they deliver communications in a way that can sound overly blunt or rude.

Awkward people can improve their ability to show empathy toward others, but doing so requires some self-awareness from the awkward person about why he finds emotions difficult to read. It also helps if other people can have some empathy for well-intended awkward people who are prone to empathy malfunctions. When awkward people take the responsibility to work hard to improve their empathic capacity and others show some patience and encouragement, awkward and socially fluent people can find an unusual brand of emotional connection.

An Intense World of Emotions

I REALIZED THAT my emotions operated differently from most kids' after my fourth-grade Valentine's Day party at school. The day before the party, my parents took me to choose a box of Valentine's Day cards at the Hallmark store. When I saw the messages printed on the cards, such as "You Are My Valentine!" or "I Love You Lots!" I felt a panic. I asked my parents to drive me around to other stores so that I could look at different cards. When my parents asked me what I was looking for, I replied, "Something less emotional."

I eventually settled on a pack of cards that were relatively low in emotional expressiveness, but once I started to complete the "To" and "From" blanks, I still felt uneasy with all of the feelings conveyed by the cards. Perhaps as a compulsive calming mechanism, I began to organize the cards on a continuum from those with the highest emotional intensity on the left to the least amount of emotional intensity on the right. Then I began to match classmates to the cards based on the dose of affectionate messaging I thought they could tolerate.

Of course, most of my classmates would not have a problem with even the cards highest in emotional expressiveness. On Valentine's Day, it's socially expected that people will throw around words such as "love" and "Valentine" in the same way they would say words such as "like" or "buddy" the other 364 days of the year. My inability to readily adapt to this daylong shift in cultural expectations left me spinning my emotional intelligence wheels. I decided to take matters into my own hands. I picked up a permanent marker and began to strike the most disquieting verbs such as "love" and modifiers such as "lots." Sometimes I substituted words of lower intensity, such as "like" or "quite a bit."

The next day, my dad asked me if I had finished addressing my cards and I told him yes, never thinking twice about telling him about my extensive edits. At school, my classmates and I dropped our cards for each person in their decorated paper bag that hung from the chalkboard. While we sipped on Capri Suns and ate Valentine's Day sugar cookies, we opened our cards. After I had read a few of the cards given to me, I noticed that no one else had made annotations. It was one of those moments when you realize too late in the game that you have completely misread a situation. My extensive efforts to avoid being awkward were having the opposite effect. Although my classmates were gracious not to remark about my annotated Valentine cards, surely they found it odd to read, "I ~~Love~~ Like You ~~Lots~~."

Socially fluent people are understandably vexed by awkward people's emotional lives because there is this apparent paradox of awkward people being emotionally disengaged at times, but then emotionally over-reactive at other times. Awkward people can be described as robot-like because they have an aloof air about them and are less likely to show appropriate empathic responses to other people's emotional distress or excitement. This lack of emotional congruency from awkward people makes them appear uncaring about the situations underlying other people's emotional reactions. But awkward people can also be emotionally over-reactive to minor situations, such as their daily routine being broken or setbacks in their work that appear minor or transitory to others. How does one explain this apparent paradox of awkward people being both emotionally over- and under-reactive?

Kamila Markram and Henry Markram at the Laboratory of Neural Microcircuits in Switzerland have developed a theory that provides a compelling explanation for awkward people's atypical emotional lives. Their intense world theory arose from their early lab studies with rats that had been bred to display behaviors such as low social motivation, repetition, and high anxiety. When they looked at the brain activity of these rats, they found that their social deficits and repetitive behaviors corresponded to unusually high levels of activation in brain areas associated with perception, attention, and emotion.

This led the Markrams to wonder whether the brains of these rats perceived their surroundings with greater intensity than other rats did. Maybe these rats displayed high levels of anxiety because their strong perceptual responses made their environments over-stimulating. Maybe the rats showed less social behavior because they were trying to temper the intensity of their environment by engaging in repetitive behaviors that helped them avoid the intensity of social interactions. By analogy, they were like humans who opt to spend their Saturday night watching Netflix reruns or knitting a scarf instead of going out to deal with a crowded restaurant or chaotic nightclub.

In a research review of intense world theory, the Markrams found a number of studies showed parallel findings with people who have a high level of autistic symptoms. For example, when children with social and communication deficits view emotion-rich stimuli such as faces and eyes, their brains show hyperactivity in the amygdala, an area of the brain associated with emotions such as fear and anxiety. Although intense world theory has mostly been investigated with autistic subjects, the theory seems logically consistent with how awkward people process and cope with emotions.

If you think about the vibe that characterizes your interactions with awkward people, there is often an agitated energy that underlies the interaction, which can make them appear nervous, irritated, or generally upset. But if you view the awkward person as someone who is experiencing the interaction as particularly intense, then the unusual vibe they give off starts to make more sense. For the awkward individuals, their perception of emotion is like stepping into the sunshine after having your eyes dilated.

As a coping mechanism, awkward individuals learn to temper this intensity by avoiding things that trigger strong emotions. When awkward people do not look someone in the eye, it's not because they are incapable of making eye contact or disinterested in the conversation. Avoiding eye contact helps them avoid the strong emotional cues conveyed by faces and especially the eye region. Awkward individuals may sidestep emotional conversations about uncomfortable situations or they might even feel overwhelmed by praise from others. All of these efforts by awkward people to dampen the emotional intensity of interactions can make them appear aloof. For awkward people who experience the world of emotions as too intense, it does not really matter whether the emotion is negative or positive; even people as young as Ellie know that any strongly felt emotion could spin out of control.

One of the unfortunate paradoxes for awkward people is that there are few emotions more acute in intensity than the feeling of awkwardness, and this intensity can easily overwhelm the awkward person's mind. Awkward moments feel like walking nose first into a glass door. It's an entirely unexpected moment of disorienting alarm and this flood of emotions is the first psychological response we experience, which is to say that we *feel* awkward before we *think* about the fact that we are in an awkward situation. But awkwardness is a powerful emotion that makes it difficult for people to think clearly about what has gone wrong and how to remedy the social misstep.

Awkward feelings do serve an adaptive function, but awkward people have to figure out what their awkward feelings are trying to tell them.

The Function of Feeling Awkward

CHARLES DARWIN PROVIDED some of the early scientific insights about why humans would be wired for emotions. Darwin hypothesized that in the survival of the fittest, people had to respond quickly to circumstances that threatened their safety or well-being. People did not have the luxury of conscious deliberation when they were under attack from a predator or fighting for scarce resources. Emotions are reflexive and involuntary, like the kick of your leg when a doctor hits your knee with a rubber hammer. In the same reflexive way, when you feel emotions like anger your mind instantly triggers physiological reactions like an increase in blood flow and muscle tension that prepare you to respond to the threat. Strongly felt negative emotions narrow your focus on the threat, and anger catalyzes fight responses while fear catalyzes flight responses.

Awkward feelings are also accompanied by strong physiological reactions—a pounding heart, speeded up breathing, and tensed muscles—but unlike fear and anger, which are triggered by threats to our safety or resources, feeling awkward occurs in response to small deviations from social expectations. Although undone zippers and calling your friend's wife by his ex-wife's name are not ideal, they are not dangerous situations or something that stem from malicious intent. So why would the relatively innocuous social faux pas incite such a strongly felt emotion?

On some subconscious level, we know that too many violations of small social rules can lead to social exile. Our minds have an overly sensitive emotional trigger when it comes to alerting us to unmet social expectations because our need to belong is so essential to our well-being. June Price Tangney is a professor of psychology at George Mason University who has found through an extensive program of research that there is a cluster of "self-conscious emotions" that occur following social missteps and each has a different function. These self-conscious emotions include embarrassment, guilt, shame, and, I would add, feeling awkward.

I used to hate it when I blushed during times of embarrassment. It felt bad enough that I had committed an awkward act, but my blushing felt like a public acknowledgment of my awkwardness that made things worse. Matthew Feinberg and his colleagues from the University of California, Berkeley, conducted a series of studies to test the idea that embarrassment serves the social function of demonstrating to others that they hold prosocial values, which is to say that they care about the well-being of others and are generally motivated to avoid harming or inconveniencing others. Feinberg found that people who showed more embarrassment while recounting one of their most embarrassing moments were rated by others as more prosocial and more trustworthy. Importantly, observers reported that they would be more interested in affiliating with people who showed high levels of embarrassment compared to people who showed low levels of embarrassment. In other words, people who demonstrated embarrassment became more socially valued.

Another emotion related to awkward feelings is guilt, which makes you feel bad about your behavior and motivates you to repair the social damage: to apologize, clean up a spill, or pay for something you have damaged. All of these responses to your social missteps help you assure others that you understand what you have done wrong, you feel remorseful, and you are taking action to make things right. Both embarrassment and guilt help us recover from awkward acts because they show others that we "get it." That is, there are outward signs that we are aware that we have violated a social rule and we feel bad about any inconvenience to others.

The problem is that awkward people do not always clearly

understand which social expectation they have violated. Sometimes awkward people know their behavior is off base, but they
are not sure exactly which social expectations need to be met. The
function of feeling awkward is to alert us that social expectations
are being violated and to get it together before we burn more social
capital. But unlike embarrassment and guilt, which are responses
to our knowledge of the specific expectation we have not met,
awkwardness leaves us with no clear diagnosis of what is wrong.

Until the person committing the awkward behavior shows embarrassment or acts with intent to fix the situation, others do not
see any indication that the person is aware of her faux pas and its
potential impact on others. Awkward people tend to be less emotionally expressive, which can make them appear unremorseful
when they inconvenience others or hurt others' feelings.

Embarrassment signals remorse, guilt encourages behaviors that
repair social damage, and awkwardness alerts someone to expectations being violated, but shame plummets one's self-esteem to
the point of immobilization, making it harder for people to admit
their missteps or repair the effects of their behavior. People can find
ways to cope with their feelings of awkwardness, but when someone
starts to feel ashamed about their awkwardness, then it becomes
tough to find a way forward. Although emotions are reflexive, people can have some choice about whether they choose to reframe
their response to an awkward moment. I have found that people
can benefit from simply asking themselves, "Does this mistake
mean that I'm a bad person or just someone who made a mistake?"

If one becomes accustomed to accurately seeing fleeting social
missteps for what they are and not an indication of one's overall
worth as a person, then there is a chance that one will begin to
reflexively respond with more adaptive emotions. Sometimes, if
you're lucky, something as small as saying you're sorry with a quick
blush can be enough to spark a graceful response from others even
during our most awkward moments.

THE MEANING OF SIX EMOTIONS AND HOW TO RESPOND

EMOTION	WHAT IT MEANS	WAYS TO RESPOND
Anger	This was unfair.	Apologize if it's you, clarify if it's a misunderstanding, say, "I'm sorry, that's unfair," if someone else is responsible.
Distress	This is going downhill.	Mirror their emotional state, express your concern or willingness to help.
Embarrassment	That was inappropriate.	It depends . . . sometimes you can minimize the event, "It's not a big deal," other times you can commiserate, "I did that before."
Joy	This went way better than expected.	Do *not* temper the mood, just go along with being happy.
Pride	This achievement was important to me.	Do *not* say anything that starts with, "Yes, but . . ." Simply say, "I'm happy for you."
Hope	This is bad, but it could get better.	Do *not* try to suggest that contrary to what they hope, things will continue to go poorly or get worse.

Broadening a Narrow Focus

ELLIE'S PARENTS HOPED that I could help her gain some control over her emotional life and help her express her displeasure with emotions that were more socially acceptable. Ellie's parents knew that her temper tantrums scared other kids and eventually other kids' fear of Ellie's explosive potential would make them leery about befriending her. Whether they're experiencing depression, anxiety, or anger, clients usually hope that therapists can help them decrease their negative emotions. But what happens when psychologists see therapy not only as a way to decrease negative outcomes, but also as an opportunity to help people leverage the functional nature of emotions to facilitate positive outcomes?

Ellie's aloofness and disarming cuteness made her a covert form of awkward, but her spotlighted attention and emotional dysregulation were among many of her quintessentially awkward qualities. Her intense focus on how to render drawings allowed her to appreciate form, shape, and color in ways that most adults will never know. She did things that most people never learn to do, such as draw portraits with her subjects standing at pleasing and meaningful angles or drawing clothing with rich texture that gave her subjects depth. But her spotlighted attention on form made it easy for her to lose sight of the bigger picture, and her intense energy while pursuing something she wanted made it easy for her to launch into a tirade when her expectations were not met.

Ellie and I worked to improve her identification of emotions and managing those emotions, but I also had a hunch that we could leverage positive emotions to broaden her attention to the bigger picture in social situations, namely her impact on others when she went on a tirade. Positive emotions also have adaptive functions, but they are very different from the fight-or-flight responses associated with negative emotions.

Emotion researchers like Alice Isen at Cornell University and Barbara Frederickson at the University of North Carolina at Chapel Hill have found that positive emotions do more than just create a pleasant feeling. Professor Frederickson's broaden-and-build theory of emotions suggests that positive emotions facilitate more expansive thought processes, make us more likely to notice atypical pieces of information, and allow us to hold more information in our conscious mind. This broadened thought process and availability of more information give us an opportunity to see creative solutions because the number of possible combinations grows exponentially with each additional piece of information we notice or hold in our mind. These creative insights can help us achieve professional outcomes that build financial or political resources, but they can also help us see new ways of handling complex social conundrums that build our social capital.

In this way, positive emotions can broaden the awkward person's tendency to remain narrowly focused. For awkward people whose creative potential relies upon their ability to put together information in a unique way, positive emotions can be a catalyst to bring together disparate ideas into unusual combinations, which is one of the hallmarks of innovative thinking.

Although there are exceptions to the rule, the best odds for achieving creative breakthroughs happen to people who figure out how to be the opposite of the tortured artist. This data paints a picture of people who are grateful for their specific talent, mindful of their limitations, driven to better themselves, and their affable nature builds social resources that help them feel a sense of belonging.

Evidence for the long-term benefits of positive emotion comes from a study by LeeAnne Harker and Dacher Keltner at the University of California at Berkeley, who conducted a fascinating study of positive emotional dispositions and social outcomes. They looked at data from the thirty-year Mills Longitudinal Study of one hundred women who graduated from Mills College in 1958 and 1960. Harker and Keltner applied a clever methodology to answer a relatively straightforward question: Would women who smiled in their yearbook photos have different social outcomes during their lifetimes from women who did not smile?

How could a seemingly insignificant act of smiling in a college yearbook photo be predictive of so many important life outcomes? There is no reason to smile in a photo with a photographer you will meet for one minute and probably never see again, yet some people sat on an uncomfortable stool, in front of an earth-tone tie-dyed backdrop, and flashed a genuine smile for the photo. They were probably the same people who smiled while shoveling snow or who sat in rush hour singing along in their car with a smile. They did not need a reason to be cheerful; it was in their dispositional nature to be cheerful. People who are disposed to being cheerful are strange in their own way, but their enthusiastic weirdness is magnetic and energizing, and people cannot help but feel deep down that they want to shovel snow or sing along in the car with these cheerful souls.

What Harker and Keltner found was that compared to women who were not smiling in their yearbook photos, women who smiled were more likely to report more positive emotions, lower negative emotions, more pleasant interpersonal behaviors, and more competency (e.g., productive, responsible). These associations held decades later, when the women were assessed at age forty-three and fifty-two. Women who were smiling in their yearbook photos were still higher in dispositional positive emotion, lower in dispositional negative emotion, and scored higher on measures of occupational competence. They were also more likely to be married and to be satisfied in their marriages.

These findings suggest that when people become narrowly focused on ameliorating the negative they can miss a key foothold. Positive emotions can do more than just get us out of a negative emotional rut. They have the potential to facilitate new insights that can help one see new ways of approaching social situations and build durable social resources. Although awkward people are prone to appearing aloof to others, they are also capable of joy and enthusiasm for the things they love. Positive emotions may be particularly useful for awkward individuals because they could broaden their spotlighted focus and allow them to see a broader perspective.

The data we have reviewed in this chapter suggest that awkward people are prone to appearing aloof, but we have also seen that this may be because they perceive their world so intensely that they become leery of being overwhelmed by their capability to manage intense emotions. For someone like Ellie who could easily lose control of her temper, her expression of unbridled negative emotions was a punishing experience that began to make her fearful of her general capacity for emotions. But awkward people can also become apprehensive about expressing positive emotions. When they gush with enthusiasm and joy about their achievements at the highest level of a video game or explain at great length their fascination with an unsolved mathematical proof, they can get social feedback that makes them feel as if their intuition about when to feel joyful is wrong.

I knew that I needed to have a sense of urgency about helping Ellie get a handle on her temper tantrums, but what made me feel a profound sense of fear and sadness was that she was also at risk for tamping down all of her emotions, including her wondrous joy about a world that she already saw differently from most people. What I eventually learned was that well-intended adults were constantly telling Ellie to stop doodling, pay attention, or hurry up. The adults in Ellie's life kept telling her to stay on task.

Ellie was paying attention and she was very task oriented, but her spotlighted attention was drawn to unusual things and this led her to choose to solve intangible tasks, which took the form of artistic renderings or wildly creative fictions. Even at her young age she was already more interested in drawing new boundaries than

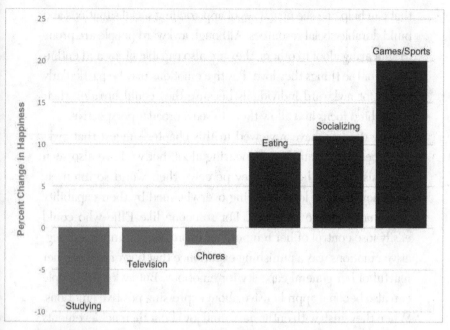

Figure 4.1 What can you do to boost your positive emotions? In an experience-sampling study that tracked changes in moods based on people's daily activities, Csikszentmihalyi and Wong found that games, socializing, and eating were the activities associated with boosts in positive emotions. They also found that activities done with other people were consistently associated with more positive emotions.

coloring inside the lines, and she preferred imagining new stories of what could be rather than recitations of the same old tales.

What Ellie and I eventually discovered was that her temper tantrums occurred when she was lost in her rich imagination. When adults barked at her to eat some more of her dinner or unexpectedly pulled away her sketch pad, she felt sharply annoyed. I explained to her parents that it would be like someone talking during a critical scene in a movie or someone interrupting them during an important call. It's understandable that Ellie may have felt frustrated in those interruptions, but she needed to learn how to express why she was frustrated instead of launching into temper tantrums.

Why Are You Making That Face?

WHEN I OPENED the door to the waiting room, I found Ellie standing right in front of the door. She had been waiting for three days to get an answer to her unanswered question, "Ty. Did you find out what your angry face looks like?"

During the three days between my appointments with Ellie, I casually asked every friend I saw two questions: First, do I have an angry face, and second, what does it look like? Although I am easily prone to some negative emotions such as frustration or anxiety, I have always been unusually slow to anger, which made it difficult for me to recall specific instances when I felt angry. While most people could not recall seeing me angry, the two people I asked who knew me best reported that there was indeed an angry face.

My girlfriend said, "Your angry face is not so much angry, but dismayed." Instead of my eyes narrowing, they grew wide and jumped around, as if physically searching for an answer as to why the other person decided that it was a good idea to do something so upsetting to me. My lips did not purse, but rather my mouth fell agape, which conveyed a sense of disbelief. My cousin told me that others probably perceived my facial expression as "more dumbfounded than upset." I also learned my upset was made worse by the fact that I never vocalized an explanation for why I was upset, but rather moved on to another topic, as if the moment never happened.

I made my angry face for Ellie. She gave me a quizzical glance. Then I made my self-conscious face. Ellie was aware that she was far from being an emotional expert, but she knew that there was something odd about my angry face. She flashed her emotional intelligence potential when she delivered surprisingly diplomatic feedback, "That's not a very good angry face. But you have a good smiley face."

We went back to my office, where we sat on the floor and casually doodled with crayons on an oversized sketch pad. I asked

Ellie if she had any temper tantrums since I last saw her. As she told me about her three temper tantrums over the past three days, her gaze turned downward, her posture slumped, and before the last ounce of cheerfulness escaped I suggested a positive take. Even though she had not changed her temper tantrums, at least she could start to identify her emotions.

Awkward people eventually become aware that they have trouble naturally picking up on signals that someone else is distressed, but in other situations they might feel their anger rise in response to nonthreatening circumstances. This puts awkward people in the counterintuitive position of needing to do something other than what their emotional reactions dictate. Awkward people figure out that sometimes they need to use a secondary response that follows the logic: If situation A, then I feel B, but most people feel C, so I should react as if I were feeling C instead of B.

It's a tough bind because it highlights the ongoing question of being true to yourself versus the motivation to improve your ability to meet social expectations.

Most people cannot feign embarrassment by blushing on command and you cannot take action to remedy a social transgression when you cannot identify how you have deviated from what was socially expected. A functional way for awkward people to handle a mismatch between their natural emotional reaction and the expected emotional reaction is to verbalize the message that is not being communicated through their expressions by saying something like, "I'm sorry, I probably should have handled that differently" or "I hope I did not offend, I think I'm having a hard time saying exactly what I mean." It's an imperfect solution, but these kinds of phrases following a social transgression allow the awkward person to convey three important things that are likely missing from their emotional response: I didn't act with bad intent, I'm sorry, and I would like to fix it.

There are things that awkward people can do to mitigate the

effects of uncomfortable emotions, but it's interesting to consider whether awkward people's lack of emotionality in some circumstances and intense emotionality in other situations might serve a purpose. Maybe awkward people's emotional lives should not be looked at as dysfunctional, but rather as different and potentially adaptive in some situations.

When one stops to think about the high probability of failure in ventures such as start-ups (90 percent within five years), restaurants (60 percent during the first three years), or the repeated failures in scientific endeavors, the vicarious anxiety alone can be enough to dissuade someone from ever getting involved. What kind of a person is all right with taking on enormous tasks that are more likely to fail than succeed, and what kind of person does not implode during the weekly failures in these types of ventures?

Maybe there are some circumstances when it's helpful not to absorb all of the emotions in a room, when being relatively immune to emotions like panic or demoralization that quickly spread through groups could be good for the group. It's not to say that only awkward people take on high-risk projects or that they don't experience negative emotions in the face of major failures, but their unusual emotional wiring might insulate them from becoming panicked after the failure of a major product launch or relatively indifferent after a nasty review in the newspaper.

Conversely, some awkward people get upset when seemingly trivial details are out of place. In some circumstances, awkward individuals' agitation with details not being exactly as they wish can be misguided or unnecessarily stubborn. But in some very high-profile success stories, whether of CEOs of successful tech companies, chefs of Michelin-starred restaurants, or scientists who make important breakthroughs, one of the common themes is that they insisted on a passionate attention to details and remained unusually calm when it seemed as though their ship would go under.

5

Carson sat alone, atop a weathered oak stool, in the middle of a theater in the round and watched as some of the top physicists in the world encircled him. In a few minutes, Carson would present his latest research at the applied mathematics symposium, an honor usually reserved for well-known senior faculty, but Carson was already making a splash in the world of physics as a twenty-five-year-old doctoral student. He had recently published a paper in a leading scientific journal that had generated a great deal of commotion and researchers around the world were eager to learn more about his work. As the auditorium began to reach capacity, Carson felt the gravity of the situation begin to weigh on his slight shoulders.

Carson had unruly blond curls and big blue eyes that were always darting around the room. He dressed in a semiformal manner, but his oxford shirts and slacks were always a tad too long. He looked like an adolescent who was perpetually on the verge of trouble. Although he had a boyish appearance, his scientific mind was mature beyond his years. Carson was an abrasive brand of awkward. His incisive observations and lack of mental filter made him too unruly for most people's tastes.

I knew Carson better than most people. We met during a music appreciation course as undergraduates in which he frequently offered mathematical observations about the music. His comments were accurate and insightful, but in a group of people who were looking for an easy elective, his remarks usually incited eye rolls from other students. I thought that Carson meant well, but he had a hard time showing it to other people. Most people saw him as disrespectful or even malicious and I can see how they reached those judgments. Carson had a sense that others perceived him as overly blunt, yet he felt as if he did not have time to beat around the bush with diplomacy or sugarcoating the facts. Carson was task-oriented rather than people-oriented, but this way, of approaching the world had made him a lonely person for twenty-five years.

After Carson received a glowing introduction from the chairperson of the physics department, he stepped to the podium and pressed the space bar on his computer to begin his presentation. He looked over his shoulder to be certain it was projected on the floor-to-ceiling screen behind him and saw the red letters, in all caps, of the title he had chosen to make a preemptive strike on the presumptive haters in the room:

EVERYTHING YOU THINK YOU KNOW
ABOUT GRAVITY IS WRONG!

When he turned back around, Carson noticed for the first time that there was an unusually large turnout for his talk and knew that this would not be an easy crowd to win over. While most people would have felt their anxiety skyrocket with this realization, Carson felt his nervous energy channel into a hardened resolve to shoot past the expectations of his audience. It's an uncommon killer instinct, but this instinct is common among people like Carson, who are bursting with a rare mixture of exceptional talent and sharply focused ambition. Such people are captivating to others because they give off the feeling of a nuclear potential, that any day that potential will explode and launch them toward greatness.

For Carson, this would not be that day.

The presentation we speak of took place in 2002, a time in computing history when antivirus software was porous. It was commonplace for viruses to take over people's operating systems and Trojan horse viruses were particularly menacing. They patiently waited inside computers for days before unleashing destruction or unwanted pop-up windows on a computer. I guess Carson contracted a Trojan horse virus.

As he advanced to the hypotheses slide of his presentation, the Trojan horse deployed its first attack, an autonomous launch of an Internet Explorer pop-up window. The window displayed a photo of a naked woman, her nurse uniform casually thrown onto a surprised patient's head, with a caption that advertised: *Naughty Nurses!* A few seconds later another pop-up appeared: *Exotic Asians!!* Then a third: *Ménages à Trois!!!* A fourth, a fifth . . .

Carson was not known for his ability to pick up on social cues, but even he noticed that there was a collective shift in his audience's nonverbal cues. The idea that emotional expressions are universal was on full display as everyone from punk rocker undergraduates to stodgy senior professors sat with their mouths agape, eyes wide, and a crinkle in the middle of their brows. As the pop-up windows continued to proliferate, some of the audience members began to slump in their chairs while others shot into hyper-straightened postures. Carson looked over his shoulder just as the seventh pop-up appeared: *Horny Coeds!!!*

Carson stood motionless for a few seconds, immobilized by his flood of emotions. Then he lurched toward the mouse pad and began a frenzied effort to close the windows, but it was too little, too late. He looked like someone trying to behead a Hydra, with each pop-up window closed sprouting two or three more. As this panoply of pornographic windows proliferated like fireworks, Carson's desperation shifted to resignation. Then, the projection screen suddenly went dark.

Carson looked to the left of the podium. His advisor, a stately professor emeritus in the department of physics, held the cable that had connected Carson's laptop to the projector. Everyone knew that Carson's advisor did not gladly suffer foolish behavior. The advisor's glare demanded that Carson look him straight in the eye. While Carson's advisor stared him down, everyone else tried to avoid looking at Carson, or anyone else in the audience, which is awkward when you are seated in a theater in the round.

The professor asked only one question, "Do you not get it?" This was the most helpful question anyone had ever asked Carson and one that would guide him toward a more likable manner of interacting with the world around him.

Theory of an Awkward Mind

ONE OF THE best feelings is to find someone who just gets you. People who get you not only understand your quirks, they are oddly endeared by them. It's the rare breed of individual who bursts into uncontrollable laughter when no one finds your inappropriate jokes funny or who sends your cat a birthday card because they know you love your cat just a little too much. When someone gets you, she sees the world through your eyes, she experiences your joys and sorrows as her own, and sometimes she knows what you are thinking before you do. People who get us are also the people we find most likable because who's better than someone who fully understands your good, bad, and weird qualities, but decides to love you anyway? Conversely, we can be hurt or offended when people misread what is on our minds. Teenagers and their parents are the classic case of two groups of people with a high probability of misunderstanding each other and at some point most parents will hear their teen exclaim, "You just don't get it!"

When people get you, psychologists would say that they have formed an accurate *theory of mind*. The term refers to developing an organized framework (theory) about how other people think and feel (mind). As people get to know each other better, their theories about that person usually become more intricate and accurate, which allows them to predict what the other person might be thinking or how they might feel in various situations. Theory of mind is similar to character development in books or movies. Readers make inferences about characters' characteristics and beliefs by picking up on telling details about those characters, such as their style of dress, habits, or responses to pressure. For example, a character with shifty eyes who presents contentious PowerPoint titles written in red font could give readers the sense that this character is edgy or aggressive.

As stories of our real lives unfold, it's human nature to form theories about the characters we encounter along the way and try to read their minds to gain a deeper understanding of their personality and values. We are all scientists conducting single-person case studies on each person we encounter. We constantly make observations about other people's behaviors to formulate theories about whether they are likely to act as a friend or adversary.

Socially fluent people form theory of mind so quickly that they are often unaware of how they reach their conclusions. It's remarkable that they are capable of triaging dozens of social cues in a split second, then quickly assemble those cues into patterns that allow them to intuit whether someone is happy, angry, or impatient. Yet many times a day, socially fluent people formulate theories of mind and adjust their style of interaction to match the mood. Within seconds of the Monday-morning meeting at work, they can judge whether their boss is feeling agitated or laid-back and use that judgment to inform whether this is the day to ask for the extra vacation days.

Carson's book smarts allowed him to quickly pick out relevant data and organize those observations with existing physics theories or algorithms. He did these complex computations without pen and paper or a calculator; they somehow came naturally to him. But Carson had trouble picking out the right social cues and organizing that data to figure out what was going on in other people's minds. He is not alone because numerous studies have demonstrated that awkward people have trouble forming theory of mind. Colin Palmer at the University of New South Wales and colleagues investigated how awkwardness was related to theory of mind in a sample of more than two thousand adults from the general population. Palmer found that people who were more socially awkward were much more likely to have trouble forming theory of mind about other people's intentions, thoughts, and feelings.

Given what we know about awkward individuals' processing of social cues, it's not surprising that they have difficulty with theory of mind, but this difficulty can leave them feeling as if they have lost the plot in social life. When people have difficulty with theory of mind, it's hard for them to create continuity across repeated interactions with the same person. When people are slow to form an organized understanding of how someone else's social mind works, they feel as if each social interaction is unfamiliar even though they have interacted with that person many times before.

Socially fluent individuals instantly recognize what is on other people's minds by seeing recognizable patterns from the social cues available. Consider the following thought experiment from eighth-grade algebra. The layout of the problem on the next page implies you should solve for x on the left side by adding the neatly organized numbers on the right side:

$$(x = 3 + 2 + 1)$$
$$(x = 6)$$

The problem becomes unsolvable when a variable becomes unknown on the right side of the equation: $(x = 3 + 2 + c)$. Likewise, awkward people have social difficulty because of those variables that are unknown in social situations. They are likely to be missing some key social cues because they have trouble remembering to look at people's faces for those cues or do not naturally hear cues from people's intonation as they try to solve the mystery of what other people are thinking or feeling. But if someone provides the value for x, then it's possible to solve the problem by working backward: $(6 = 3 + 2 + c)$.

It's not as easy to see how everything fits together in the second problem because with the missing value for c, it's not as neatly organized as the first problem. But with some mental maneuvering the problem is solvable if people can find out the answer to x. In the same way, awkward people take longer to add up social cues while they try to solve what is on other people's minds because they may have missed a key social cue, and social information does not appear neatly organized in their minds. Fortunately, researchers have figured out the x-factors that govern most social interactions, which creates an opportunity for awkward people to reach the same conclusions as non-awkward people, but the order of operations to reach a solution looks a little different.

A Theory of Being Likable

IF YOU HAD a superpower that gave you mind-reading abilities, what would you discover on the minds of the most likable people? The first task would be discerning the right targets because there is a difference between people who are likable versus people who are popular. Developmental psychologists define likability by how much others perceive someone to be a cooperative and pleasant person. They define popularity by how much others perceive someone to be influential or powerful. When researchers analyze social perceptions among middle school and high school students, they find that likability and popularity are only weakly related to each other.

Both popular and likable people tend to be socially fluent, but people motivated by popularity use their mind-reading skills to boost their social status or protect their position in the social hierarchy. Conversely, likable people are more likely to use their mind-reading skills to ensure that they act in fair and collaborative ways. Put differently, people driven by popularity approach situations thinking, "What's in it for me?" whereas likable people are thinking, "What can I do to contribute?"

People who are motivated by popularity tend to focus on short-term social gains, but these grabs for power come at the cost of burning social capital. They are more likely to use tactics that erode social capital such as manipulation, gossip, and degrading others for personal gain. Although likable people may not always win the contest for having the most Instagram followers or win the nomination for homecoming king or queen, they are more likely to be happy, have higher self-esteem, and find more reliable friendships. Likability is like trying to achieve financial security through investing in a blue-chip stock portfolio whereas popularity is like trying to achieve financial security by investing in trendy, high-risk companies without a sustainable business plan.

If people who are likable are more likely to find sustained belonging, then it's worthwhile to take a look at what runs through their minds. Thomas Berndt at Purdue University has spent his career researching how people form and maintain friendships. In his reviews of research on friendship, he reports that likable people hold distinctive views of friendship that influence their social perception and behaviors. If you search #friendship on Facebook or Instagram, it's easy to find hundreds of memes with heart-warming hypotheses about what makes someone a good friend, but the empirical answer turns out to be pleasantly straightforward. Likable people are driven by three core values: be fair, be kind, and be loyal.

Fairness is one of the first social expectations children develop. Whether it's taking turns during a game or sharing toys of similar desirability, fairness is about the perception that things are equal. When a peer takes two turns in a row or hoards too many of the best toys, kids respond with tears or tantrums because they are upset that their expectation of equity has been violated. In adulthood, fairness is still expected about concrete things like taking turns doing the dishes or sharing the remote control for the television. In adulthood, fairness can be more complex because the things being exchanged can be abstract concepts such as empathizing with people who have shown you empathy or forgiving someone who previously forgave you. Adults grow tired of friends, coworkers, or romantic partners when they feel like their empathy or thoughtful gestures are unreciprocated.

Children eventually understand that relationships can be viewed as more than a one-for-one exchange. They begin to see the limitations inherent in the mind-set "I'll scratch your back, but I'll only scratch your back again if you scratch mine in return." Children begin to proactively offer more than what is fair by saying things like, "You can go first," or "You can play with the best toy." They learn that these small sacrifices have a way of moving relationships forward and subtly send a message that they are invested in the well-being of others in the social group. Kind children and adults give freely early in relationships because they start with the assumption that most people can be trusted to be fair. Kind people hold a karmic belief that when everyone proactively looks for opportunities to contribute, there are more benefits for everyone in the group.

When we appreciate people who exceed our expectations of fairness we feel grateful. The function of gratitude is to direct our attention to people who exceed expectations, and this emotion motivates us to reciprocate the kind act. Sara Algoe is a social psychologist at the University of North Carolina at Chapel Hill who has found that people who experience gratitude tend to overshoot when they give back. People probably give more to make sure that they restore a sense of fairness, but giving more than expected is an act of kindness as well. Gratitude creates an upward spiral of helping behaviors because people feel grateful when we reciprocate kind behaviors, which motivates them to be kind in return.

Kindness begets the third characteristic of likable people: loyalty. Friendships exist in an open social market. People are free to enter and leave relationships at their convenience, but a loyal person will stick with you through the times when it would be easier for them to exit the friendship. When our life circumstances take a downturn, whether it's hitting a low point in your career, getting dumped by a boyfriend, or getting shunned by a group of friends, even the best of us can feel bad about our self-worth. Yet when our views of our self-worth take a dip, some friends refuse to change their valuation of us and some even increase their investment. This seems illogical from a short-term perspective because the amount each person has to offer in the friendship is unequal, but the logic behind being loyal is not always readily apparent.

Here's what loyal friends believe about you. Loyal friends believe that you contribute something unique to their lives. They value you not for extrinsic things like wealth, social status, or power. They believe that you will rise from your toughest times. They trust that you will emerge through adversity as a better person. They have faith in not only who you are, but who you will become. There are few things better in life than having loyal friends,

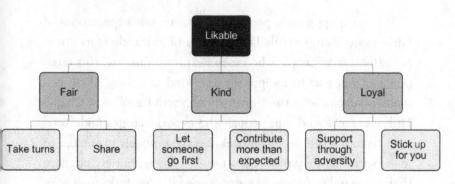

Figure 5.1 Network representation of friendship quality

people who have stubbornly committed to making a long-term investment in you for who you are.

If we had mind-reading superpowers, then we would see that the minds of likable people are organized around three pro-social values: be fair, be kind, be loyal. These three core values are what likable individuals use to evaluate other people. They also drive likable people to act in ways that are consistent with these values. Of course, this empirical approach to friendship is only one way of searching for answers, and there are many other spiritual or cultural traditions that might prescribe a different set of values. But these three pro-social values seem to transcend spiritual and religious traditions across cultures.

For awkward individuals who are trying to solve the problem of what is running through other people's minds, these three core values provide a way to work backward in the problem. Instead of piecing together individual cues to formulate an idea of other people's intent or underlying meaning, awkward people can begin with the assumption that likable people are evaluating them through these three criteria, and that the likable person is acting with the intent of embodying fairness, kindness, and loyalty.

But not everyone is invested in being likable. Some people are driven by power or greed, or try to take advantage of others' goodwill, and this creates some complications that deserve careful consideration.

The Surprising Social Skill of Bullies

BULLIES EXIST AT all ages. The prototypical playground bully pushes other kids out of the way in line, steals their lunch money, or mocks their differences. In adolescence, bullies might publicly insult peers lower in social power or spread gossip about those higher in power. Even in adulthood, there are bullies who try to take more than their fair share, manipulate others for their personal gain, or pick on people they perceive as less powerful. A survey by the Workplace Bullying Institute found that 35 percent of employees had been bullied at work and another 15 percent witnessed workplace bullying, which was defined by repeated mistreatment and included behaviors such as threats, humiliation, and sabotaging employees' work.

One of the most disconcerting findings about bullies of all ages is that they are not naive. The results of a number of studies suggest that bullies have a better-than-average capability to mind-read and use their social fluency to manipulate others to achieve selfish ends. Gianluca Gini and colleagues at the University of Padova investigated the assumption that bullies have poor moral reasoning, which is to say that they have trouble differentiating right versus wrong. In a sample of more than 700 nine-to-thirteen-year-old children, they looked at the differences in moral reasoning among bullies, victims, and defenders who intervene with bullies. They found that bullies' moral reasoning capabilities were just as sound as defenders' and that both groups had moral reasoning scores that were higher than victims'. However, bullies showed significantly lower levels of compassion and they were more likely to rationalize away their immoral behavior by seeing their selfish gains as taking precedence over the emotional costs incurred by victims.

Bullies use their social fluency to target people who are less likely to retaliate. In a meta-analysis of 153 studies, Clayton Cook from the University of Washington and his colleagues from the University of California, Riverside, reviewed dozens of risk factors for being bullied, including gender, race, low self-esteem, and stressful family environments. Although a number of factors were associated with the risk of being bullied, the strongest risk factors were low social competence and low peer status. For the awkward kid with low social competence and low peer status, it's an unfortunate circumstance because even though bullies might not be well liked by their peers, they often possess a good degree of social power and influence and tend to have a good understanding of social dynamics and the ability to be selectively charismatic.

Awkward kids already have trouble navigating normal social expectations, so to go against the sophisticated manipulations bullies incorporate can feel entirely bewildering to them. Awkward children may not speak up about being bullied because bullies use methods of harassment that intentionally blur the lines between right and wrong. The awkward child might be uncertain about whether she is being wronged and even more uncertain about what to do.

If bullying victims are lucky enough to have a defender stand up for them, then it's important they acknowledge the social capital the defender risked. Rashmi Shetgiri at the University of Texas Medical Center found in a study of 354 sixth-to-tenth-grade students that defenders significantly increased their risk of being bullied by the bullies they confronted. This suggests that there are likely a limited number of times peers can intervene with people being bullied before they put themselves at risk for being bullied as well. It's important for victims to consider that the defender selectively spent his social capital. This means that awkward kids cannot rely upon defenders to continually absorb the social costs of defending them. The awkward kid has to figure out how to bolster his social competence and peer status, which is easier said than done. Also, in the interest of fairness and showing gratitude, awkward individuals would also do well to find subtle ways to return the favor or at least privately express gratitude to their defenders.

Bullies don't go away in adulthood. Although some people who were formerly bullies change their ways, there is a growing body of research that shows that kids who were bullies tend to grow up to be adults who are bullies. They manifest as manipulative managers in the workplace, emotionally abusive partners, or criminals who steal or aggress to get what they want. The severest form of adult bullies are sociopaths who look to exploit others' goodwill for their personal gain while feeling no remorse for the people they harm. About 1 percent of the general population can be diagnosed as sociopathic, but roughly another 10 to 15 percent can be categorized as selfish rather than pro-social. Some people are prone to being self-absorbed, greedy, or power hungry and will readily take more than their fair share from others.

Of course, people who want to be kind and loyal have to be cautious about who they trust because bullies' actions can produce consequences that are heavily weighted. Yet people also need to be careful about becoming overly guarded or too pessimistic about human nature. This can be particularly true about awkward kids who have been on the receiving end of extensive bullying. It's easy to understand how children who are chronically bullied could develop a jaded view of others or become proactively aggressive to protect themselves, but that global resolve makes it hard to connect with the good people. For awkward and non-awkward people alike, it's tough to figure out how to protect themselves while also preserving their commitment to making themselves vulnerable through kindness and loyalty.

The risks one takes while trying to strike a balance between self-protection and proactive kindness can be minimized by thinking about altruistic or kind behavior being delivered in measured doses while people get to know each other. This approach gives kind and loyal people a way to protect themselves while starting the positive cycle of altruism and gratitude with potential friends.

The Devil Is in the Details

JOHN GOTTMAN OF the University of Washington and his colleagues have conducted observational studies of positive and negative behaviors with married couples and grade-school children for decades. The focus of many relationship scientists has been on negative behaviors such as resentment or withdrawing from conflict, but the trick to understanding interpersonal behavior is about the ratio of negative to positive behaviors. It turns out that positive behaviors can be as small as telling someone he looks handsome, attentively listening to a friend's small triumph of the day, or surprising a coworker with her favorite cupcakes.

Gottman has found that people keep an informal count of behaviors. He calls this ratio of positive to negative behaviors an emotional bank account. To stay in good standing with others, people need to keep a balance of about four or five positive behaviors to every one negative behavior. Imagine that you do four good things during an interaction with a friend: give an enthusiastic greeting, compliment his outfit, share some french fries, and respond empathically to a concern. Then you inadvertently insult this friend by forgetting that today is his birthday. You would probably come out of this interaction with $0.00 in your emotional bank account with him, which is not bad considering that you could have left the interaction in the red had you not been so nice at the start of the interaction. It's good to think about leaving interactions without a negative balance because people's emotional bank accounts charge interest.

Gottman finds that negative balances are not wiped from other people's minds at the end of the day, but instead carry over to your next interaction. This is bad news if you end the day in the red with someone, but good news if you end the day with money in the bank. When people leave interactions with a negative balance, it has a way of building corrosive resentment in others' minds, which essentially adds interest to their emotional debt. The good news is that leaving interactions with a positive balance tends to build trust, which is like gaining interest on your deposit.

One strategy is to avoid mistakes, but a focus on trying not to make a mistake has a way of creating persistent anxiety, which is both unpleasant and unhelpful. The best way to leverage the concept of the emotional bank account is to commit to making small deposits of positive behaviors on a consistent basis. Instead of viewing the dozens of social situations and hundreds of cues that one encounters every day as an opportunity for failure, the mindset shifts to capitalizing on routine situations by contributing a little more than expected. Sometimes others view heroic efforts as a disproportionately large contribution, but typically positive efforts both big and small have about the same effect.

When you become the kind of person who first thinks about how to help people rather than how to get something from people, it builds a positive balance in your emotional bank account with others. Over time, that positive balance begins to build trust and eventually faith that you are a good-natured person. The key is to be subtle about your contributions. Most people feel tremendous gratitude when their grandparents slip a ten-dollar bill into their birthday card, but if their grandparents slipped a check for $10,000 into their birthday card, it would actually feel awkward for most people. Subtle deposits could be as small as being more specific when you say thank you or letting others go first when a line forms at a buffet. As a supplement to face-to-face deposits, it's easier than ever to make "mobile deposits" through a kind text the day of someone's big test or a follow-up message after dinner to say, "That was fun, thanks for getting together."

CLOSE FRIENDS	TEACHERS AND PARENTS
1. Understand my feelings	1. Explain things when I'm confused
2. Stick up for me when others don't	2. Try to answer my questions
3. Accept me when I make a mistake	3. Are fair to me
4. Make me feel better when I mess up	4. Help me when I want to do a better job
5. Spend time with me when I am lonely	5. Praise me when I do a good job

Table 5.1 Top five supportive behaviors from close friends and teachers/parents. Data comes from researchers at Northern Illinois University, who pooled data from more than 1,600 elementary, middle, and high school students. These students all perceived acts of loyalty and companionship from close friends as the most supportive behaviors. They perceived solicited advice and praise for good work from teachers/parents as the most supportive behaviors.

The reality is that awkward people are more likely to make small withdrawals from their emotional bank accounts with others because they are prone to mishandling minor social expectations. Awkward people may not notice that their large backpack swung into their friend's head as they turned to sit down on the bus or they may accidentally disclose the surprise birthday party to the birthday boy. These awkward moments are done without premeditation or malice, but they are still negative and even if people do not say anything, their automated mental accounting system deducts a little bit from the emotional bank account.

These unexpected or accidental withdrawals make it imperative that awkward individuals make a concerted effort to maintain
a positive balance through consistently making small deposits that
move their balance farther to the positive side in others' minds.
It's like contributing a little bit every month for social insurance.

Awkward individuals should not let their clumsiness with minor social expectations define them. As both awkward and non-
awkward people get older, most of them will care less about
surface qualities and instead evaluate people on their willingness
to be fair, be kind, and be loyal. So long as good people feel as if
you are trying your best to consistently contribute, then they are
willing to overlook a little awkwardness. Whether it's a commitment to a familial relationship, friendship, or romantic relationship, when awkward people make sure that they find a way to
contribute to the broader good, it is the best strategy for creating
sustainable social capital.

	MEET EXPECTATIONS	DO NOT MEET EXPECTATIONS
Care	Likable	Awkward
Don't Care	Manipulative	Malicious or Reckless

Table 5.2 The consequences of expectations when others perceive good intent versus bad intent

The Value of Social Equity

CARSON'S ADVISOR, PROJECTION cord in hand, maintained his death
stare as he waited for Carson's response to his rhetorical question,
"Do you not get it?" Carson replied, "I don't get it, I don't know
why, but I'm sorry." That's all Carson had to say to keep the faith

of his advisor. Carson's advisor was a wise man, someone who had learned an important distinction through his years of mentoring students who were talented, but often awkward. Yet while Carson's advisor was unfazed by his students' awkwardness, he did not see Carson's tiny acts of self-absorption as awkward, but as willfully selfish. Carson's narrow focus on becoming an academic star meant that he had showed little awareness about how he could contribute to the people around him. His advisor had noticed his unwillingness to help other students and his abruptness with the administrative staff in the department; therefore, the pop-up catastrophe was the last straw in a string of withdrawals Carson had made from his emotional bank account with his advisor.

I suspect that Carson's advisor saw the goodness in him and he knew that Carson's abrasiveness was a protective mechanism. From his earliest days in school, Carson had been an awkward kid and a loner who was frequently bullied. Like many awkward kids, Carson tried his best to figure out how to fit in, but despite his best efforts, he didn't get what other kids wanted from him. He was given the standard advice, well-intended sayings from adults like "Just ignore them" or "You will be very successful someday while they are flipping burgers." But ignoring bullies does not always work because bullies have a relentless mentality, and telling their victims that they will be "better" than their tormentors instills an adversarial "them against me" mentality. Telling awkward kids that they are better than other kids also implies that achieving academic or professional status is equated with being a better person. Awkward kids' best chances of finding a meaningful and happy life are unlikely to come from being more professionally accomplished than their peers. Their best chance of eventually finding happiness comes from a patient focus on becoming someone who is inclusive and fair even when other people are not treating them the same way.

In college, a confluence of events turned Carson's fortunes around. By the luck of the draw he was paired with an incredibly kind roommate who genuinely enjoyed Carson's intellect and sharp wit. In the lab where Carson worked, a group of older graduate students took him under their wing, which provided a place where he could talk as much as he wanted about physics with peers who were enthralled rather than bored. Carson felt less threatened in college and as a result was more himself, which made him a much more likable guy.

But Carson quickly found that being a graduate student at an elite program came with a more competitive environment. It was a dog-eat-dog world and when older students caught glimpses of Carson's potential, some of them began to plot against him. They thought that his success could threaten their positions in the academic hierarchy, and this insecurity manifested in behaviors that re-created Carson's playground nightmares of being teased and degraded. He was quick to raise his old psychological guards. From this protective position, he zeroed in on being competitive in his work, but by doing so lost touch with the people around him. Although it was true that Carson's work was important and he needed to work hard to succeed, it was also true that his myopic focus and hyper-ambition had become so intense that he had turned into someone who was entirely unlikable.

Carson's advisor knew that Carson had no intent to embarrass him at the applied mathematics symposium, but he also knew that this misstep would carry significant consequences for Carson's reputation. This was a hit that Carson could ill afford, given his negative balance with most people in the department. If Carson had been a kind soul who had earned the social respect of his peers, then people who witnessed the pop-up fiasco would have seen this awkward moment as an aberration and attributed the incident to faulty antivirus software. But Carson had no social cushion, and his advisor knew that if Carson did not make deliberate efforts to be more likable, he would never form the social ties necessary to reach his full professional potential.

In the wake of the pop-up disaster, Carson took a hard look at what he "didn't get." He eventually concluded that he got physics, but did not get people. For the first time in a long time, he tried to see the world through other people's eyes and considered what his classmates might say when asked about what they don't get. Full of good intent, Carson set out on a social science investigation around the department, asking a handful of his peers what they "didn't get" in graduate school. Some of his classmates didn't get advanced statistics and some of the foreign-born students didn't get all of the nuances of the English language. Although this was probably frustrating for them, those who struggled with advanced statistics went for additional tutoring, and some of the English as a second language students consistently went to the writing lab for extra help with papers. As Carson sat in his dorm formulating theories from his interviews, he realized that his classmates were doing things to figure out what they didn't get, but he was doing nothing to improve how to get along with other people.

Carson made a genuine effort to examine his attitude. He began by visiting his advisor's office, where he gave another apology for good measure, then asked for a "candid and uncensored" critique about what exactly he didn't get. He took meticulous notes as his advisor told him in great detail about why Carson could not afford to move through his graduate studies and professional career with blinders on: because science is a collaborative discipline. He recited case studies about how many of the greatest scientific discoveries resulted from collaboration and sometimes scientists being open to people with wildly different perspectives. The detailed feedback and concrete examples made sense to Carson, and he left that meeting on better terms with his advisor and a determination to shift his perspective about what it would mean to be successful in graduate school.

Carson had hoped that his academic status would carry over to his social relationships, but he realized that 99.99 percent of people were not going to determine his likability based on the prestige of his professional credentials or publication record. It's an understandable fantasy because physics was what came naturally to him, but he realized that small behaviors like taking the time to lend a helping hand with a colleague's experiment or showing up for a colleague's marathon to cheer him on carried far more weight in people's minds than professional status or power. His shift to approaching interactions with an intent to contribute first and worry about his self-interest second might sound like common sense, but it's a perspective that some people never learn and even the best of us can lose our grip on.

During his last year of Carson's doctoral program, I had a chance to catch up with him on his campus. I had not seen him since we had graduated from college and he was as awkward as ever, but as he showed me around his department I could tell that he was well-liked and there were people who were clearly drawn to him. What Carson had come to understand about the pull between two people in a friendship is that one does not become more magnetic by launching higher than the other, but instead by adopting pro-social values that really matter in the long run. When Carson decided to be fair, be kind, and be loyal, he became a more substantial person, which had a way of attracting other people of substance into his orbit.

PART II

THIS IS GETTING AWKWARD:

———

HOW MODERN SOCIETAL SHIFTS
ARE MAKING EVERYONE FEEL
MORE AWKWARD

6

NURTURING AWKWARD CHILDREN

By my last year of junior high, I was a serious academic under-achiever, a below-average two-miler on the track team, and my social progress had definitely hit a point of diminishing returns. At a family dinner toward the end of my final semester, my parents informed me of a decision "we have reached as a couple," which was their way of saying that this decision was a nonnegotiable executive order. They had decided to send me to a different high school from the one my junior high classmates would attend. I staged the obligatory adolescent protest, but I knew in the back of my mind that a change of scenery might provide some traction to get out of my rut.

After learning that professionalism and maturity were not the keys for junior high social success, I was reluctant to make decisive moves to prepare for high school social life. I began high school with the social aspirations of many awkward kids, which was to avoid doing anything that would get me harassed by bullies and make a few reliable friends. Things turned out better than I had hoped because I caught a few early breaks. One of my early child-hood friends had grown into a six-four man-child by the time we were fifteen and was the star running back on the football team.

We were locker partners and he was a good friend to me. He took me under his wing and a few of his friends from the offensive line followed suit. Suddenly my fortunes had changed from being a skinny kid with no social capital who was always in danger of being thrown in a locker to being a skinny kid with some borrowed social capital who was well guarded. By high school standards, this was a vast improvement.

Although high school was going extremely well on the social front, I continued to underachieve in many of my classes. This fact escaped many of my teachers, who had bigger problems than a relatively well-behaved C student like me, but my low academic expectations caught the sharp eye of my chemistry teacher, Mr. Z. He told us on the first day of school that he went by Mr. Z because he had no patience for students mispronouncing his Eastern European surname. Legend had it that Mr. Z had worn the same outfit for all twenty-five years he had been teaching high school chemistry, a sweater-vest, a starched shirt, khakis, and polished brown oxfords. He was always on time, never conducted a show-a-video-and-worksheet class, and was one of the top triathletes in his age group in the state of Colorado. He was a self-proclaimed nerd before it was common to reclaim a derogatory term by using it as self-description. He was an awkward guy, but his awkwardness was overshadowed by his strict expectations of excellence for himself and from his students. It was a philosophy that struck most high school students as overly earnest.

One day Mr. Z called my parents to tell them that I was "in jeopardy of doing very poorly in chemistry" even though I was a solid C-plus student in his class. Sure, I was underachieving, but I was far from failing. When Mr. Z informed me that I would need to come in after school to redo the problems I had missed on my chemistry homework until I started fulfilling my potential, I became incensed. The idea of missing after-school socializing was unthinkable. I was gaining social momentum and Mr. Z's detentions would surely infringe upon a critical window to socialize with people at the end of the school day.

The first time I showed up to Mr. Z's after-school detention to fix my homework problems, I realized that no other student had been sentenced to this punishment. As I stood at the chalkboard fixing a problem, I found it difficult to steady the chalk in my hand, which shook with anger. As I plugged in values and balanced equations, shards of chalk were flying off the chalkboard like sparks—until I would make a mistake and Mr. Z would stop me with the same phrase: "careless mistake." My eyes would grow wide and my mouth would fall open as I tilted my head to the side and felt my face grow hot.

One Friday afternoon, I missed the opportunity to spend a weekend with some friends at someone's mountain home on account of my chemistry detention. To a high school student these kinds of lost social opportunities feel like the end of the world. My dad picked me up from school and saw that I was making my angry face. He knew exactly what was on my mind: "If Mr. Z was not in the way, then this never would have happened." My dad was the vice principal at my high school and had known Mr. Z for years. My dad decided that I needed some context to understand Mr. Z's intent. He asked, "Did you know that Mr. Z grew up without a mom and dad until he was a teenager?"

I had not known. None of the students in Mr. Z's classes knew anything about him except that he was evangelical about chemistry and a self-proclaimed nerd. My dad explained that Mr. Z was raised in an Eastern European orphanage and was adopted around age three by a family in the United States. His adoptive parents decided after a couple of years that they could not keep him, which left him bouncing around foster homes throughout his childhood. When he was thirteen years old, an older couple permanently adopted him. The husband and wife were both successful science professors and they saw Mr. Z not as a misfit, but as a boy with a precocious scientific ability who was bored with his schoolwork and who needed a great deal of structure to guide his high energy toward something positive.

Mr. Z's adoptive parents provided a systematic approach to life, which was something that he desperately needed. He also loved the casual dinnertime stories his parents told about scientific discoveries or legendary scientists. By the time Mr. Z graduated from high school, he was at the top of his class, a state champion distance runner, and was accepted to the Naval Academy for college. After graduating with a science major, he quickly rose through the ranks as an officer while working as an engineer on top-priority military projects. At the end of his commitment, Mr. Z could have continued his fast rise with the navy or he could have accepted lucrative job offers from private companies that worked on defense projects. Instead, he decided to pursue his teaching certificate to try to motivate kids like me who were trying to do the bare minimum to get by in school.

After telling me Mr. Z's story, my dad offered a hypothesis about why I was in those detentions: "Mr. Z is hard on you because he cares about your future. I know you don't love chemistry. I know you're not interested in the scientific method or statistics. But you have to understand that science was Mr. Z's way to a better life. This is his way of trying to help you out." I contemplated this conversation about Mr. Z for many weeks. It made me less upset about the detentions, but it also made me wonder how a guy like Mr. Z managed to achieve so much, at such a high level. I wondered about classic questions of nature versus nurture and how much Mr. Z's inherent nature versus his adoptive family influenced who he became. Years later, as a graduate student in psychology, I would learn that these answers are not dichotomous, but rather suggest a dynamic interplay between genetic influences and the people who modify our psychological trajectories along the way.

The Nature of Awkward Families

WHEN I SAW teenagers as psychotherapy clients, they would often tell me, "My parents totally made it awkward." The "it" could refer to their father's style of dress at a baseball game, their mother's intervention with a teacher at the child's school, or an attempt by a parent to be cool when a teenager's friends came over to the house. When I heard these stories, I would first acknowledge that their parents' black dress socks with shorts or use of the phrase "homey" with their friends was indeed awkward, but then I would ask the teenager, "Do you think your parents ever feel awkward about what you do?"

It's risky to come back with this kind of reflective question to a teenager, but I found that they appreciated the play. Teenagers would recall with a degree of amusement times when their parents must have felt awkward, like the time when the teenager chose a family movie that had an unexpectedly long and graphic sex scene. By the end of these therapy sessions, we would usually conclude that being part of a family is inherently awkward.

While family life naturally presents awkward moments, there are unique challenges for the modern family when it comes to defining expectations for each member. Alison Gopnik is a leading child development researcher at the University of California, Berkeley, and during a presentation to the Association for Psychological Science she provided an insightful overview of some shifts in familial expectations. Throughout most of human history, families were part of a network of extended family who lived close by or even in the same household, which meant that kids not only received guidance from their parents, but also from aunts, uncles, grandparents, and older siblings or cousins. This arrangement also meant that kids learned to take care of other children while they were growing up because they usually had to tend to younger siblings or relatives. But that changed in the late 1900s when kids were more likely to be isolated from rich networks of extended family, were less likely to actively care for other children, and were more likely to learn how to "be an adult" through experiences in school or the workplace.

Numerous intellectuals have pointed to an interesting shift in the expectations held by the modern family. The expectation used to be that parents simply provide a safe, supportive environment for their children, but that shifted to an expectation that parents intensely manage their children's progress toward discernible achievements in the classroom or on the playing field. The average child now is under constant surveillance and her free time is much more structured, which means that parents have a level of involvement in their children's lives and a personal stake in their children's achievements that is unprecedented in recent history.

In some ways this intensive parenting has conferred certain protective advantages that are important for children's safety and emotional well-being, but the pendulum of protectiveness has swung so far that the modern family has also removed some of the exploration and learning that occurs through children's free experimentation and the corrective action of natural consequences. Part of the job description of being a child is to do some things that are socially inappropriate or foolish, to learn what the consequence of those actions are, then to take responsibility for correcting course. Part of being a kid is: be inappropriate, find out the consequence, revise, repeat.

When this natural progression becomes hindered through parental interference or overinvolvement, interactions between family members can get awkward. Parents try to be cool, kids try to be adult, and everyone has a sense that the expectations for parent and child have become blurred.

Our first lessons about how to be social come from our families. For much longer than infants in other species, human infants rely upon their caregivers for protection, nourishment, and mobility. Human infants are completely reliant on their caregivers to meet their physical needs, protect them, and teach them how to navigate the complexities of social life. Caregivers teach their children how to make friends, work collaboratively with others, and manage conflict. They provide direct instruction about how to behave in social situations, but children also learn by observing how their caregivers navigate social interactions. Although caregivers have direct and indirect influences on whether their children became socially fluent or socially awkward, the strongest influence biological parents have on their children's social fluency is genetic.

John Constantino and Richard Todd at the Washington University School of Medicine investigated the heritability of awkward traits in the general population with a sample of 788 pairs of seven-to-fifteen-year-old twins. Identical twins are more genetically similar to each other than fraternal twins, which allows researchers to infer genetic influences on traits if identical twins' scores are more similar than fraternal twins' scores on tests measuring certain traits. Constantino and Todd wanted to investigate whether identical twins would show more similarity than fraternal twins on a measure of social skill deficits called the Social Responsiveness Scale. While they were interested in genetic influences, they were also interested in how much social skill deficits were influenced by non-familial social influences such as teachers and friends.

Constantino and Todd found that identical twins were far more similar to each other than fraternal twins on the measure of social skill deficits. Their analyses suggested that boys' awkwardness was 52 percent heritable and that girls' awkwardness was 39 percent heritable. They also found differences between boys and girls regarding environmental factors. Girls' awkwardness was more strongly influenced by their family environments (43 percent) than boys' (25 percent).

This study and others suggest that awkward characteristics are heritable, but it's important to note that awkwardness is neither 100 percent heritable nor 100 percent environmental. This is the kind of outcome most behavioral genetic researchers find intriguing. The goal of behavioral genetic researchers is not to tell us that there is nothing we can do about our psychological fates; rather the goal is to discover what is attributable to genetic influences and environmental influences in hopes of one day figuring out which environments might reduce individuals' genetic risks and maximize their genetic strengths.

For caregivers, teachers, or other mentors of awkward children, these behavioral genetic findings suggest that some kids will show a stronger biological disposition toward awkwardness than others, but they also suggest that family environment and non-familial environments have a substantial influence on how children's awkward characteristics manifest.

The question is how caregivers can provide environments that minimize the potential negative outcomes of, and maximize the strengths of, children's awkward dispositions. We will see that awkward children can be coached to think through social situations and encouraged to make good use of their unique perspectives. But this approach needs to be tailored to awkward children's unusual ways of seeing the world. This can mean a war of attrition between awkward children's impulses and their caregivers' attempts to impose social rules that channel those impulses. To start thinking about how this battle plays out, let's take a look at an updated version of one of the most influential theories of the twentieth century.

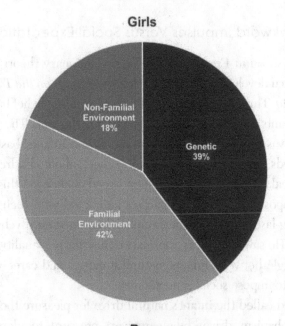

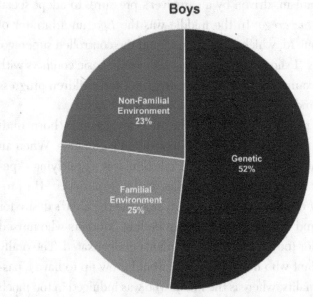

Figure 6.1 Genetic, family, and non-familial effects for boys' and girls' social ability

Awkward Impulses Versus Social Expectations

IN 1905, SIGMUND Freud presented a revolutionary theory of psychological development in the book *Three Essays on the Theory of Sexuality*. Through the early 1900s, the prevailing belief had been that infants were incapable of purposeful thought. The general advice was that parents needed to meet their infants' basic physical needs, but did not have to worry much about children's psychological needs until after infancy. Freud challenged this notion and proposed that the way parents interacted with their infants had long-lasting psychological implications for their psychological health. He saw infancy as a formative time for personality, a time of struggle between infants' natural impulses and caregivers' attempts to impose social expectations.

Freud called the infant's natural drive for pleasure the *Id* and the mechanism, driven by a caregiver's pressure, to adopt social rules the *Superego*. In the middle was the *Ego*, an arbitrator of the desirous Id, which says "I want," and the controlled superego, which says "I should." He elaborated on these basic conflicts with detailed examples of stages that caregivers and children progress through, and that's when things started to get weird.

Freud proposed that from the time an infant is born until about eighteen months, its main motivation is to nurse. When an infant is hungry and his mother feeds him, it is a gratifying experience, or what Freud called a pleasurable experience. He proposed that mothers need to properly regulate the child's desire for pleasure and this began with breastfeeding. Mothers who nursed too much or too little made their infants orally fixated. The orally fixated infant who nursed too little would grow up to have a passive personality, whereas the infant who was indulged in too much breastfeeding would develop a manipulative personality. Freud suggested that one tangible sign of this underlying psychological neurosis was a tendency to chew on pencils, bite nails, or other orally oriented behaviors.

After the oral stage, Freud postulated that the basic parent-child conflict shifted from whether an infant was breastfed too much or too little to a showdown over toilet training. Infants in diapers do not have to "hold it' until they find a restroom; they have the luxury to let things go whenever they want and it feels good, even pleasurable, to relieve themselves. This unrestricted expulsion is all fun and games until caregivers come around with their Superego ideas. They impose expectations about when and where children should relieve themselves, which is atop an enormous porcelain hole in the ground. To infants, this looks like an instrument that might be capable of whirling all kinds of things into an unknown abyss. If you put yourself in a child's mind, then you can imagine not wanting to buy into any of this ridiculous social expectation. Children wage a battle against these restrictions with one of two strategies: withhold or expel.

Anally retentive children sit on the toilet, look their parents in the eye, and do . . . . nothing. Anally retentive kids will sit there for hours in willful disobedience. By comparison, anally expulsive children look their parent in the eye while they soil themselves. They are daring their parents to stop them from doing what they want, when they want. Both tactics are remarkably effective ways to agitate parents. Freud thought that the anally retentive child grew up to become overly controlled, a sort of obsessive-compulsive type of adult. Conversely, the anally expulsive child developed a loosely controlled personality, a risk-taking type of adult who would let bad decisions flow freely in the face of cultural norms that prescribed constraint.

I like to imagine Freud in the starched air of Victorian-era modesty. I imagine him at elegant dinner parties in downtown Vienna where the other guests would politely try to engage in small talk with him, asking Dr. Freud what he did for work. I imagine Freud engaging in uncensored discourse about his theory of psychosexual pleasures and elaborating upon how infants' frustrated psychosexual pleasures might result in oral fixation or anal expulsion. The awkwardness in those salons, stuffy with Superego, must have been priceless to observe. A collective self-consciousness must have infiltrated the remainder of the evening as guests privately wondered how to deal with the bratwurst on their plates or their after-dinner smokes.

Although some of the specific examples Freud gave about the oral and anal stages seem absurd, his core ideas were a revolutionary way of thinking about child development. Researchers have found little support for Freud's proposed link between nursing and oral fixations, or toilet training and orderliness, but they have found support for Freud's core idea, which was that there could be long-lasting psychological effects from how early parent-child conflicts were handled.

Take the oral stage as an example. Infants are without language or mobility, which means that they are completely reliant upon their caregivers to meet their needs. Consider what happens when infants cry because they are hungry, but learn that they cannot rely upon their caregivers to respond. Conversely, a parent who is smothering, who does not allow a child enough independence, could also negatively influence the child's development. Kids need their parents to strike this balance between attentiveness and freedom throughout their lives, whether the context is nursing during infancy, summer camp as a kid, or a child's setting off to college as a young adult.

An anal stage of development sounds absurd now, but once again Freud's core idea is useful. Anyone who has tried to toilet train an infant or watched others try to do so can tell you that the process can be a real struggle. There are many struggles for power between child and parent besides toilet training that take place on a daily basis, such as those around a parent's exhortations not to hit, to be gentle, not to kick, to be nice, not to eat your snot. But these are only a few among hundreds, if not thousands, of expectations parents try to impose. Kids need to learn to say please, wait for their turn, and resist their impulse to throw a fit when they don't get their way. Most parents push these social expectations upon their kids as soon as possible because they know that their children's ability to meet these expectations will be critical to their children being seen as a team player and a valued group member.

This battle between parents trying to build the children's Superego and kids who would prefer to indulge their Id can be awkward at times in all families, but some families are more awkward than others. We will see that awkward children present some unique challenges to parents because they have hyperactive Ids, or supercharged Superegos, or both, which leaves these children's Egos overwhelmed by a world that feels very intense. Despite these challenges, the underlying story line in awkward families is the same as that of any other family: parents are searching for a way to help their children pursue their natural interests while also giving their kids the structure necessary to play well with others.

The Pleasure in Being Awkward

BEFORE I LEARNED about Mr. Z's childhood, I had felt my resentment growing with every passing detention. I began to notice little things about him that annoyed me and that I took as further evidence that he was worthy of nemesis status. I seethed while he solved chemistry problems on the chalkboard because he could not help but grin in a way that suggested he was delighted by doing the work. Smiling! I couldn't believe that someone would take pleasure in such a torturous endeavor.

Before Mr. Z proudly self-proclaimed that he was a nerd, most of us suspected that he was an awkward guy. The dead giveaway was his inability to hide this intrinsic joy he experienced while doing chemistry problems. When awkward people turn their spotlighted attention to their interests, they become fully absorbed. If you catch awkward people while they are unaware that anyone else is watching, while the bookworm reads an engrossing book or a virtuoso practices her violin, you will see the childlike joy of those lost in doing what they love.

When awkward people are fully absorbed in something and it results in high performance, it's a state that psychologist Mihaly Csikszentmihalyi calls *flow*, which is like being "in the zone" or "on fire." A runner in a state of flow flies effortlessly through the twenty-fifth mile as other runners move with a heavy stride, or a ballerina in flow moves through the most difficult parts of her performance with remarkable strength and grace. When athletes or performers get into a state of flow and are asked afterward what was going through their minds, they say, "Nothing." When people are in flow they do not have to think about the mechanics of their craft or devote effortful thought about what they have to do. They act on instinct or impulse.

When most people think of someone who is driven by his impulses, someone with a hyperactive Id, they envision the archetypal rock star who indulges in too much drinking, ill-advised sex, and dangerous drugs. Although some awkward people are at risk for overindulging in these traditional vices, they tend to lean toward different types of nonsocial excesses. They might play video games until their fingers blister, read about mythical creatures until the early morning hours, or tinker obsessively with inventions like the personal computer in their garages.

Just as people with a genetic disposition toward nicotine or alcohol dependence experience more pleasure when they smoke or take a few drinks, awkward people seem to get an unusually strong sense of pleasure from engaging in their nonsocial interests.

This fixation comes with an opportunity cost, which is that they are less likely to pay attention to important social expectations.

For example, all of us know the feeling of having a lot on our minds and how this can distract us from giving people the full attention they deserve. When the awkward child is working on a project or daydreaming about an idea, his impulse is to remain fixated and absorbed on that task or idea. If someone begins a spontaneous conversation during these moments of intense focus, awkward people have trouble shifting gears into social mode. This difficulty means that they are more likely than non-awkward people to continue following their impulse to finish the project or finish their thought. To achieve this, awkward people might subconsciously send social cues that others clearly perceive as signs of disinterest or annoyance. This can leave the well-intentioned person looking to engage in some small talk feeling hurt or offended, and he or she has every right to feel that way.

Caregivers who see their awkward children blow off people in this manner are usually appalled by their behavior and try to correct it, but it's just one of many specific examples of awkward kids having a hard time controlling their impulses. Awkward children's impulses manifest in other unusual ways, whether it's correcting people's grammar or pointing out other shortcomings that are better left unsaid. Awkward kids tend to be overly blunt. They are more likely to see social situations in concrete terms rather than as relational transactions that require letting some things pass or delicate phrasing of sensitive topics. That's why they tell their teenage babysitter that her face has really broken out or tell the pastor at communion that Mommy uses much larger cups to consume her wine. Awkward kids are slower than non-awkward kids to realize that factual comments can be hurtful or get other people in trouble; for them, it's just reporting the facts.

Of course, awkward children cannot expect a free pass to disregard social graces just because social graces do not come naturally to them. The solution for parents is not to ask for special treatment for their awkward child's social missteps. The most helpful thing a parent can do is to let his or her children suffer the natural consequences from their missteps, then explain in concrete terms why an interaction went poorly and provide coaching about how to handle it better in the future. If awkward children do not learn to control their impulses and follow important social expectations, then they will likely pay a significant social price as they get older. Caregivers faced with helping their awkward children develop a less porous mental filter have to sell them on the notion that they need to follow seemingly arbitrary societal expectations and refrain from saying or doing things that others perceive as overly blunt or harsh.

During moments of frustration, caregivers have an impulse to admonish their awkward child: "Control yourself!" But they have to be careful what they wish for.

A Supercharged Superego

MR. Z HAD an unusual number of classroom rules that were strictly enforced. You had to staple your papers at a 45-degree angle because that ensured neatly folding pages. Your book needed to be open to the proper page before class started because he did not want to hear the "grating sound" of papers rustling during class. You were not to lean your head against the back wall because he didn't want another head lice outbreak like the one in '89. These precise rules along with many others were enforced with a military-like vigilance that struck many of us as odd.

Mr. Z also imposed a number of strict rules upon himself. The few times I saw Mr. Z in less formal settings, once at a baseball game on a hot afternoon, another time at the grocery store on a Saturday, he was always wearing the same thing: sweater-vest, pressed shirt, and polished brown shoes. Every morning, Mr. Z arrived at school precisely two and one-half hours before the first bell, to push through his regimented triathlon training, which he meticulously tracked in a graph-papered notebook. When he solved chemistry problems at the chalkboard, he was precise with every step, and took care to show each operation on separate lines, even though he probably knew the answer just by glancing at the problem.

The rule I consistently broke in Mr. Z's classroom, which bothered him more than rustling papers or papers not stapled at 45 degrees, was my stubborn refusal to show all the steps of my work. I didn't see the point in showing every step because I thought the final answer was all that mattered. I have to admit that if I had been less stubborn and took a few extra minutes to do each step of my homework problems, I would have spent a lot less time after school working on problems that had been marked down for "vague process." A few years later, when I became a professor and began grading students' papers, I realized that Mr. Z had to grade every step, of every homework problem, for every student in the class. It must have been an extraordinarily tedious task and I wondered, "What kind of person would impose that kind of task upon himself?"

Awkward people love rules and systems. Their routines are usually built around specific times, locations, and meticulously defined methods. Although most people have a preference for their daily routines, awkward people are unusually precise and inflexible about their own. Try to interrupt or change a few details about an awkward person's routine and you will see someone who has become extremely agitated and uncomfortable. When awkward individuals cannot rely upon their routines, they are like smokers who have run out of smokes.

Freud may have observed that awkward people are inflexible about their routines because they are anal-retentive, but I think that is an overly pessimistic view. Awkward people's routines and rules can be a positive quality in the right contexts. For example, many awkward people thrive in fields that require systematic procedures and persistent pursuit of repetitive tasks that would quickly bore most people. With the requisite talent, awkward individuals' methodical nature can be especially helpful in fields like computer science, finance, and chemistry, in which rigorous adherence to a set of rules and systems is essential to mastery and avoiding costly errors. Mr. Z understood his systematic nature and it helped him channel his impulsive energy through well-thought-out routines and mental rules, which was an adaptive skill he applied to everything in life and that helped him succeed as a great student, military officer, engineer, and chemistry teacher.

Instead of thinking about awkward individuals' obsession with routines as a neurosis, a more helpful perspective is that this obsession comes from their strong tendency to look for rules that govern systems. This love for linear order and logical rules is what Professor Baron-Cohen calls *systemizing*. It's the mental process of looking for what is predictable in a situation and establishing rules about how things work. In the simplest form, these rules follow the script, "If A occurs, then B will occur." When you understand awkward individuals' systemizing nature, then their interests and the pleasure they derive from their interests make more sense. "If I run 5.5 miles today, then tomorrow I will run 6.0 miles"; "If I press 1–1–1 on the microwave instead of 1–0–0, then I can be more efficient about programming the cooking time": these might not sound like immensely pleasurable thoughts to the non-awkward person, but to the awkward person this kind of systematic ordering feels strangely gratifying.

Although systemizing can help an awkward person persist through triathlon training or save him 1.5 seconds when he programs the microwave, highly systematic thinking is not as well matched to figuring out phenomena that are less systematic and predictable. When awkward people's minds work in highly systematic ways, what one might call hyper-systemization, then it can be difficult for them to deal with situations that are not easily corralled with linear rules. To people with a hyper-systemizing view of the world, there are few things more variable than other human beings and seemingly less systematic than social interactions. Why do people eat something loud like popcorn in movie theaters, where people are trying to listen to a dialogue-driven movie? Why do people fall in love with partners who treat them poorly? Why do people tell each other "sweet dreams" if people cannot control their dreams? These are the types of situations that flummox the awkward person's systemizing mind.

Awkward people have a harder time seeing the systematic patterns in social information and for that reason, social situations can feel like a hot, unpredictable mess. But the reality is that common social situations follow relatively predictable scripts. Cognitive psychologists like Mark Baldwin at McGill University and others have found that people develop "if-then" scripts in their minds to make sense of social information. Some of these scripts are situational, such as, "If you are a man, then you should not lecture women about how to conduct their lives," or "If you are a man on the subway, then you should not indulge your impulse to spread yourself out across two seats." When people follow these socially accepted "if-then" scripts, it prevents them from engaging in socially undesirable mansplaining or manspreading.

"If-then" scripts operate outside of our conscious awareness, like lines of code operating in the background of a website, which is why awkward people have a hard time picking up on these scripts. Society assumes that everyone will figure out the "if-then" code running in the background of social interactions, but this is not a sound assumption with awkward people. After awkward people violate a social script, you might hear them say, "But no one even told me!" It's not an excuse, it's genuine exasperation about all of the hidden "if-then" scripts that no one has taught the awkward person to recognize. Socially fluent children naturally pick up thousands of these scripts through social observation, but awkward children usually need more direct instruction to do so.

If awkward people are willing to memorize social scripts and have some flexibility about how they and others execute these scripts, then they can navigate a number of routine social situations with far more ease. Both awkward and socially fluent children thrive when they have a routine to follow and parents consistently and fairly enforce the rules embedded in those routines. Well-functioning families look like well-oiled organizations in which each team member knows his role, trusts that everyone will fulfill their roles, and that these actions will coalesce into a well-coordinated effort. Families who have clearly defined and enforced routines are able to get to school on time, clean up after dinner with little conflict, or readily jump to support each other during times of need. A myriad of self-help books about parenting offer all kinds of conflicting advice, but one of the robust findings across decades of developmental psychology research is that children raised with firm, consistent enforcement of reasonable expectations are those most likely to become centered, healthy adults.

Of course, parents' ability to get their families running like well-oiled machines is easier said than done. Even high-functioning families go through consistent growing pains and conflicts, whether it's a parent badgering a child who has a hard time getting up in the morning or a parent who has to explain why dishes cannot wait to be done until tomorrow. This battle of wills can be particularly intense when awkward children are as stubborn as their biological parents, who share some of the same genetic dispositions.

Parents of awkward kids need to convince them that the *process* of social interactions matters, that taking the time to make subtle gestures and statements accumulates into something that adds important value to social relationships. Parents need to calmly show empathy about their awkward children's tendency to become overwhelmed by social situations and find ways to coach their reluctant children about social scripts that help them fit in seamlessly to social situations. For parents hoping to raise children who end up being well liked and respected, they are faced with a painstaking process of making their children show their work in every social situation.

Helping Awkward Kids Build Social Fundamentals

ONE OF MY vivid memories from childhood was a recurring incident that begins in the Wendy's parking lot. My parents would park our station wagon, turn to the backseat where I sat, and one of them would say, "Let's get mentally prepared." Maybe it owes to my father's military background, but these mental preparation drills of my childhood had the feeling of a sergeant's remedial efforts with a soldier who has trouble marching in step. My parents' series of well-orchestrated questions led to Socratic dialogues about how I would engage with others.

These mental preparation drills took place in parking lots all around the city and in the privacy of our home before going to a restaurant, the grocery store, a birthday party, or a church event. The drills would go on for as long as needed, which on one of my bad days meant that we could be in the car for ten minutes trying to prepare for a two-minute interaction with a cashier. My parents wanted to make common social situations, like ordering at a restaurant or riding public transportation, become second nature to me through deliberate practice. These drills might sound pedantic, and at the time I was certainly not an enthusiastic participant in these Socratic dialogues, but as a socially awkward kid I needed this level of detailed instruction. I'm sure my parents disliked these mental preparation drills as much as I did, but they

PARENTS' QUESTIONS	MY ANSWERS
Why are we at Wendy's?	To eat.
Where should we go when we enter?	I should find the back of the line.
What will you do at the front of the line?	Order something.
How should you prepare to order?	Decide what to order, get my money ready.
How do you speak to the cashier?	Eye contact. Project my voice. Say please.
What do you say when you're done ordering?	Pay. Wait to hold out my hand for change. Say thank you.
Where do you stand after you order?	Move to the side so others can order.

Table 6.1 Mental preparation before entering a Wendy's

saw them as necessary exercises to help me learn the unspoken rules of engagement, and ultimately they were right.

My parents' strategy to help me navigate the social world was to turn my spotlighted attention on three social cues at a time. That's how they came up with the "big three" that I discussed earlier, and they framed these social expectations as "if-then" statements: "If we are at Wendy's, then we are here to eat," and "If we are here to eat, then we need to figure out what to order," and "If we are going to order, then we should get our money ready to pay." The "if" referred to the social expectation and the "then" referred to the behavior I needed to execute. I would walk toward the door at Wendy's while silently rehearsing the big three in my mind: "Back of the line, decide on an order, prepare your money." Once my money was in my hand, then another script of three behaviors would kick in: "Eye contact, project voice, say please."

I began to see that these chunks of three social behaviors linked together into bigger systems, such as the system for ordering at a restaurant, and I eventually generalized these systems to navigate interactions at the movie counter or ticket office at the ballpark. I began to see why saying please or thank you in all of these situations communicated things like politeness and respect, which were essential to smooth interactions. These insights might sound like common sense to non-awkward people or like extremely straightforward, easy situations to navigate, but they were entirely nonintuitive to me.

With time and persistent effort, I began to build social proficiency as I learned to anticipate the social rules required to navigate common social situations. Eventually, my confidence to engage in these common interactions reduced my social anxiety about upcoming interactions and made me come across as calmer and more confident in the interactions. When I was able to automate the first few steps in an interaction, it freed my mental resources to handle unexpected wrinkles in social scripts and created opportunities for me to add social accoutrements such as compliments or a humorous comment.

If parents present social expectations in "if-then" language for their awkward children, they capitalize on their children's systemizing nature. As awkward children begin to master individual "if-then" statements, they begin to connect expectations and see the benefits of following those rules that string together into social scripts. When parents get their awkward kids to the point that they start to see how systematic execution of social scripts can produce tangible results, such as people responding in a friendlier manner or wanting to talk to them for longer, then these kids might reach an inflection point where they become naturally motivated to learn the rules of social engagement on their own.

Although this social-skill coaching can be extremely valuable to awkward individuals, I have observed that it is rarely practiced.

It's difficult for parents to get a kid to pay attention to social graces that are not interesting to the child and are frustrating to understand. But I also wonder if some parents might feel self-conscious, that having to engage in this remedial social-skill coaching means there is something wrong with their kid or that their parenting has been subpar. In the age of the Pinterest-Perfect Parent, there is so much pressure for parents to keep up appearances that they are cruising through the arduous task of raising their children. As my parents watched other kids seamlessly pour their own milk or confidently place their order at a restaurant, it's understandable if they felt a little self-conscious about coaching remedial social skills to their own kids.

It is important that parents do not feel embarrassed about their need to coach their awkward kids because the kids will pick up on that hesitancy in a heartbeat. Mentally preparing kids for social interactions is no different from the parents next door having to give extra help to a child who is slow to read or who struggles with math. When parents try to gloss over their awkward children's rough social edges, they lose an opportunity to make meaningful change by coaching them in concrete skills that actually make a difference in their ability to smoothly navigate social situations and form meaningful ties.

Personality psychologists have a perspective that is helpful for parents who worry about their awkward children's unusual dispositions, which is that most personality traits are not uniformly good or bad. Awkward children's obsessive focus or routines may be challenges in some contexts, but strengths in others. A kid who seems distractible may see unusual things that lead to creativity in certain contexts, or a kid who is stubborn will look determined in other contexts. But awkward kids have to bump around more than other kids to figure out how their own minds work and to find an outlet for their unusual interests. When things go well for awkward kids, they grow up to be focused, determined, disciplined, and able to communicate their unique views of the world.

I fought against the mental preparation drills my parents imposed on me, but their stubborn commitment to give me a systematic way to develop concrete skills allowed me to persist in showing other people that I was considerate and thoughtful. They also modeled these skills themselves. This was important, because parents need not only to instill a core set of pro-social values in their children, they also need to model the specific behaviors that communicate pro-social intent to help their children become adults who are fair and thoughtful.

NEGATIVE MANIFESTATION	AWKWARD TRAIT	POSITIVE MANIFESTATION
Asocial	Narrow interests	Focused
Low empathy	Nonsocial focus	Notice unusual details
Compulsive	Obsessive interests	Determined
Rigid	Need for sameness	Disciplined

Table 6.2 Negative and positive manifestations of awkward traits

Bake a Second Batch

WHILE MR. Z was bouncing between orphanages and foster homes during his childhood, there must have been little in the way of predictability and stable routine. For a kid who was probably genetically disposed toward needing routines more than the average child, this must have been a particularly unnerving way to grow up. One day during a chemistry detention, I asked Mr. Z why he loved chemistry so much. He took a pause and then showed a rare moment of vulnerability as he told me the story of his adoptive parents.

I could see the profound respect and deep gratitude he had for his parents as he told his story. His parents were stern but fair and thoughtful caretakers who channeled his rebellious energy through clear expectations and redirected his active mind into the sciences. When Mr. Z fondly recalled the structure his parents gave him and their support for his passionate interests, I realized it must have been like oxygen for a boy who had been underwater for too long. Not all teens are so enthralled with their parents' discussions about work matters, but for Mr. Z, the topic fit perfectly with his scientific interests. He eventually began to see how his parents' systematic approach to scientific matters also informed their approach to social propriety: how they wrote thank-you notes if they received a kind gesture or followed up with a phone call if they heard about friends who were facing a challenging or joyous life event.

Chemistry is a precise science. Mr. Z loved the idea that if you did your part by following the necessary steps to solve a chemistry problem, then you would get a predictable outcome. One had to be precise with each step of the process because small mistakes would yield an unpredictable solution. After our conversation, I realized that science and the systematic thought embedded in the discipline had been a life raft for a kid who had spent his childhood struggling to stay afloat.

Not all awkward kids face these kinds of extraordinary circumstances, but Mr. Z's family life illuminates what awkward kids need from their own families. His parents did not try to reduce his impulses or energy, but rather thought about channeling his energy into generative outlets. They laid out clear expectations, gave him a sound rationale for their rules and routines, and they were fair about enforcing these expectations. Science was one outlet that they provided, but they also expected that he be open-minded about other subjects, and they wanted him to be active in at least one extracurricular activity of his choice.

Freud generally thought that people's traits were baked into place by late adolescence. This deterministic view that pervaded psychotherapy throughout much of the twentieth century motivated parents to try to not mess up their kids for life. But personality researchers now know that the way our traits influence our adult lives is far more nuanced than what Freud suggested. Even though awkwardness shows heritability, its manifestations across a life-span as strengths or weaknesses rely heavily on environmental influences. It is kind of like those reality television shows about cooking competitions: participants are given a set of ingredients they have to use in a dish, but they are also given discretion about the other ingredients they use and the method to create their dish.

For most people, their personality traits will stabilize around late adolescence, but there are exceptions to this rule. Some people become more talkative or reclusive as they age, while others become more pleasant or unpleasant. Researchers are still investigating why these changes occur, but many personality psychologists suggest that influential relationships are one of the most likely candidates for why some people's traits improve or worsen over time. Although we may appear "baked" into a way of being at any point in time, the people we encounter with every new school year, new job, or new social interaction represent a chance to remix our psychological ingredients and to bake a better version of ourselves.

For Mr. Z, the influence of his adoptive parents was the inflection point in his life trajectory. They did not simply impose their way of living on him, but instead were thoughtful about who he was and collaborated with him to build a set of routines and expectations that worked with his characteristics. Throughout his lifetime, Mr. Z remained high energy, relatively rigid about certain routines, and a little awkward in social situations that fell outside of his normal daily routine. But he had learned how to channel his personality and abilities into outlets that amplified the positive impact of his natural disposition. Mr. Z was not what you would have called charismatic or comfortable in all social situations, but his commitment to being thoughtful about how he interacted with other people made him one of those teachers kids deeply respected and eventually grew to like.

I never became an A chemistry student, but I did get much better and, more importantly, I eventually understood the deeper lesson Mr. Z was trying to get into my stubborn head. He wanted me to understand that process is important, that people want you to show your work in both scientific and social matters. Mr. Z had picked up on my unusually high energy and saw that when it went unbridled I became distractible and careless. In social situations, my intense energy sometimes caused people to wince, and he saw that would be costly for me if I couldn't find a way to contextualize it for people.

As a kid, I was so focused on outcomes that I skipped niceties such as saying hello or taking the time to ask people how they were doing, which are critical steps in achieving the correct social outcomes. Other times, I would decide to leave a social situation or abruptly shift to a new topic of conversation without explaining my thought process leading up to those decisions. This non-contextualized behavior understandably gave people the impression that I was bored or disinterested in their company, when in fact I had simply failed to communicate the innocuous reasons for my social actions.

Mr. Z taught me to trust the process and procedures in chemistry. If you learn to trust your ability to make the right moves at each step of the process, then eventually you discover that the basic elements with which you started produce new solutions. But if people become impetuous or falter in their confidence to execute each step, then they end up jumping to unreliable conclusions. In this way, the act of doing chemistry is a practice of faith. You need to have faith in your ability to execute each step, be willing to let others see those steps, and have trust that the order of operations will reveal a solution which may be different from the constituent elements. For awkward people, social life relies on this same kind of faith. Until they gain experience repeatedly seeing how eye contact, mirroring others' postures, and a pleasant vocal tone add up to abstractions such as a good first impression, they need to have faith that their attention to social details will produce a social compound that is greater than the sum of its parts.

I say that I am awkward by nature but socially proficient by nurture. My parents and mentors like Mr. Z found a way to install a customized software in my mind that allowed me to use my unusual mental hardware to find work-arounds to most social situations. When it comes to any awkward child, the trick for parents and teachers is to provide a clear system of expectations and a framework for how those "if-then" rules link to the broader values of the household or class. For parents, this is particularly important while preparing children for modern social life because in the midst of a fast-changing technology and information age, it's harder than ever to find answers about how to behave in a well-mannered way.

7

THE AWKWARDNESS OF MAKING FRIENDS

Brock had never picked up a tennis racket in his life, but Coach Martinez saw the raw elements of a great player. As a speedy point guard for the basketball team and a scrappy shortstop for the baseball team, Brock had shown tremendous athleticism, but also an exceptional level of grit and mental toughness. These latter qualities had inspired Coach Martinez to recruit Brock for his varsity tennis team, which could use a good dose of mental toughness.

On the first day of practice, most of us wore white, five-inch-inseam shorts and white tennis shoes, which was not a style of dress that made Brock comfortable. He wore baggy basketball shorts and black high-tops that left long scuff marks on the court. He swung with both hands on his forehand and backhand, and his swing started with his fists swirling around by his back shoulder, like a batter getting ready to crank out a fastball. Brock's personality was also rough around the edges. He played with an intense scowl and cursed in creative ways that astonished the country club crowd. While Brock did not look the part of the archetypical tennis player, he could sure play the game of tennis. No one had ever seen someone move so recklessly on a court, dive for so many shots, and hit the ball with such fury.

After the first week of practice, Coach Martinez decided that Brock and I would be paired as doubles partners. I am pretty sure Brock threw his head backward and rolled his eyes when he heard this announcement; I was not exactly a vision of mental toughness and athleticism. I also had some trepidation about his intense personality and wondered whether we would find common ground.

I was intrigued that Brock was so unapproachable at practice, but well-liked among everyone who had known him through grade school and middle school. He rolled with the popular crowd, but he didn't seem to care about any of the artifice involved with achieving or maintaining popularity. Cool clothes and cool cars were of little interest to Brock; he preferred to focus his efforts on his academics. He met few of the social expectations that were usually applied to people in his social group, and his intense focus on his schoolwork rivaled that of the nerdiest kids at school, which meant that Brock should have technically been classified as a nerd or socially awkward. Yet if you asked anybody at school what they thought of Brock, they would have said, "He's a really cool dude."

During the second week of practice, I had an off scrimmage. A few bad shots turned into a few more bad shots and eventually I couldn't do anything right. I was choking under the pressure. Eventually, Coach Martinez sent me to run laps around the track while the rest of the team finished practice. It was a smart move on his part because it stopped me from doing further damage to my eroding self-confidence, but I felt like I had embarrassed myself. No one else on the team had practiced badly enough to be exiled to the track.

After Coach dismissed the rest of the team, he forgot that I was running laps at the track until he was in his car driving home. He drove down to the track and found me staggering around the bend and apologetically told me that I could stop now. He gave me a few encouraging words and told me tomorrow was a new day. It was a long, contemplative walk back to the locker room, but when I ascended the hill from the track I saw Brock waiting by the gate of the tennis courts with a bucket of tennis balls. In a matter-of-fact tone he said, "Hey, partner, let's hit a little more."

Among teenage boys there is a primal survival-of-the-fittest mentality that even crops up in the cushy confines of the suburbs. Boys have an aversion to aligning themselves with the weakest link in social groups because mere association can threaten one's position in the ever-competitive social hierarchy. Brock was socially proficient enough to understand that I was clearly the weakest link that day, but he was not interested in protecting his social capital. Although he had not chosen to be partnered with me, his family had instilled an ideal in him that dictated his choice in that situation: "If someone is at their lowest point, then that's when you give them the most."

We hit in silence for about forty-five minutes. I started hitting the ball well and eventually I was hitting with confidence. At the end, Brock said, "Stay tough, man, we'll get there," and took off on his brisk run home. In just forty-five minutes, I saw why Brock was universally liked and revered as a "cool guy" among people who knew him well. He had formulated a theory of social life that heavily weighted fairness, kindness, and loyalty, and by doing so he was able to bypass a lot of minor social expectations. Brock didn't have to worry himself with as many social expectations as other likable people because he was able to exert tremendous leverage on his friendships with relatively few actions. It was a valuable lesson for me, and one that is more important than ever in the midst of a social landscape that is undergoing dramatic changes.

How Many Friends Are Enough?

KIDS STARTING THEIR first day at a new school, middle schoolers going away to summer camp, and teens headed off to college all feel anxious about making new friends. It's human nature to worry about fitting in, and many schools and social clubs intentionally create infrastructure to help individuals feel like they belong. Extracurricular activities in schools, group projects, and even bonding activities at camp provide a social infrastructure to facilitate interactions and spark potential friendships. These are worthwhile efforts because students with strong friendships perform better in school, are less likely to drop out, and in the long run are able to learn lifelong lessons about how to build social capital that will be essential to their personal and professional success.

But when people enter adulthood, they are finding social environments that are less structured than those of previous generations, and this has made it challenging for both awkward and non-awkward people to find and navigate new friendships. This is a concerning trend because the importance of friendship does not diminish once people become adults. As John and Stephanie Cacioppo of the University of Chicago point out in their review of social relationship research, people who feel like they have strong friendships sleep better, are far less likely to be depressed, have better cardiovascular health, and live about 26 percent longer than people who are chronically lonely.

Friendships are integral to social life above and beyond the benefits we derive from our families, work colleagues, and romantic partners, but adults are finding that making friends feels a little more awkward and elusive these days. This chapter explores the changing state of modern friendship for both awkward and non-awkward people, and how our social ties have been affected by the demise of traditional social institutions, more diverse expectations, and casual attitudes toward etiquette. I'll also take a brief look at the few studies that have examined social awkwardness and friendship, but there are broad social forces that can make friendship formation feel more awkward for everyone.

The contemporary notion that social life is undergoing dramatic changes was brought to light in the 2000 book *Bowling*

Alone. The author, Robert Putnam, is a professor of public policy at Harvard University, and in *Bowling Alone* he cites evidence from large-scale surveys that suggest there has been a sharp decline in civic participation in the United States since the 1960s, which has corresponded to a growing sense of isolation. Putnam's message that people were finding it harder to belong in society struck an emotional chord and received widespread attention from academics, policy makers, and the general public.

The name of the book came from an illustrative finding that the number of people bowling increased by 10 percent from 1980 to 1993, while participation in bowling leagues declined by 40 percent over the same period. Although some of Putnam's conclusions have been debated, there was strong support for his conclusion that people were leaving traditional institutions such as churches, political parties, and social clubs, which removed structures that once facilitated social connectedness.

In the sixteen years since *Bowling Alone* was published, there have been further participation declines in traditional social institutions. These seismic social shifts have created a new social terrain that remains relatively uncharted, which makes it worthwhile to take a look at how the social changes of the past two decades have influenced the way people find social ties and how they navigate those relationships. If you feel like making friends is more awkward these days, then you might take some comfort in knowing that you are not alone.

To begin our investigation of whether close friends are harder to find, it's interesting to begin with a simple question: How many friends do people have and has that changed over time? Cornelia Wrzus at the Max Planck Institute for Human Development and her colleagues provide some answers to this question from their investigation of 277 different studies about the number of friends and family members people reported across different age groups. Their results suggest that people have the largest social groups from ages ten to twenty-four. The average teenager has about nine friends they interact with on a regular basis, but that shrinks to about seven friends by age thirty, and continues to decline throughout older adulthood. The number of family members people reported seeing on a regular basis was stabler over time, with all age groups reporting regular contact with about seven family members.

If people need about three or four reliable relationships to satiate their need to belong, then the average thirty-year-old with seven friends and seven family members would seem to have plenty of close relationships. But being able to see people on a regular basis is not the same thing as feeling a sense of connection with those people. Although the feeling of connectedness is somewhat related to the total number of friends, it's more strongly influenced by their perceptions that these interactions are gratifying. One interaction that leaves someone feeling understood and supported carries far more psychological weight than ten interactions that fall short of one's expectations. This is why it's common for celebrities who are surrounded by adoring fans or CEOs who are inundated with meetings to often feel painstakingly lonely in the midst of constant social interaction.

The United Kingdom's Mental Health Foundation published a 2010 report that provides some clues about how many people feel lonely. They recruited more than two thousand people across a wide range of age groups and found that 11 percent of respondents reported that they "often" feel lonely, which is notable, but far from epidemic. They found a different pattern when they asked people about other people's loneliness. Thirty-seven percent of respondents said that a close friend or family member was "very lonely" and 48 percent agreed that ". . . people are getting lonelier in general." It's possible that the stigma associated with loneliness led some people to underreport their personal loneliness, but these same participants were more willing to report loneliness when it did not apply to them.

Although these overall rates of loneliness are substantial and concerning, it's interesting that they have actually decreased over the past two to three decades among teens and young adults. Matthew Clark and his colleagues from the University of Queensland analyzed the results of forty-eight studies of loneliness among U.S. college students and found that loneliness scores declined from 1978 to 2009. In a second study, they analyzed data from a representative sample of more than 300,000 high school students and found small but steady declines in loneliness from 1991 to 2012.

Although the general trend was for loneliness to decrease among teens and young adults, Clark and colleagues also discovered a few anomalous findings. From 1991 to 2012, high school students became less likely to report that there was someone they could turn to if they needed help and also were less likely to feel that they could usually get together with friends. These findings echo the results of another study by Miller McPherson at the University of Arizona and his colleagues, who found in a representative sample of more than fourteen hundred U.S. residents that the number of people who said they have no one to talk to about important matters tripled between 1985 to 2004.

Overall, these results about friendship suggest that the average teenagers and adults are satisfied with the number of friends they have and that this quantity is enough to keep them from feeling lonely. But there are indications that not being lonely is not the same thing as being satisfied with one's friendships. Although the size of our social groups has not changed, people may be feeling a diminishing sense of real connection with the friends they do have. Sociologists and psychologists have been intensively studying what accounts for this slowly growing malaise in friendship, and the results of their studies can help us map the new social landscape of friendship and identify where opportunities for friendship reside.

The Demise of Social Institutions

SOCIAL PSYCHOLOGISTS HAVE studied hundreds of possible factors that predict why people become friends. After decades of testing elaborate theories, the answer has repeatedly come down to three factors: proximity, similarity, and reciprocated liking. In other words, we end up being friends with people who are close by, who are similar to us, and who are willing to tell us that they like us. These results might sound like common sense, but many people find that it's challenging to translate these principles into practice.

For most of the twentieth century, social institutions brought people together in churches, offices, or social clubs. People in these groups were more likely to share similar values and interests that were disseminated by their religion, company culture, or social organization. Membership implied that people shared a common affinity with one another and were bound together as brothers, sisters, colleagues, or friends. If people were eligible for inclusion, then members found that these social institutions facilitated proximity, a shared sense of similarity, and literal belonging to a group.

The first major shift in the social landscape began in the 1960s, when people began to lose faith in social institutions and their participation rates plunged. Paul Taylor and his colleagues at the Pew Research Center released a 2014 report that showed the turn away from social institutions has been particularly pronounced among millennials, those born between 1981 to 1996. Taylor and his colleagues found that compared to older adults, millennials were far more likely to identify as political independents, less likely to affiliate with a specific religion, and significantly less likely to enter the institution of marriage by the age of thirty-two.

Some pundits decried millennials' declining participation in traditional institutions as a consequence of their laziness or an erosion of moral virtues, but it's hard to blame millennials for developing some skepticism. For example, they watched big banks' deceptive lending practices nearly collapse the U.S. economic system in 2009, then saw CEOs from these failed institutions collect millions in severance pay while middle-class families with subprime mortgages struggled to stay afloat. They also observed that some religious institutions were slow to reject sexist or homophobic views, which did not sit well with millennials' inclusive attitudes. The wave of highly publicized sexual abuse scandals in the Catholic Church added further damage to the overall perception that religious institutions could be trusted.

Of course, it's unfair to make blanket statements about groups or institutions. There are far more good people than bad apples in

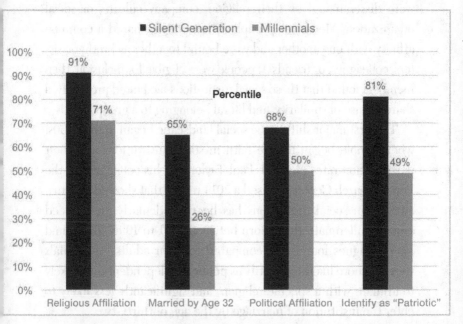

Figure 7.1 Generational difference in institutional participation and attitudes

big corporations and religious institutions, but the actions of a few have had far-reaching consequences. While millennials showed the strongest mistrust and decreased participation in traditional institutions, all generations reported declining institutional trust and participation rates.

When group members were less likely to question their political party's platform, church mandates, or company mission statements, there was less confusion about how members should behave. People were simply expected to act in accordance with their institution's prescribed expectations, which could include things as specific as how to dress, when to speak, and even what to say. Although institutional expectations were relatively easier to understand, the appeal quickly faded once people did not agree with the expectations or simply wanted the freedom to negotiate those expectations. One would be hard-pressed to find many millennials who will gladly join a workplace where they have to follow strict dress codes, speak only when spoken to, and whose default response when spoken to should be "yes, sir" or "right away, sir."

Eventually corporations began to ditch the suits, employees were encouraged to speak their minds, and at some Silicon Valley companies "yes, sir" was replaced with valuing people who were willing to challenge the status quo. Churches replaced staid organs and hymnals with electric guitars and contemporary lyrics. The new pope even posted a few papal selfies with church members. But turning around the culture of a large institution is like trying to turn around a large cruise liner, which has meant that institutions and individuals have been caught in an awkward cultural limbo while everyone tries to figure out how to come together in new ways and with a revised set of standards.

Most people probably prefer this freedom from institutional control, but freedom has a way of provoking anxiety about whether one's personal decisions are socially acceptable. This paradox between society's desire for freedom versus society's desire for imposed standards from institutions is a sociological version of Freud's impulsive Id against the rule-governed Superego. Our societal Ego has been caught in the middle, trying to figure out what it means to "be yourself" while also showing respect for a set of societal standards that seem to be constantly on the move.

The other major shift in the social landscape has been the relatively rapid transition to more inclusionary views about diversity. Although millennials have led the way, all age groups are more likely to be open to people of different races, sexual orientations, and more likely to support gender equity. When the Pew Research Center asked randomly sampled adults whether teachers should be fired for being gay, 51 percent agreed in 1987, but by 2007 the agreement rate dropped to 28 percent. Overall support for gay marriage rose over the past decade from 35 percent to 55 percent.

Pew also reported that racial attitudes have also shifted toward more inclusionary views. When white respondents were asked whether "our country needed to continue making changes to give blacks equal rights with whites," 36 percent agreed with the statement in 2009, but agreement rose to 53 percent just six years later in a 2015 poll. When Pew asked respondents whether they agreed that "it is all right for blacks and whites to date each other," 48 percent of respondents agreed in 1985, and by 2010 the rate of agreement jumped to 83 percent.

These shifts toward more inclusionary societal attitudes have occurred alongside rapid demographic changes, including the racial composition of the United States and the gender composition of the workforce. For example, the U.S. population was 15 percent nonwhite in 1960 and 36 percent nonwhite by 2010, the percentage of interracial marriages more than doubled from 7 percent in 1980 to 15 percent in 2010, and women's labor force participation rose from 44 percent in 1970 to 57 percent by 2012.

Some people see this increased willingness to embrace diversity and opportunities for marginalized groups as signs of cultural erosion while others see these shifts as clear signs of cultural progress. I am one of those who strongly believes these social changes, particularly more inclusionary attitudes toward traditionally marginalized groups, have been positive and long overdue. I think it's important to make clear that I hold a supportive view of these changes because I would also suggest that these societal shifts have come with some societal growing pains. These significant shifts in the social landscape have created a post-institutional social world where traditional expectations have faded away and new expectations have yet to be clearly defined. It's all right to admit that social progress comes with a little confusion about what to do next.

Many people are also discovering how much work it takes to truly embrace diversity. It's one thing for people to say that they support racial diversity, gender equality, or gay marriage, but being fully open to negotiating different attitudes and expectations takes a tremendous amount of social awareness and effort.

Anyone who has immersed herself in an unfamiliar culture knows how hard it is to learn about hundreds of new social expectations and how easy it is to say something awkward. Even politicians with cadres of aides who specialize in foreign relations can find themselves in some awkward cross-cultural moments. There was the time Richard Nixon flashed the "A-OK" gesture upon his arrival in Brazil, which was essentially like flashing everyone the middle finger by Brazilian standards. Howard Dean inadvertently let out a bobcat-like scream while delivering a speech after the 2004 Iowa caucuses and he became one of the first public figures to experience their awkward moment going viral on social media. President George W. Bush was notorious for misspoken phrases while abroad, including the time he thanked Australian premier John Howard for the Austrian troops in Iraq.

Curt Clawson, a freshman congressional representative from Florida, found out that you don't have to travel overseas to experience an awkward multicultural moment. During a hearing

with the House Foreign Affairs Committee, Representative Clawson and the other committee members were introduced to two
U.S. senior officials, Nisha Biswal from the State Department
and Arun Kumar from the Commerce Department. Representative Clawson, who is white, must have missed this key social
cue because he proceeded to address Biswal and Kumar, who are
American-Indian, with well-intentioned phrases such as, "I'm familiar with your country; I love your country," and "Anything I
can do to make the relationship with India better, I'm willing and
enthusiastic about doing so." When Representative Clawson asked
for the cooperation of the Indian government, Biswal gracefully
replied, "I think your question is to the Indian government. We
certainly share your sentiment and we certainly will advocate that
on behalf of the U.S."

It's easy to see how well-intentioned people could misunderstand or mishandle minor social expectations when they are unfamiliar with people from diverse cultures. Although it can be
uncomfortable when expectations between people are less certain,
these growing pains produce people who are more open-minded
and enlightened. During the process of people reaching a mutual understanding about how to interact or even how to become
friends, they need to be open about learning new expectations,
but it is also imperative that minor missteps are met with grace
rather than indignation.

The real work of embracing diversity will be easier if people
look toward the intent behind actions instead of reflexively acting
offended by what they perceive as someone's ignorance. Representative Clawson's awkward moment was probably not his finest,
but he sounded like someone trying to convey respect and a cooperative spirit, even if his read of the interaction was off from the
start. Biswal could have said that she was offended, but it seems to
me that much more was achieved with her graceful reply. In fact,
it may be our decency and social graces that are our best bet for

navigating the uncharted social landscape ahead of us. Manners and etiquette can provide solid footing when you are unsure of other people's expectations.

Never Mind My P's and Q's

SOMETHING UNEXPECTED BEGAN to happen as these societal shifts occurred, which was that teenagers began to actively search for people who could teach them manners. While Boomers and Gen X teens rolled their eyes at parents who tried to impose social graces, millennials appear hungry for some guidance about how to handle common social situations. During the past few decades, people have also begun to take a more casual approach toward manners, and somewhere along the way some caregivers forgot to teach their kids how to tie a tie, which fork to use at a nice restaurant, or what to bring to a dinner party. While this casualness works at home, adolescents begin to encounter situations where they find themselves poorly prepared to engage in appropriate behavior and that can lead to some awkward moments.

In a 2013 *New York Times* article, Alex Williams reported about a curious case of millennials and manners. Williams found a viral genre of YouTube videos that were how-to tutorials about manners, and discovered that millennials were the demographic most interested in viewing these videos. If you search on YouTube you will find hundreds of manners videos that include how to punctuate a business-related email, what to do when you fart in a crowded yoga class, and how to use appropriate table manners. There has also been a surge in companies who pay manners consultants to teach their young-adult employees about proper business etiquette and a renewed demand for books about social etiquette.

One of my favorite books about manners is Amy Alkon's *Good Manners for Nice People Who Sometimes Say F°ck*. It's a modern guide for people who want some advice about modern conundrums such as whether it's all right to leave a voice mail or how to politely deal with people talking loudly on their cell phones at a quiet coffee shop. Alkon provides a number of tips about how to manage specific social expectations that are newly created due to technology or casual attitudes, but even more useful is what she says about why we use manners in the first place. Her core message is that good manners are important because they are a mechanism for showing other people empathy and respect.

For example, when you go outside to take a phone call you convey to the other people that you respect their work and privacy. When you leave a text instead of a voice mail it's a subtle convenience that says you value someone's time. Most manners are actions that convey your understanding and respect of what other people value and that you are invested in people getting what they need. Some awkward people tend to view manners as nuisances or pointless routines, but manners are important social signals while unacquainted individuals form impressions about each other. When people are perceived as ill-mannered, people can assume that they are unlikely to be cooperative and fair in a friendship or social group.

Manners are like the secret code word or secret handshake to gain provisional entry to the clubhouse. Once inside, there are certainly other expectations to be managed, but manners can be enough to get your foot in the door and generate some positive momentum. When people are well-mannered, it suggests they share the social values or morals of the group. Jonathan Haidt, a leading morality researcher, suggests that "morality binds and builds" people together. Haidt finds that people make split-second judgments about other people's moral behavior or moral character based on intuitive reactions to whether people meet or deviate from social expectations.

Most manners are related to five broad categories of morality, which in plain terms are: do no harm, be fair, support your friends or group, respect authority, and don't be gross. With these categories in mind, it's easier to see the rationale behind various social expectations. For example, when people gossip negatively about someone, the commiseration with others may forge a temporary bond, but gossip also sends an unspoken signal that they are willing to harm another person's reputation among group members and threaten the integrity of the group.

When people show up on schedule, dress appropriately for an event, or bring flowers to a friend's recital, they can usually count on these behaviors meeting expectations and know that the behaviors convey respect for other people. This premeditated effort shows other people that you are thoughtful and willing to act in ways that support and facilitate the efforts of other people, which is the kind of message that is particularly helpful for awkward people to send.

Manners provide a way for awkward people to anticipate some of the early moves in an interaction and the systematic nature of social graces are well-suited to their structured style of thought. This makes manners a promising foothold, but for awkward people to gain mastery over these subtle rules of social engagement, they need to make concerted efforts to shift their attention.

Making Friends While Awkward

MANNERS ARE SUBTLE and usually fall outside of awkward people's spotlighted attention. Awkward people are less likely to attend to fashion rules, table manners, or the caveats necessary to temper the bluntness of their comments. In some situations, awkward people may consciously disregard etiquette or niceties because they see them as impediments to achieving a more important outcome. But in many instances awkward individuals are genuinely unaware about proper etiquette or are unsure about why their behavior was perceived by others as rude. This has a way of getting

MORAL CATEGORIES	MANNERS RELATED TO EACH MORAL CATEGORY
Do no harm	Don't bully, don't publicly call out a mistake.
Be fair	Share, take turns doing favors, don't cheat.
Support your group	Don't gossip, celebrate people's successes.
Respect authority	Be on time, dress appropriately, respect tradition.
Don't be gross	Shower, chew with mouth closed, don't groom in public.

Table 7.1 Five categories of moral behavior and examples of manners that show compliance with those moral expectations

awkward people off on the wrong foot with new acquaintances because the early social expectations are put into question, which can distract from awkward individuals' good qualities such as a fair or kind attitude.

From the few studies available about awkward people's friendships, the results generally suggest that awkward people have a harder time making and maintaining friendships in childhood and early adulthood. In one study of awkward individuals' friendships, Lisa Jobe and Susan Williams White at Virginia Commonwealth University surveyed a group of university students to investigate whether awkward individuals were any different from non-awkward individuals regarding close friendships and loneliness. Jobe and White found that the length of awkward participants' close friendships was significantly shorter (4.5 years) than those of non-awkward participants (8 years), which suggests that it takes longer for awkward individuals to form close friendships, sustain them, or a little bit of both. They also found that participants' degree of social awkwardness was strongly associated with higher degrees of loneliness, which was explained by their difficulty understanding social situations and social skill deficits.

The good news for awkward people is that manners are like most social scripts and follow "if-then" rules that can be applied to common social situations. If a friend makes dinner for you, then you should offer to bring something and offer to help clean up. If you are a woman going to a wedding, then you should not wear white. Being well-mannered provides a relatively unambiguous way to navigate the early stages of social interactions, which are usually the parts that are toughest for awkward people. Unlike the challenge to be charismatic or funny, manners are predicated upon predictable rules that can be studied and rehearsed in between social interactions.

For awkward people, the study of etiquette provides a structured way to improve their social skills, but more importantly, to think ahead about what will be fair or kind in a situation. If awkward individuals turn their natural preference for routine and systems to the task of mastering etiquette, then they gain a method for anticipating the early stages of an interaction that might alert them to questions about how to handle those expectations. Etiquette decreases the proportion of unpredictability in social situations, which allows awkward people to focus on actually being in the moment and frees mental resources to better improvise the unpredictable aspects that eventually occur in most social interactions.

Some manners are antiquated or vary across different subcultures, so people want to find the sweet spot between considerate versus overdone. Anthropologist Frank Boas captured this notion well when he wrote, ". . . what constitutes courtesy, modesty, very good manners, and definite ethical standards is not universal." You may encounter awkward people whose awkwardness owes partly to their rigid application of formal behavior when the expectation is to be casual. They may show up to beach parties in overly formal attire or use phrases that sound like they came from the 1950s. Sometimes you discover that they use those phrases because they actually picked up a book about manners without considering the publication date and that some of the advice might be outdated.

Perhaps the biggest omission from manuals about manners published even fifteen years ago would be how to handle online socialization. Email, social media, and other online platforms have made social interaction through our cell phones and computers ubiquitous. This ever-emerging way of socializing has come with a new set of expectations to learn and has created some confusion about how to merge what others expect of us in real life and online. But online socializing has also opened up new opportunities for awkward people to connect with those who share their unique and passionate interests.

In 2011, there were 372 million monthly users on Facebook, and by 2015 that number grew to over one billion daily users. Over one-third of the world is on Facebook and about half of millennials check their Facebook page as soon as they wake up. Although people sometimes lament our reliance upon social media, many of us cannot help but pull up the latest Facebook, Twitter, Instagram, or Snapchat post for fear of missing out. Social media has made an unprecedented amount of social information available, which can feel like a lot for someone who has a hard time sorting out which information is relevant and difficulty knowing exactly how to respond.

The primary complication with online socialization is that many of the social cues humans have relied on for thousands of years are absent online. It's commonplace for us to wonder exactly what people are trying to tell us when a message is delivered online versus face-to-face. You may have wondered whether you did something wrong when a friend who always ends her text messages with "!!!" suddenly decides to end a message with a period. At work you may have wondered whether your boss wrote a word in caps for EMPHASIS or to express that he is feeling PISSED. Justin Kruger at New York University and his colleagues found that when people were asked to discern whether someone else was being serious or sarcastic in email messages versus spoken communications, participants correctly differentiated serious versus sarcastic intent only 56 percent of the time when the message was sent through email, but correctly differentiated intent 73 percent of the time when messages were spoken. There is nothing wrong with the evolution of social networks, but like any new frontier there are clearly unknowns about how to best use this medium for socializing with others.

But the Internet has also been a boon for awkward people who felt passionate about interests that were less common before widespread social media. Gaming, comics, and other interests were once considered fringe and people could have difficulty finding others with like-minded interests and passion for them. For example, kids in rural areas who wanted to learn about filmmaking or how to code were hard-pressed to find world-class advice or supportive communities, but online communities allow people to gather troves of information and make connections with others. When one's Internet life is working well it can be a place of affirmation and spark feelings of connection. Some awkward individuals find initial meetings more comfortable online because they do not have to deal with the social cues, such as nonverbal cues, vocal cues, and facial expressions. When these social cues are removed for everyone, it can actually simplify interactions for awkward people because there is less social information that needs to be processed.

But online mediums are not enough to satisfy our need to belong. Most people need to get face-to-face with their friends to feel truly connected and like they have found a place to belong. The emerging research regarding online socialization suggests that online mediums work best as catalysts for getting face-to-face with people or as supplements for people who have gratifying in-person interactions with friends. The best practice is to use online communication to get things going or augment ongoing friendships, but to turn off the devices used for online communication once you get face-to-face with someone. Although online socialization has been a great way for awkward people to find new friendships, online interactions have a set of expectations that need to be learned and followed.

Once we open a text, email, or go on social media we are faced with a relatively vague set of social expectations that are not yet clearly established and tend to vary among different platforms. For example, a stream-of-consciousness post is permissible on Twitter but annoying on Facebook; the oven mitts you want to buy are good to post on Pinterest, but not so fun on Instagram; and the bikini selfie from the foam party in Cancun is great for Instagram, but potentially career ending on LinkedIn. In the early years, Facebook users needed a few years to realize that posting about their household chores, check-in at the gym, or daily commute was not the kind of social information other people in the online community really wanted to know. Instagram came along as a different social media context with different expectations: it was all right to share a picture of the healthy dinner you made (#nom), your abs that were now visible after months of those healthy dinners (#blessed), or a photo you took of the sunset while you commuted home (#dangerous).

While people struggle to figure out their online identities, they also struggle with understanding how their online life relates to off-line friendships. Even though it's socially desirable for people to say they do not care much about social media, the truth is that most people nervously check their phones every minute after they post a photo or link, hoping for a respectable number of likes or comments. The implication is that they believe their posts' likability is reflective of their social status with their friends or might influence their social status. But is there any evidence that online popularity translates into being likable in real life?

The early research findings regarding people's online behavior and their off-line social lives have produced surprisingly nuanced results. Among the studies I reviewed, I found the most interesting results were about the association between online behaviors and popularity versus likability. We already know that being seen as influential is not the same thing as being seen as pro-social, but this rule can be easy to forget when one gets lost in the social media universe.

Zorana Ivcevic and Nalini Ambady conducted an interesting study of social dispositions and social media. They wanted to investigate whether users' Big Five personality traits—extroversion, openness, agreeableness, conscientiousness, and neuroticism—would be associated with their Facebook behavior. They recruited ninety-nine college students who allowed the researchers to monitor their Facebook activity for three weeks. Ivcevic and Ambady found that participants who were high in agreeableness, a trait that corresponds to pro-social views, generally posted less frequently on Facebook, except in one circumstance: when they wanted to show emotional support for their friends. They also found that people were more likely to initiate social media interactions with participants higher in agreeableness.

These findings and similar results from other studies suggest that being likable in real life and being likable online stem from the same underlying factor, which is being someone who maintains a pro-social disposition toward being fair, kind, and loyal.

Trickle-Down Social Economics

BROCK ENDED UP becoming a great tennis player and an even better friend. Sometimes I wonder how he would have dealt with
the significant social changes of the past two decades. He might
have tossed around a few curse words about the slow decline of
traditional manners or the constant barrage of selfies, but I cannot
imagine that it would have changed his proclivity to be a generous,
fair, and loyal guy and to do his best to find those qualities in others. When I have come up against adversity in my life, I oftentimes
wonder how Brock would have handled similar situations or try to
imagine what kind of encouraging words he would have offered.

Brock was one of those friends who upended the way I approached social life. Instead of trying to think about how I could
nickel-and-dime my way to social inclusion through meeting small
expectations, I began to see that if I approached each situation
asking, "How can I contribute?" that the specifics tended to take
care of themselves. If I was consistent about maintaining these
pro-social attitudes, then I built some cushion for those times
when I inadvertently bungled some social situations or mishan-
dled an expectation in ways that offended others. But I also saw
how giving other people the benefit of the doubt and proactively
investing in them created more social capital for everyone and
that pro-social attitudes had a way of trickling down through social groups and bound them together.

I think that it's not a good idea to expect that friendships will
change you, but once in a while you are lucky enough to find
friends who end up being surprisingly influential and create last-
ing change in how you see the world. Brock helped me change
from being someone who was always reactive to social situations
into a guy who thought ahead about how to proactively give.

They say that you can tell the true character of a person by
watching how he treats people when he has little to gain from

them and by how he conducts himself when he is faced with adversity. When Brock was diagnosed with terminal cancer when we were juniors in college, I guess that I was able to see his true character.

During this extraordinary difficult time in Brock's life, the adversity seemed to make his way of valuing others even more readily apparent. He never complained about the hospital food or when nurses had trouble drawing his blood. He joked about the sleekness of his new bald look and remarked that the awkward-fitting hospital robes were a step up in his fashion game. Whenever I walked into Brock's hospital room, he always expressed how grateful he was that I had taken the time to visit and in his weakened state he always tried his best to sit up to pour me a glass of water. He was supremely interested in hearing about my small triumphs at university even though he had no chance to experience similar victories from the confines of his hospital room, and he was sincerely invested in hearing about my challenges even though his were far greater.

Brock respected the fact that people held social expectations that he might not care about, and even though his behavior could be odd at times, no one really cared much because they knew that he was governed by a simple set of values: be fair, be kind, and be loyal. In the end, those guiding principles were more than enough to make him the kind of guy people wanted to befriend and hoped to emulate.

8

DATING AND SEX ARE SO AWKWARD

During the spring of my ninth-grade year, Coach Arfsten scheduled a four-week golf unit and so we walked around the football field and soccer field with our putters and three-irons. We would have been turned away from most real golf courses for wearing our standard 1980s physical education uniforms. The five-inch red nylon shorts were too short and too tight, and the tight white T-shirts stopped right at the top of our shorts.

By the eighth month of the school year and the third week of playing golf we had grown bored with a game that was too slow paced for adolescents who were looking for more excitement. The novelty we sought was delivered one cloudy afternoon when my group teed up on the fifth hole. Two large dogs approached each other by the tee box and began to circle around each other like yin and yang. We immediately saw the promise that something entertaining was about to happen, and by that I mean inappropriate.

The dogs eagerly sniffed each other and it was exactly the type of crude act for inducing adolescent giggles of delight. When the male dog became excited by the female's intoxicating scent, something in his hindbrain reflexively initiated the launch of his red rocket. We burst into raucous laughter, a mix of amusement and horror, which resonated around the course like the call of wild animals summoning their pack. Everyone dropped their clubs and ran to the fifth hole to see it firsthand. We stood around the spectacle pointing and giggling with crude delight until the sniffing stopped and the dogs broke from the yin and yang formation. You could have heard a golf tee drop on the grass as our giggles turned to nervous anticipation.

The climax of this experiential biology lesson occurred when the eager male pit bull finally mounted the female dachshund, who looked surprisingly disinterested. We were stunned by the duo's combination of odd shapes and unexpected agility, and the silence among us became louder as the male pit bull's enthusiasm turned into a more workmanlike persistence.

Chrissy Silus let out a shriek. Her bulging green eyes were so wide that her horror looked cartoonish. Her hand was over her mouth and her index finger eagerly pointed to the source of her dismay. Our eyes followed the direction of her finger and the trajectory landed our attention on Timmy Johnson's tight red gym shorts. Timmy had launched his own rocket and then Chrissy Silus gave the announcement that no one needed: "Timmy got a boner!"

The fifth hole of the golf course was far from any kind of refuge for poor Timmy, who took the most dignified response available. He did a slow, 180-degree turn and stood motionless with his hands crossed in front of his red shorts. After an awkward pause, a moment of group indecision, the rest of us simultaneously felt a renewed interest in the game of golf. It was a surprisingly empathic response from the class, an unspoken agreement not to make this awkward moment any worse. People briskly walked back to their respective holes and all eyes were focused on drives and puts as Timmy slinked back to the locker room.

I am sure that Timmy did not know why he pitched a red tent at that moment. He may have wondered whether he was wired to be one of those sexual deviants we heard about on the Dr. Ruth radio show late at night. Timmy's ill-timed excitation, which happened to co-occur with the doggy mating spectacle, was probably just an example of correlation not equaling causation. But part of what makes puberty so awkward is that our onset of romantic interest comes with trying to learn the toughest set of social expectations most of us will encounter in our lifetime, while our physical and psychological changes are happening with an intensity that feels unbridled.

During puberty, the world feels very intense, fast-paced, and unpredictable. It gets better as our hormones calm down and we become accustomed to a more complicated set of social expectations, but one social domain that all of us are slow to understand is how to navigate our romantic relationships. In fact, even as grown adults we can feel like the world of dating is overwhelming in intensity, too fast-paced, and unpredictable as ever. Part of the awkwardness of dating is inherent to this unique type of relationship, but there is a new awkwardness that stems from the technological age of dating, in which the rules of engagement are less clear than ever before.

What Happened to the "Romantic" in Romantic Relationships?

IF YOU FEEL like dating is awkward, then you are certainly not alone. In fact, dating and sex have become so awkward that it's tough to tell whether awkward people have a harder time dating than non-awkward people. The confusing nature of modern dating begins with the fact that the traditional endgame for dating, which for thousands of years was marriage, has changed dramatically in just a few decades. Lifelong commitment has become a moving target and that has made it harder to plot a course from where single life begins to where it ends.

Take the simple message you want to convey after a good first date: "I had fun. I would like to see you again." But for the modern single, sending that simple message has become very complicated. Should you text, send a message through the dating app, or risk the audacity of a phone call? If you text, then should you use an emoji? Should your text end with a period, an exclamation point, or should you leave the end naked? Should you send the text when you get home, the next day, or in the middle of the next week far enough from the date, but not too close to the upcoming weekend? All of these minor details have a way of gaining psychological momentum in our minds, each becoming a monumental decision that could signal that you are disinterested or conversely a stage-five clinger. Because there is so much ambiguity around the proper move, the situation starts to feel forced instead of fluid. In other words, the situation feels awkward.

In 2013, across all age groups, the percentage of people who are not currently married has never been higher, with 48 percent of adults categorized as single. Part of the reason for this high rate of singlehood is attributable to 41 percent of first marriages ending in divorce, but also due to a higher proportion of never married people. A report by the Pew Research Center found that in 1960, 68 percent of young adults ages eighteen to thirty-two had married. That rate of marriage had dropped significantly by 1997, to 48 percent, and by 2013 the rate of marriage among eighteen to thirty-two-year-olds had dropped to 26 percent.

Although some sociologists speculate that millennials are simply waiting longer to get married, I find that assumption is far from guaranteed. A 2010 report from the Pew Research Center found shifting attitudes toward marriage when they compared millennial respondents ages eighteen to twenty-nine to boomer respondents ages fifty to sixty-four. Millennials were more likely to say that marriage is becoming obsolete (44 percent) compared to boomers (34 percent) and millennial respondents saw new family arrangements as a good thing (46 percent) more often than boomers (28 percent). I'm fairly agnostic about delayed marriage and young adults' far less eager position on marriage, but these shifts do raise a practical question: If adults are not busy doing married things, then what are they doing?"

In an age of dating apps and friends with benefits this may surprise some people, but Pew and Gallup researchers find that most people still want a romantic relationship with substance. The majority of millennial singles say that they hope to marry someday (70 percent) and across all age groups about 87 percent of singles hope to marry or remarry. Most people still want to find a love story that ends happily ever after. But most singles—whether it's a divorcee who is getting back into the dating game or a millennial trying to Tinder or Bumble their way to a decent guy or gal—will tell you that it's pretty tough out there.

Gerrymandering the Friend Zone

BEING IN LOVE is a categorical variable. You do not hear people say that they are "kind of in love." When people fall in love, they fall hard and they fall completely in love. Although it happens only a few times during the course of one's lifetime, the recipe is surprisingly simple. There are two ingredients: liking and lust. If there are sufficient amounts of both, then there's a good chance that people might hit the tipping point where they fall in love.

When marriage by age twenty-two was the endgame and people decided who to marry based on whether they were in love, then the goal of dating was relatively clear: only date people with whom you might fall in love. However, when the goal is to defer marriage until the late twenties or early thirties, then an awkward pocket of time is created during the twenties. If someone starts dating at age fifteen and is likely to be married by age twenty-two, then they essentially have seven years to lock someone down, but if someone starts dating at age fifteen and is likely to be married at age twenty-nine, then the number of years to date doubles to fourteen years.

Modern dating is like hosting a dinner that has been pushed back from 7:00 P.M. to 9:00 P.M. You do not want to put the duck in the oven too early and you don't want to eat a full meal while you are waiting for your late dinner, but you also get hungry in the meantime. You decide to snack. You start out pretty healthy with some baby carrots, then decide that those carrots need some Ranch, shift to something more substantial like a Hot Pocket, and next thing you know you are eating Nutella out of the jar. The decline in the quality of the food does not sit well with you and suddenly you are wondering why you decided to snack in the first place.

Such is the life of the modern single who hopes to find love, but not too soon. Personally, I think it's great if people get the best of single and married life, but striking this balance is difficult. Like our finicky host of the dinner party, singles don't want to start cooking the pièce de résistance too early, which means that they might try to delay falling in love, because falling in love leads to commitments, and commitments can infringe upon one's independence. When people fall in love there is a natural progression, which includes talk about whether there is an "us," joint ownership of pets, living together, and eventually the M-word. When people try too hard to delay the natural progression of commitment, the relationship can be like a duck that was put in the oven too early and now suffers under a heat lamp that robs it of flavor and dries it far past well done.

To avoid this kind of lame duck relationship, people who want to date while they forestall falling in love have three strategic options, but all three strategies involve carefully treading a slippery slope called commitment. The first strategy is to find someone for whom you feel some liking and lust, but not too much of both. This is a perilous strategy because it starts you off with the two necessary ingredients in place, which leads some people to try a lust-only or liking-plus-benefits strategy of dating.

The lust-only approach is adopted by the single who recognizes that people have physical intimacy needs and who aims to have those needs met not by a full-time boyfriend or girlfriend. The advent of online dating apps has made this easier because the main filter for most technology-based dating is the profile picture, which is the primary way that users gauge a potential partner's physical attractiveness. If someone is on the lust-only dating plan, then some dating apps are an ideal medium for efficiently finding a temporary partner not only because of the interface, but also because the app provides a seemingly limitless number of options in metropolitan areas. The third strategy is the liking-without-lust route, which involves redistricting the friend zone by turning a friend into a friend with benefits.

The problem with the lust-only or liking-plus-benefits strategies is that the lust zone and friend zone are not perfectly distinctive. They are not like counties neatly divided by a wide river, but instead are like the crooked lines you seen drawn on a map that demarcate counties or voting districts in a state, unintuitive divisions drawn to optimize a political party's voting base. When the safe friend who was to fill a romantic void by providing dinner companionship, make outs, and spooning may start to look more physically attractive, it's tempting to rearrange the dividing line between friendship and sex. People who go with the lust-only strategy might think that it's easy to separate emotional intimacy and sex, but many people find that physical intimacy can stir sentiments of fondness that were supposed to remain dormant.

I'm sure that dating and sex have always been awkward to some extent because they require a unique social skill set, but one can easily see how dating could be more awkward than ever, given the dramatic cultural shifts in how we choose partners, when we hope to marry, and the technological advances that make new dates easier than ever.

For most of the time that marriage has existed, you did not have to worry about who you were going to marry because it was chosen for you. Free choice of marital partners introduced new complications, but most people were on board with the endgame of "let's fall in love and get married when we graduate from high school or college." But now the expectations of dating are much more diverse, which means more freedom, but also more ambiguity regarding what the other person expects. For the single who is trying to navigate whether someone is just a friend, a friend with possible benefits, or someone looking to fall in love, he or she needs to learn a different dialect of social cues that are unique to romantic relationships—and the language of love is now spoken in more dialects than ever.

Online Dating Can Be an Awkwardness Incubator

WHEN I WAS in junior high the quintessential creepy behavior was to ride your bike by a girl's house. While I rode by I tried to look nonchalant in case the girl or her parents happened to be looking out the window, but based on how often I heard my female classmates discuss these ride-by incidents from non-awkward guys, I'm sure that I was not as smooth as I thought. Sometimes I thought about circling around again for another ride-by, but in my eleven-year-old mind I thought that only a crazy person would be that obsessive about a love interest.

The modern single uses the Internet like an invisibility cloak for doing the equivalent of the ride-by. The relative anonymity of the Internet allows people to do deep dives into potential dates' eHarmony or OkCupid profiles or research someone's social history on

Instagram or their relationship history on Facebook. They top off this covert creepiness by Googling potential dates for incriminating information or clues to their character that might exist in the deep archives of their long-abandoned Myspace profile. This would be like you riding your bike by someone's house, walking around the house, then sneaking inside to go through their photo albums and journal. Online stalking is about the closest you can get to feeling awkward in the absence of anyone there to witness your socially unacceptable behavior. It's one of those shameful things that we all do, but don't talk about, like peeing in the shower.

Sometimes, after you conduct these undercover intelligence-gathering operations, you might decide to send a message. After you carefully craft a message and hit *send*, an anxiety instantly begins to build while you wait for a response to this message in a bottle. A minute passes, then two minutes, and there is not a response or even so much as texting bubbles to show an effort . . . Now you start to convince yourself that your message was fatally awkward. Maybe it was too long or there were not enough exclamation points or you should have sent it in the afternoon instead of the evening; then, when you least expect it, she responds.

It's the best thing that happens all day, but you need to pull it together. Play it cool. To guard against looking overeager, you suddenly devise an arbitrary algorithm that doubles the time until you respond back to her. The intentional waiting game is a bad decision because now you are ruminating about the "xoxo" she used to sign off. Maybe that's just a friendly "xoxo," kind of like a European kiss on each cheek exchanged among friends. But maybe it's something else, and now you can't stop yourself from looking at your phone, at that dating app, at that message, while you deliberate the philosophical meaning of four letters that are not even a word: "xoxo."

All of it is totally crazy and it's the new normal. Although researchers are still in the early stages of understanding online dating behavior, it's clear that socializing through technology can produce a significant amount of anxiety. In 2015, online magazines geared toward young adults such as *Elite Daily* and *Buzz-Feed* began running popular stories about the benefits of taking a break from dating, being alone, or commiserative articles about the alarm that arises from unsolicited sexts. In 2016, an app appeared for people who had grown weary of texting their romantic disinterest to potential online dates by using bots to send vague and unsatisfying messages. For people who had given up on dating, another app appeared to help lonely people hire people to do nothing more than spoon for a fee. There are certainly success stories, however, with online dating accounting for about 25 to 30 percent of marriages. But many singles feel like online dating has become a game for some people, and it can be hard to tell the differences between the players and people looking for something more substantial.

We have seen that online communication involves a high degree of uncertainty because it's devoid of social cues such as gaze, facial expression, personal space boundaries, and touch, which is unfortunate because nonverbal cues are particularly important when it comes to flirtatious cues. Only face-to-face can you find out if you like their scent, the way their voice resonates, or their crooked smile. Only in person can your date cast a telling glance your way or let his hand linger for a second longer on your back.

If someone has managed to get through the dating apps and decipher flirtatious games, then things can get physically intimate. Eventually, things can reach a point when both people are ready for sex, which is about as face-to-face as you can get, and that makes sex a situation ripe for awkwardness.

FOUR FACTORS TO MAKE DATING LESS AWKWARD

Relationship scientists have repeatedly found that there are four factors that consistently predict interpersonal attraction: proximity, similarity, liking and reciprocity, and physical attractiveness. These factors might sound like common sense, but researchers also find that people only sporadically enact these behaviors in real life. Awkward people tend to be more reclusive, have unique interests, and may be hesitant to express their interest in someone, so I put together a few ideas about ways to enact the four factors of attraction.

PROXIMITY

- Sign up for online dating to establish virtual proximity.
- Hang out where the type of partner you want would spend time. Foodies hang out at specialty stores, comic book lovers are at Comic Con, writers hang out at coffee shops . . .
- There is some validity to "don't be a wallflower." Figure out a non-creepy way to position yourself by high-traffic areas. Maybe volunteer to sign people in at an event or offer to help serve drinks at a friend's party.

SIMILARITY

- Try being specific instead of broad about your interests. Instead of saying, "I enjoy sci-fi," you might say, "I enjoy Marvel Comics." People like it when someone happens to have the same exact interests.
- Once you start talking with people, be sure to ask them about their interests to see if there are any points of commonality.

LIKING AND RECIPROCITY

- At the right time, someone needs to find a way to say, "I'm interested in you," or "I really like you," or else a burgeoning love can die on the vine.

- Be subtle. Awkward people tend to be eager when they are interested in someone. If you are thinking about buying jewelry or plane tickets within the first month, there's a 99 percent chance it's going to get awkward.

PHYSICAL ATTRACTIVENESS

- It's harder to control this, but there are obvious things that go a long way, such as getting cleaned up and wearing something flattering.
- Research from Tinder suggests that one can boost online attractiveness by smiling, wearing a non-muted color, and not posting shots with groups of people.

Sex Is Super-Awkward

MICHAEL WAS HAPPILY married and undersexed. This lack of sexual activity was no one's fault, but rather a symptom of Michael and his wife, Tracy, being people who were busy with their demanding careers while they also dealt with sleep deprivation as parents of an eight-month-old infant. For Michael and Tracy, sex had become one of those things they used to enjoy, like staying awake for the ten o'clock news or a good night of sleep.

They met during their senior year at MIT, where Michael majored in mechanical engineering and Tracy majored in psychology. They were an odd couple, but somehow perfect for each other. Michael stood six feet eight inches tall with broad shoulders and a husky build. Despite his powerful physical stature and experience as a former defensive lineman in college, you could take one look at Michael and sense that he was clumsy. He was renowned for having a poor sense of where his body parts were in relation to the things around him, which led to various accidents that Tracy somehow found endearing. Tracy was petite and coordinated in every way. She was a gymnastics prodigy who was nationally competitive until she decided at age thirteen to follow her intellectual pursuits instead of making a run at the Olympic team. She was far from clumsy, physically or socially, but she loved Michael for his affable nature and sharp analytical mind.

Recently, their infant put together a string of three good nights of sleep and this had left both of them feeling well rested and more than a little frisky. After they completed their side-by-side night routines by the bathroom sinks, Michael walked into the bedroom and pulled the sheets close to his chin. After three months of a sexual drought, Michael was surprised when Tracy emerged from the bathroom without her traditional flannel pajamas on or anything else. This excited Michael.

I will not bore you with the details of what followed. There is not much to report because after their long dry spell, Michael and Tracy were not interested in compulsory pleasantries. They were two former athletes who had locked into their game-time zone of intense focus. They rushed through their rehearsed sequence: make out side by side, heavy petting, Tracy on top first, then Michael on top. It was the passionate, raw kind of sex that had swung both of them into some *Kama Sutra*–like zone, and in the heat of the moment Tracy yelled, "Oh Michael, get awesome!"

Oh yeah! Get awesome indeed! But wait. What does that mean?

Michael had never been told by anyone to get awesome during sex, but then again his experiences were based on a very small sample size. Maybe this was a common phrase among the sexual elite or an idea from one of those *Cosmo* listicles about "Seven Ways to Please Your Man." His awkward mind furiously tried to think about a behavior to meet Tracy's "awesome" expectation. In his analytical mind, Michael reasoned that the sex was already awesome by any objective standard, which led him to deduce that

Tracy's competitive spirit was urging him to be the best that he could be, to push him to the limits of his sexual potential.

Michael pushed himself up into a yoga-like upward dog. He raised his right arm perpendicular to his body and with all of his might flexed his right bicep. He knew that Tracy liked his muscular arms and he reasoned that flexing them would take them all the way to awesome. Once he was done gazing at the crown of his bicep, he looked at Tracy to gauge her delight with the sexual spectacle before her.

Tracy looked befuddled. In a terse tone she asked, "What are you doing?" Immediately after her accusatory question, Tracy felt guilty. She wished that she could take back what she had said, but in the heat of the moment she had lost her mental filter. With a gentler tone, she repeated her earlier request, "Sorry, Michael. I was trying to say could you please get off me?"

Michael had put on a few pounds, actually it was about twenty pounds, since their last sexual encounter, which had become too much weight for Tracy to comfortably bear. In his enthusiasm, Michael had heard Tracy's request to "Get off me" as "Get awesome." After a tense moment, while Michael and Tracy lay side by side flushed with embarrassment, they burst into laughter. Even for elite athletes, sex can get pretty awkward.

Although most people can recall awkward sexual moments, there's reason to believe that sex has become more awkward compared to previous sexual eras. In the United States and many other countries there have been changes in sexual attitudes and societal changes in how sex is portrayed by mass media, which might be associated with individuals' changing their sexual expectations. Brooke Wells and Jean Twenge examined generational differences in sexual attitudes and behaviors with data from the General Social Survey, which is a nationally representative sample of more than 33,000 U.S. adults. They were interested in whether they would find generational differences in attitudes toward premarital sex and casual sex, but they also looked for generational differences in sexual behaviors such as the total number of casual hookups and of sexual partners.

They compared boomers', Gen Xers', and millennials' responses from when they were ages eighteen to twenty-nine regarding attitudes toward premarital sex. They found a steady rise in acceptance of premarital sex during the eleven-year period for each group: 47 percent of young-adult boomers, 50 percent of young-adult Gen Xers, and 62 percent of young-adult millennials said there was nothing wrong at all with premarital sex. Attitudes toward adolescent sexual activity became slightly more accepting across generations, whereas acceptance of extramarital relationships actually declined. When examining reports of sexual behavior, the researchers found that young-adult Gen Xers reported having more sexual partners than boomers, but millennials actually showed a decline in their number of sexual partners compared to Gen Xers. Collectively this data suggests that attitudes toward sex have become significantly more open over time, but this has not corresponded to the stereotypical belief that millennials have more sexual partners than did previous generations.

Although the total number of sexual partners has not changed much across these three groups, there are reasons to believe that people have become more open and willing to engage in a wider variety of sexual activities in the bedroom. One of the highest-profile cases of widespread sexual curiosity occurred when the erotic novel *Fifty Shades of Grey* was published in 2011. Integral to the plot was a sadomasochistic sexual relationship, which had unexpectedly widespread appeal. By 2015, over 125 million copies of the book had been sold in over 52 languages, and in 2012 the author, E. L. James, was named one of *Time* magazine's 100 Most Influential People. Couples in suburban areas who had grown tired of the same old sexual routines were exposed to a whole new world of possibilities, and their expectations for a little more excitement in the bedroom shifted to the adventurous side.

Although *Fifty Shades of Grey* focused on a sexual relationship with sadomasochistic rituals, it was more fantasy than instructional manual for novices. Sex toy sales rose dramatically and couples excitedly put their new purchases to use. Neophyte couples of all ages began cuffing, tying, and whipping with little idea about the nuances of how to properly meet their wild sexual expectations, and that's how things got awkward. In many countries where the novel was popular, fire departments and ambulance services reported an explosion of emergency calls to uncomfortable bedroom situations. The London fire department issued public service announcements before the *Fifty Shades of Grey* movie was released in 2015, in which they pleaded with moviegoers to be careful about their reenactment plans. London firefighters had spent the previous year racing to 393 *Fifty Shades* book-related emergencies, including freeing twenty-eight couples who had lost the keys to their handcuffs and a variety of injuries from improper use of sex toys.

Beyond the *Fifty Shades of Grey* craze, more people have been exposed to a broader range of sexual practices through pornography being more readily available. In the era of big data, there are also readily available analyses about what people search for the most on pornography sites. I won't go through all of the awkward findings here, but one of the most popular sites, Pornhub, reports that there was an 845 percent increase in demand for bunny pornography around Easter and an 8,000 percent increase for leprechaun pornography around St. Patrick's Day.

Whether pornography causes deeply problematic attitudes or behaviors is still unclear from existing studies; there are some studies that suggest higher-than-average pornography consumption is associated with concerning sexual attitudes and behaviors, but others find it to be relatively harmless in moderation. But another matter is whether this wider exposure to different sexual behaviors makes sex more awkward for the average couple. One possibility is that increased pornography consumption by both men and women has made couples more flexible regarding their sexual expectations, which would mean that new behaviors would be seen as intriguing rather than awkward. But the other equally plausible possibility is that one partner's expectations of sex could significantly differ from the other partner's expectations, which could create some uncomfortable situations. There's just something about being naked that makes awkward moments feel extra-awkward.

Intimately Awkward

WHEN IT COMES to awkward people and their experiences with dating, there are a few studies that provide insight. The intuitive hypothesis is that awkward people should have more trouble picking up subtle, flirtatious cues and might struggle with executing subtle flirtatious behaviors themselves. If reading romantic situations and executing the needed behaviors is more difficult for them, then awkward people should also be less likely to be in romantic relationships.

Flirtation is like the double-black-diamond ski slope in the world of social skills. There is no one flirtatious signal that means someone is romantically interested, but rather romantic interest is decoded by individuals taking in multiple signals and searching for a pattern that indicates romantic intent. For example, someone who squares their body toward you, looks you in the eye, and smiles is probably just a socially fluent person who is being affable. But if someone squares toward you, leans into your space, casts a number of long gazes, giggles while touching her hair, touches your leg, then there is a reason to suspect that she might be romantically interested. But the probability never reaches 100 percent; it's a maddening asymptotic rise that falls short of complete certainty. That means that there is always room for error or misinterpretation of how the cues add up and some of us are more prone to misinterpretation than others.

An interesting study about awkward people's romantic relationships comes from a graduate thesis by Kojo Mintah at Carleton University. Mintah surveyed 124 university students to investigate whether awkward participants were more likely to misinterpret romantic interest. Mintah found that they were more likely to misinterpret platonic social cues as flirtatious. Awkward participants' misperception of platonic cues was associated with a greater likelihood of engaging in inappropriate dating behaviors such as obsessional interest or making inappropriate comments.

It's understandable that awkward individuals' difficulties with interpreting social cues would be particularly problematic in the context of romantic relationships. It's always awkward when someone remains romantically interested in someone who clearly does not reciprocate the same feelings, but it's also problematic because barking up the wrong tree comes with an opportunity cost, which is that awkward people are not pursuing more promising possibilities. It would seem that their difficulty in accurately interpreting these romantic cues would make them less likely to be involved in romantic relationships than their non-awkward peers.

Lisa Jobe and Susan Williams White recruited ninety-seven undergraduate participants to investigate whether this is the case. They found that socially awkward participants were actually *more* likely to report currently being involved in a romantic relationship, not because they had more dating opportunities than nonawkward participants, but rather because their average length of relationship was longer (eighteen months) than those of nonawkward participants (eleven months).

There are a few ways to interpret this result. One pragmatic explanation for awkward people's longer relationships is that they know initiating a new relationship will be particularly challenging for their social skill set, so they hold on longer to a current relationship. But another possibility is that they are able to be more selective because they do not have to deal with the same volume of dating opportunities as non-awkward people, or they want to be extra certain that they are interested in dating someone beforehand because the anxiety of communicating their romantic intent is even more intense than what most people feel.

Once awkward individuals get into a relationship, they are faced with negotiating a qualitatively different set of expectations as the initial giddiness of the first few months of dizzying passion subside. Emotionally intimate relationships are characterized by partners who readily share personal information, respond empathically to their partner's self-disclosures, and make the effort to form accurate theories about their partners' needs. These intimacy-building behaviors can be challenging to awkward individuals, who are less likely to share their interests and emotions with others and who are prone to misreading the meaning that others are trying to convey. Awkward individuals may have trouble adapting their routines to accommodate the lifestyle of another person. They are also at risk for becoming emotionally overwhelmed by the intense emotions in a romantic relationship.

These obstacles inherent in relationships that involve an awkward person are not insurmountable, but awkward people need to fix their sharp focus on the right things for a relationship to thrive. One of the keys to successful relationships lies in the expectations people hold for their partners and the effort that each partner is willing to devote to adapt their behaviors to the best of their ability to meet the needs of the other. As in any relationship, partners in romantic relationships need to have a sense that the balance of benefits and costs is equitable for a satisfying relationship.

Monique Pollman and her colleagues from the University of Amsterdam recruited 195 married heterosexual couples to assess whether awkward traits would be associated with marital satisfaction. There are at least two possible ways that awkward traits can operate in relationships: your level of awkwardness could affect your perceptions of marital satisfaction, and your partner's level of awkwardness could be associated with your marital satisfaction.

Pollman found that women married to awkward husbands and women married to non-awkward husbands showed no differences in marital satisfaction. Awkward wives and non-awkward wives also reported similar levels of marital satisfaction. For women, their levels of awkwardness and the awkwardness of their husbands did not adversely affect their overall levels of marital satisfaction.

For husbands the outcomes were mixed. Pollman found no differences in marital satisfaction between men married to awkward wives and men married to non-awkward wives. But awkward men reported less marital satisfaction than non-awkward men. Pollman found that awkward men's lower levels of satisfaction were partly explained by their being less trusting and perceiving less intimacy. The pattern of results paints a picture of awkward men who are struggling to be at peace with the relationship, who are not trusting that things will work out, and whose guarded attitudes make it a struggle to feel a deeper sense of emotional intimacy.

These findings illustrate a broader conceptual point about close relationships, whether they are romantic, familial, or friendships. People generally expect that relationships become more intimate over time, but this is an expectation that can be particularly difficult for awkward individuals. Unlike initial interactions where manners and social scripts can be routinely executed, the expectations for building relationship intimacy are far less predictable. If the long-term goal in a relationship is to feel a sense of belonging that is satisfying and stable, then awkward individuals can think about achieving this goal with two separate skill sets. The first is figuring out how to navigate minor social expectations such as meeting new people, going to a dinner party, or running a work meeting. The other skill set comes into play once they forge a deeper friendship or get past the early stages of dating and begin to build intimacy, which psychologists define as a deeper sense of emotional connection and mutual reliance between two people.

Brooke Feeney at Carnegie Mellon University, a leading relationship scientist, has articulated a *dependency paradox* in romantic relationships. One of the most powerful mechanisms for building intimacy is self-disclosure and support, which begins with one person sharing a personal thought or feeling that makes him feel somewhat vulnerable. When the listener responds in an empathic and supportive way, then a degree of trust and intimacy is built, but this self-disclosure is a two-way street and the disclosures need to be shared and properly dosed. People who disclose too much, too quickly can scare people away, but conversely, people who never share private matters feel distant.

When romantic partners lean on each other for support, they are more confident about their independence. This does not refer to the needy kind of dependency in which someone cannot do anything on their own without their partner, but rather a confidence that during times of uncertainty or distress one can rely upon their partner to be supportive and loyal. When partners consistently provide emotional support when their significant others need it, those being offered support are more likely to persist and achieve goals outside of the relationship, such as school or work goals.

Awkward individuals are prone to being hyper-independent, which is partly due to their trait-like aloofness, introversion, and nonsocial interests. Awkward individuals' ability to overcome their difficulties with intimacy lies in their willingness to lean on their partner for support, which fosters a feeling of connection and builds the reassurance necessary for each partner to give the other space for autonomous pursuits and interests. But their hyper-independence makes it hard for them to believe that being more dependent on a partner can make them feel more independent.

The dependency paradox is hard to manage because self-disclosure comes with a real risk that the partner will not respond well or could eventually abandon the relationship. Romantic relationships are always a high-stakes gamble and the stakes rise the first time you hold hands, say "I love you," or share your most private thoughts and feelings. All of this can create such intense emotions that people are inclined to fold while they are ahead, based on a reasonable rationale that their emotional gambles could result in losing it all. But in matters of love, it's not an option to bring a halfhearted level of participation to the table.

When awkward people decide to do something, they really decide to do it 100 percent, and if there's anything in life that requires a 100 percent commitment to have a chance of success it's our romantic relationships. If an awkward person's partner is willing to be patient, and an awkward partner is willing to commit his focused attention and persistence to figuring out how to build intimacy and adopt a flexibility beyond what is comfortable for him, then he has as good a chance as anyone to become a thoughtful and loyal partner.

The Awkward Path to Happily Ever After

THE PROFOUND IMPORTANCE of romantic relationships in fulfilling our sense of belonging gives them an explosive potential. This amplified emotional potential accounts for why they can make us feel so emotionally unstable, which affects our ability to judiciously navigate our relationships in at least two ways.

The disorienting euphoria that accompanies being in love with someone shuts down our ability to think straight and unmet expectations can create an intensely upsetting emotional state that is ripe for our saying something hurtful that we don't believe and would never dream of saying to anyone, much less someone we love. But the explosive emotional potential of romantic relationships also gives us anxiety about setting off emotions that may push us far outside of our comfort zone. While some people are most fearful of hurting someone else through too many irritable outbursts, others are frightened that they will not be able to deliver enough intimacy, that ineffable signal that shows your partner that deep down you love him or her more than anything else in this world.

After my first book, about the search for enduring romantic relationships, came out, people often asked me, "What is the most important factor for a successful relationship?" Relationship researchers have quantified dozens of relationship behaviors that predict happy and stable partnerships, but when I have to choose just one piece of advice, I usually reply with a less quantitative answer.

When older adults lose their partner after decades of being together, they will tell you that what they miss the most are the "small things" that they sometimes took for granted in their relationship. They miss the daily habits that they shared with their partner, the quirky acts of cooperation that made two people an "us." Bereaved partners will tear up when they tell you that they miss their walks around the lake or driving to work together. A gentleman who had lost his wife of fifty years still gets me choked up when I think about him saying, "I miss that she was the only one who knew that I liked two lumps of sugar in my coffee."

What older adults miss is the spirit of cooperation that evolved between two people and the generous acts that their partner quietly carried out for them on a daily basis. As the pace of life picks up and other responsibilities outside of the marriage occupy people's minds, these subtle behaviors can be taken for granted and some people do not realize what they are missing until their partner is gone. For awkward people who can get their spotlighted attention narrowly focused on nonsocial interests, there needs to be an ongoing mindfulness to give their concentrated attention to their partner on a daily basis. Sometimes the people who love us the most are the least likely to ask for the spotlight.

Awkward people might face some unique challenges in their relationships compared to non-awkward people. They are probably more likely to misread what their partners mean or might become overwhelmed by the intensity of emotion in romantic relationships, but all partners have their challenges and all couples have difficulties to surmount. In long-term relationships, the psychological principles that carry a relationship across years or decades are fairness, kindness, and loyalty, but romantic relationships present some of the steepest challenges for enacting these pro-social attitudes and behaviors. Whether people are awkward or socially fluent, the best advice is to be unabashedly generous and ever-vigilant about their partners' acts of cooperation and kindness.

PART III

HOW THE AWKWARD
BECOME AWESOME

9

PRACTICALLY PRODIGIOUS

Prodigious: [pruh-dij-uhs] (adjective)
   (1) extraordinary in size, force (2) wonderful or marvelous
   (3) abnormal, monstrous

Ellen Winner is professor and chair of psychology at Boston College, a senior research associate at the Harvard Graduate School of Education, and author of *Gifted Children: Myths and Realities*. She is one of the world's leading experts on giftedness, and when I talked to her about the relationship between social awkwardness and giftedness, she offered a number of thoughtful insights.

Professor Winner finds that gifted individuals have a razor-sharp focus on and insatiable curiosity about their areas of interest and work tirelessly at mastering them. But she also finds that their intense focus and strong drive come with increased risks for problems with their social and emotional lives. Gifted kids have twice the risk for social and emotional problems when compared to nongifted kids. This risk is the same as the risk for chronically bullied kids to develop depression in adulthood and the same as the risk for overweight individuals to develop cardiac disease as adults.

When I asked Professor Winner about why gifted kids sometimes struggle socially, she said, "The more gifted a child is, the more rare that child is, and therefore the more difficulty the child will have in finding others like himself or herself. So I actually believe that the social awkwardness stems from the fact that they can't find other kids like themselves, and when they do they are less socially awkward."

Gifted kids often have trouble feeling like they fit in because they're different, but they also are less likely to seek out as much social interaction as other kids. Professor Winner put it this way, "These kids are more introverted than other kids, and they get more stimulation from their own minds. That might make them seem more socially awkward because they don't seek out others as much." There is also an intensity about gifted children that can strike others as odd. When I asked Professor Winner if this intensity is partly attributable to a spotlight-like focus, she agreed: "Gifted kids are passionate about their area and so they have more of a spotlight instead of a searchlight."

Not all gifted kids are awkward and not all awkward kids are gifted, but we will see that there is remarkable overlap between the two characteristics, and that giftedness and awkwardness may produce a synergistic effect that produces something that is far greater than the sum of its parts.

When Awkwardness Is Adaptive

TO BEGIN THINKING about the unique value of awkward individuals, it's helpful to begin with an evolutionary perspective: If the need to belong is fundamental, then why has social awkwardness persisted as a trait through natural selection? From this perspective, awkward individuals' difficulty meeting social expectations should have threatened their belonging to social groups, which would have decreased their chances of survival and successfully mating. If awkward characteristics were mostly negative qualities, then they should have faded over successive generations because awkward people would have been less likely to pass along their genes.

Bernard Crespi is a professor of biological sciences at Simon Frazier University who has studied why characteristics that are viewed as maladaptive might have carried an adaptive purpose. From a natural selection perspective, the primary reason why human characteristics evolve is to maximize our chances of survival and reproductive success; they do not evolve to increase our likelihood of being happy. It's not that people should not strive to be happy, but as we consider the upside of awkward characteristics from an evolutionary perspective, we want to keep in mind that it's through the lens of why awkwardness would have helped people survive or mate.

One hypothesis is that awkwardness is a trade-off. Broadly spoken, trade-offs occur when one trait increases in strength and another trait decreases in strength.

Awkward people are more likely to show a number of unusual strengths, including enhanced abilities for solving tasks that require systematic processes such as those in math or science, seeing patterns in the midst of complex visual stimuli, and an ability to persist at repetitive tasks in their areas of interest. The trade-offs are diminished abilities to intuitively empathize, difficulty developing a theory of other people's minds, and a tendency to lose sight of the big picture. The question is whether the strengths that tend to accompany awkwardness outweigh or at least balance out the social challenges that come along with being awkward.

In hunter-gatherer groups, there were people who discovered how to make better animal traps, the benefits of rotating crops, and figured out the physics of irrigation systems. These types of breakthroughs were unlikely to have occurred by accident, rather they were the product of systematic thought and persistent experimentation. Awkward people might not have been masterful hunters or could have been clumsy while carrying back containers of gathered food, but if they figured out how to preserve the meat from the hunt by salting it or designed a better system for transporting gathered food, then these innovations would be valuable to the whole group.

Unlike temporary survival provided from a successful hunt, harvest, or battle, people who made their intellectual breakthroughs available to everyone would have provided ongoing survival value to the whole group. There was also value from awkward individuals who were simply willing to continue hunting or gathering food long after everyone else went home or who never grew bored by some of the tedious tasks.

In modern contexts, food is far more abundant and life expectancies have doubled, but awkward characteristics still persist and add unique value. Society needs people to systematically generate better algorithms to solve food distribution inequalities, discover energy sources that are more sustainable, and inspire new pedagogical strategies to teach kids adaptive knowledge and skills. Modern societies also need computer scientists who will tirelessly persist to find and close tiny vulnerabilities that expose us to cyber-attacks and security experts who can identify small abnormalities in intelligence data to deter terrorism threats.

Awkwardness is adaptive because awkward individuals have the potential to add unique value through their systematic discoveries or their willingness to persist long after others have stopped working on a task. But this added value relies upon awkward people figuring out how to maximize their potential and match their strengths to the right environments. To do so, they have to figure out how to mobilize the social support necessary for turning early flashes of brilliance into prodigious achievements.

Giftedness Is Singular, Not Plural

EVEN FREUD, WHO found psychological trouble brewing where no one expected, thought that children entered a "latency stage" during middle childhood. The latency stage was a lull between the unruly years of infancy and the stormy years of adolescence. Kids in this developmental pocket find joys in things like swing sets, ice cream cones, and visits from the Tooth Fairy. Parents look forward to the relatively smooth sailing during the latency stage, but some parents begin to sense their children's unusual talents around this age. The early signs of talent are like a stray raindrop on a clear summer day and they give parents a premonition that something more potent is on its way.

Maybe it's during a family sing-along to the *Frozen* soundtrack in the car when parents hear their four-year-old daughter sing a line with perfect pitch, or while calculating the restaurant tip are told by their five-year-old son that a 20 percent tip would be $9.50. Parents look with momentary disbelief toward the backseat or to the end of the table.

When gifted children's abilities first begin to emerge, they have little sense where their abilities stand in relation to others'. The early years take place in a vacuum that is free of external expectations and pressures. When you get the chance to see a gifted child savor her newfound ability in music, mathematics, or art, the pure joy with which she engages her talent is awe-inspiring.

One of the great things about being a kid is that you are free to sing, draw, and play make-believe without external judgments about the quality of your work. Gifted kids are the same, acting on what is intuitively pleasing, but their extraordinary talent does not manifest as childlike. They sing with near perfect pitch, draw with a perspective that creates a stunning realism, and play make-believe with plot lines that build complex tensions or contain unexpected twists. Gifted children are unusual, or in psychological terms "abnormal," which has made them the subject of extensive study over the years.

In the early 1900s, Stanford psychologist Lewis Terman was one of the first to research how to quantify mental ability with standardized intelligence quotient (IQ) tests. He found that IQ was distributed normally along a bell curve, which means that most people fall somewhere around the average score of 100. People who have IQ scores below seventy are in the bottom fourth percentile of test takers and are considered to have significant intellectual impairment, while people with IQ scores of 130 or higher are in the top fourth percentile, and this is commonly used as one threshold to categorize people who are intellectually gifted.

The most frequently used IQ tests measure different subtypes of mental ability such as verbal, quantitative (math/science), or memory. One straightforward example is a memory test called digit span. Psychologists ask test takers to remember two or three numbers and ask them to remember more with each correct answer. For example, read this list of numbers:

3—1—8—1—2—2—5

Now cover the seven numbers and try to recall as many of those numbers in the order you read them. Most adults can remember five to nine digits, which is why phone numbers were created to be seven digits without the area code. The average nine-year-old, one who scores at the fiftieth percentile, correctly recalls six digits. But some gifted children in the first percentile can recall nine digits. During graduate school, I tested a twelve-year-old girl who was gifted with an incredible memory. She became so bored while she crushed the digit span test that she spontaneously recited the nine digits I read to her in reverse order.

Kids who are gifted with unusual memory capabilities intui-tively approach problems like digit span differently from other kids. Gifted children intuitively chunk the numbers into clusters without anyone having to tell them how to do it. The gifted child hears the task to remember the numbers and intuitively knows that remem-bering three instead of seven units is easier: 3, 181, 225.

The mechanisms that allow kids with exceptional cognitive ability to holistically and efficiently process nonsocial information has parallels to what we saw in earlier chapters when we looked at the mechanisms that help socially fluent kids process complex social situations. Recall that socially fluent individuals can proc-ess social cues without having to consciously consider individual cues such as intonation, nonverbal cues, and facial expressions. So-cially fluent people have the ability to intuitively cluster together individual pieces of information during social interactions. When these individuals spontaneously bump into a friend at a holiday party, they instantly recognize that they should shake hands up and down three times, stand eighteen inches apart, and use a merry greeting, given the date (12.25).

Howard Gardner is a professor at Harvard University who pro-posed that intelligence is broader than the abilities tapped by most standardized tests such as verbal IQ and quantitative IQ. Gard-ner put forth a theory of multiple intelligences, which included additional types of ability such as musical, body/kinesthetic, and interpersonal abilities. Researchers have devoted relatively less at-tention to a wider variety of multiple intelligences, but popular wisdom would suggest that individuals who are gifted with musi-cal, athletic, or social acumen possess valuable abilities that can-not be fully captured by their verbal or quantitative IQ.

There is some empirical support that popular wisdom includes a broader view of intelligence. Robert Sternberg is a professor at Cornell University who found in a study of laypeople's views of in-telligence that the average person naturally differentiates between more than verbal intelligence and math intelligence. Sternberg's participants also saw creative ability to go beyond traditional ways of thinking, wisdom from life experience, and an openness to learning from others as valid and distinctive categories of ability.

It's important to distinguish between different types of abilities to investigate whether abilities tend to be even or uneven. For example, someone with an even-ability profile might have a 110 verbal IQ score and a quantitative IQ score right around 110, whereas someone with an uneven profile might have a 135 verbal IQ and a 100 quantitative IQ. It's the difference between saying that someone is "smart" versus "really good at some things, not so good at other things." There are practical consequences to this distinction because if abilities tend to be uneven, then schools or workplaces would want to account for that when they think about how to maximize each person's potential. Conversely, if abilities are uniform, which means that individuals' subtypes of ability tend to be even across the board, then schools or workplaces could assume that someone who is above average would perform above average on most tasks.

Researchers generally find that most people have even levels of ability across the board. But when researchers look at people with IQ scores above 130, they usually see that their abilities are uneven and that this unevenness becomes more pronounced as IQ scores get higher. For example, John Achter at Iowa State University and his colleagues looked at data from more than one thousand extremely gifted seventh graders and found that more than 80 percent of them were characterized by uneven abilities and interests.

The uneven nature of gifted individuals' IQ profiles can be confusing because we usually think about intelligence as even, which is why some schools put students into typical, accelerated, or remedial tracks. But the reality is that extremely gifted people tend to be gifted in some areas and average or even below average in others. If we think broadly about multiple intelligences, then it's interesting to think about whether people who are gifted with musical ability or quantitative ability might have significantly lower capability when it comes to interpersonal ability or intrapersonal ability (knowing yourself).

A Restless Mind

NICK SABAN IS the football coach at the University of Alabama and arguably the best coach of his era. Coach Saban is known for being an intense guy, but in an interview with ESPN's Mike Smith in 2016, he told Smith a few lighthearted stories from his earlier days as an assistant coach at Michigan State University. Saban was with a fellow assistant coach on a recruiting trip in Youngstown, Ohio. After a long day of recruiting, Saban and his colleague went to a local bar to continue working into the night on some strategies for an upcoming game. In the middle of their intense session of X's and O's, a man with a shotgun entered the bar and demanded that the bartender turn over the money from the register.

Fortunately, no one was harmed during the incident, but it was a terrifying moment for everyone who witnessed it. When the police arrived on the scene, the bartender explained what had happened. After questioning the bartender, the police prepared to talk to the other people who were present during the robbery, but the bartender told the officers not to bother questioning Saban and his coworker. He said they probably had "no idea" that a holdup had transpired. The bartender was right. Saban and his coworker had become so absorbed in their game plans, so focused on doing their work, that they never even noticed that a robbery had occurred.

Technically, giftedness is defined by someone's level of ability, their raw intelligence, athleticism, or artistic ability. But Professor Winner and others have found that gifted individuals are also more likely to have a certain type of personality. Gifted people tend to be stubborn, rebellious, and perfectionistic. They show an unusual drive to master their area of interest and they are constantly trying to push the status quo, which motivates them to pursue their interest with an unusual intensity and persistence. Winner calls this constellation of personality characteristics and attitudes the "rage to master."

There is an unsettling ring to the phrase and when I spoke to Winner she said that's part of the point. It's an apt phrase because it captures gifted individuals' intensity and near-desperation while engaging their interests, but I think it also suggests that others may feel uneasy around their intense energy. Gifted people have a deeply inquisitive nature, but their relentless curiosity can come across as agitated or somewhere near the border of anger. We can see this agitation manifested in the gifted athlete trying to scratch his way back into the lead or an investigative reporter trying to get her team to meet a critical deadline.

Gifted students can feel perturbed when a parent or teacher runs out of answers, which can lead them on a hunt through the library or the far reaches of the Internet. Gifted adults are more likely to grow impatient with incompetent coworkers and managers or when the work does not move at a brisk pace. When gifted individuals' rage to master is frustrated, their agitation is palpable to others, like being around someone with an itch he cannot scratch.

When gifted individuals' rage to master is blocked, they do not perceive it as a minor inconvenience. Lauren Cuthbertson is a dancer who is the London Royal Ballet's principal and she articulated this feeling beautifully in an interview. In 2014, Cuthbertson suffered a potentially career-ending foot injury and was unable to dance for months. She remarked that the hardest moments in her life have been those when she could not *train*. It's notable that Cuthbertson missed the deliberate practice, the time spent honing her craft, rather than the exhilaration of performing for sold-out theaters. Once she was able to return to deliberate practice, Cuthbertson said it felt like she could "suddenly breathe."

Pedro Vital, at the Institute of Psychiatry at King's College, wanted to investigate abilities beyond those measured by traditional IQ tests. He looked at data available from six thousand pairs of twins who had been through assessments that included IQ tests, personality measures, and parents' observations of their twins' traits. One of the questions asked of parents was whether their children displayed a striking skill compared to children who were much older. The term "striking skill" is intentionally vague, but permitted researchers to assess a broader range of giftedness beyond verbal or quantitative IQ scores.

Vital found that 17 percent of children were identified with a striking skill compared to older children, but the most interesting findings concerned which factors were most strongly associated with having a striking skill. Although 33 percent of the children identified as having a striking skill also had high IQ scores, the factor most strongly related to their skill was the children's level of obsessive interests. Children who had high levels of narrow and obsessive interests were 61 percent more likely to be identified as having a striking skill.

The rage to master manifests in childhood, but usually persists throughout adulthood. There are two motivations that drive the rage to master: an allergic reaction to averageness and a pull toward perfection. Gifted individuals hate being bad at something, which can be a blessing and a curse depending on the situation. When their aversion to averageness works well for them, gifted individuals are not satisfied with the status quo and show an urgency to better themselves. But the reality is that gifted people will not be good at everything, which creates an angst that we will discuss in more detail later.

Gifted kids are also drawn to challenge, which might initially mean latching on to their teachers' or instructors' standards for performance, but eventually kids with a strong rage to master re-ject the traditional standards for excellence. One of the interesting qualities of many gifted individuals is that they have an unusual appreciation for the history of their area of interest and a respect for their predecessors, but seek to achieve a different standard or way of doing things. In the absence of sufficient challenge or an opportunity to move at a rapid pace toward mastery, gifted indi-viduals can appear as if they might implode.

Their rage to master is also driven by an intrinsic pleasure that comes with doing what they love. I often hear them say, "I just love to focus on the work." Gifted individuals love to work with a single-minded focus while they code, play a game, write music, or paint and they are easily irritated by anything that distracts from their obsessive work. It's understandable how someone would en-joy getting lost in her imagination when symphonies are unfolding there or enjoy singing an aria with perfect pitch. Although gifted individuals might receive praise from others for their ability or persistent efforts, they relentlessly hone their abilities even when they think no one is watching them because they find deliberate practice intrinsically enjoyable.

This unusual combination of ability, rage to master, and natural desire to engage in deliberate practice is ideal for tackling diffi-cult challenges, but these same qualities can also make it difficult for gifted children to gracefully navigate social life. When gifted kids' rage to master makes it hard for them to forge meaningful social ties, they are at risk for having their extraordinary potential stunted as well as a wide range of social and emotional problems.

The Relationship Between Giftedness and Awkwardness

TWO LINES OF research, one about giftedness and the other about social awkwardness, grew relatively independent of each other over the past few decades, but they have converged upon many of the same conclusions. Giftedness researchers originally set out to understand how extraordinary ability might be identified and nurtured, but along the way they discovered important social and emotional factors that could facilitate or impede gifted individuals' potential. Researchers who focused on studying social-communication problems and obsessive interests eventually discovered that people with social deficits and obsessive interests sometimes had unusual abilities.

The conceptual overlap between giftedness and awkwardness is easy to see. Awkward individuals have spotlighted attentions that shine on specific interests and gifted individuals are likely to narrowly focus on their specific talents. Awkward people become obsessive about their interests and gifted individuals are driven by a rage to master. Both gifted people and awkward people enjoy more time alone to engage in deliberate practice. These points of overlap and others suggest that awkwardness and giftedness may share something in common.

There is new evidence that behavioral tendencies shared by awkward people and gifted individuals might share common genetic influences. Pedro Vital and his colleagues analyzed a large sample of twins to investigate whether striking skills and obsessive interests might share common genetic roots. They found that the heritability of obsessive interests was strongly related to the heritability of striking skills. Another behavioral genetic study from David Hill and his colleagues at the University of Edinburgh included more than twelve thousand individuals who had their blood drawn and their genomes scanned for known genetic markers of psychological diagnoses including depression, anxiety, and autism. Hill found that genetic markers associated with social-communication deficits and repetitive behaviors were also associated with higher intelligence scores and higher levels of educational attainment.

Although not all gifted individuals are socially awkward and not all awkward individuals are gifted, these studies and others suggest that the two characteristics show significant overlap. When high levels of ability and obsessive interests are found in the same person, this combination is referred to as talent and researchers have found interesting behavioral mechanisms that explain how awkward characteristics and giftedness work together. Francesca Happe of the Institute of Psychiatry, King's College, has found that individuals with high levels of awkward characteristics show exceptional attention to detail and memory for those details. Simon Baron-Cohen has also found that this attention to detail might underlie some unique abilities, but also suggests that awkward individuals' systemizing tendencies help them search for patterns and logical relationships between the details of problems.

Awkward people are particularly skilled at breaking down situations into component parts, focusing on the details of those parts, and then searching for patterns that others might not see. That's why awkward kids do seemingly inexplicable things like taking apart a functional toaster "just to see how it works." Their systematic nature combined with obsessive interests drive them toward deliberate practice and help them maximize their inherent ability, potentially pushing it from very good to excellent, or excellent to exceptional.

Most people have a hunch that awkward people's interests tend to fall into certain areas such as technology, physics, or comic books, as embodied in phrases like "mad scientist" or "absent-minded professor." These archetypes of someone with an abundance of book smarts, but who seems to lack some social capabilities are counterintuitive characters. We marvel at the rocket scientist who can figure out how to get a satellite to Mars but cannot navigate his way back to his car in the parking lot, or wonder how a brain surgeon can read intricate brain scans but have no idea what is running through others' minds during social conversations.

The stereotype that techies and physicists tend to be socially awkward is found in television shows like *The Big Bang Theory* or movies like *Mean Girls*, in which the quintessential nerds were "mathletes" who competed in the Math Olympiad. These television shows and movies ultimately portray these gifted and awkward characters in a compassionate way, but part of what makes the humor work in these scripts is that people can relate to the

INTERESTS AND ABILITIES

One way to organize your thinking about your interests and abilities is using occupational psychologist John Holland's six interest types. Extensive and well-researched tests like the Strong Interest Inventory can provide in-depth feedback, but the chart below can give you some ideas about your interests and abilities. There is also extensive information available from the U.S. Department of Labor at onetonline.org.

CATEGORY	INTERESTS	ABILITIES
Realistic	Hands-on activities with tangible outcomes.	Independent, practical, produce tangible outcomes
Investigative	Ideas, theories, data	Analytical thinking and exploring new ideas
Artistic	Aesthetics, abstract concepts, creative endeavors	Imaginative, see outside the box, creative
Social	Helping people, teaching, relationships	Helpful, empathic, social fluency
Enterprising	Starting projects, leading, risk taking	Bold, assertive, persuasive
Conventional	Order, procedures, working with information	Efficient, precise, methodical

idea that those who are gifted in technology, science, or math are likely to be socially awkward. This is a good example of a situation in which casual observations overlap with the results of systematic investigation.

Simon Baron-Cohen and his colleagues at Oxford University compared the levels of awkwardness among four groups: Oxford University students majoring in the humanities, Oxford University computer science majors, winners from the high school UK Math Olympiad, and a control group that was not selected for specific interests. They wanted to determine whether participants whose interests required highly systematic thinking, as in computer science and mathematics, would report more awkward characteristics than participants in the control group or humanities group. They found that those in the control group and humanities group endorsed about a third of the awkward traits, which was significantly lower than the percentage of awkward traits endorsed by computer science majors (42 percent) and Math Olympiad students (50 percent).

Computer science students at an elite university or mathematically gifted teens likely possess an exceptional ability to apply systematic thought and logic to problems. The beauty of something like computer science is that computer chips do not have mood swings or self-doubt, which makes it easier to read the information on those chips if you work within the system. Mathematical proofs do not vacillate between logic versus intuition, which means that if someone follows an order of operations or a set of rules, then they will eventually reach a verifiable answer. But as we saw earlier, this kind of linear and systematic thinking that is so well suited to nonsocial, rule-governed problems can be an awkward fit with social problems that are far less linear and unexpectedly variable.

It's important to remember that majoring in computer science or becoming a mathlete does not cause someone to be awkward;

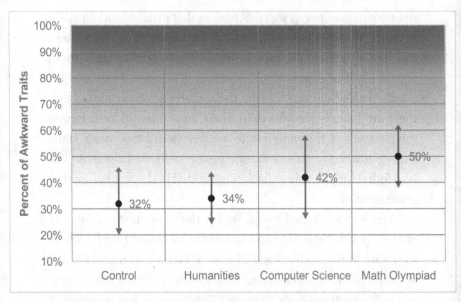

Figure 9.1 Percent of autism traits endorsed by each group. Arrows represent the 15th (low levels) and 85th percentile (high levels).

rather the data suggests that people with obsessive interests and a high degree of systematic ability tend to go into fields like computer science or mathematics. But high achievers who are compelled by an obsessive drive are found across many domains, and a systematic approach is an asset in many fields. Consider the obsessive nature of elite athletes like swimmers who wake at four-thirty to train for two hours in the morning and return in the evening to do the same training all over again. Or consider the need for elite dancers to attend to detailed movements and repeat those movements thousands of times, and the violinist who practices the same scales for so long that the skin under her chin grows tough to protect itself against the repeated abrasions. The strongest link between giftedness and awkwardness appears to be this predisposition to engage in deliberate practice, but this kind of obsessive drive can get in the way of people's social lives.

Professor Winner has found that talented individuals' rage to master can manifest as social behaviors that make it hard for them to fit in. While talented individuals are happy to spend solitary time honing their skills, their isolationist behavior can make them appear aloof or disinterested in others. The narrowness and intensity with which they pursue their interests usually means that there are few people who share their same interests or certainly the intensity of their interest in a topic. Recall the young Hans Asperger, who loved the nihilistic poetry of Franz Gillparzer, but who found his peers were far less interested in this kind of morbid contemplation.

Even when talented people share the same areas of interest as their peers, their rage to master can be off-putting to others who want to have fun instead of rage. When talented people cannot approach their interests with the intensity or pace they prefer, you will sometimes hear them say, "This person has no sense of urgency!"

As outsiders, it's easy for us to see the bigger picture. Talented people need to compartmentalize their rage to master and understand that sometimes they need to temper their intensity or do something just for fun. They need to understand that most people will not be as obsessed about their interests and will probably hold interests in other areas. Awkward people should try to pay attention to the big picture and focus less intensely on narrow areas of interest, but the reality is that it's not as easy as flipping a switch.

All of this seems obvious, but so are most psychological liabilities when viewed from an outside perspective. It's obvious that the alcoholic should not drink so much, the anxious person shouldn't worry too much, or the depressed person should not be so glum; but everyone has struggles that make it hard for them to keep themselves away from themselves. The trouble for parents, friends, managers, or psychotherapists who try to get people to get a grip on their obsessive interests is that the more they push, the more the people they are trying to help dig in their heels.

It's tricky for parents and teachers to help talented kids realize that their chances of success will rely upon an ability to relate to other people. A brilliant computer scientist might realize that she needs sharper emotional intelligence to communicate her ideas to others, or an exceptionally talented singer may realize that he will have to develop a rapport with his fans online or onstage. The awkward computer scientist may not intuitively understand how to be more persuasive or the awkward singer may not know how to let himself show his emotions during a performance, but these kinds of social skills are usually important for fully realizing one's potential. For talented kids with social deficits, it's tempting to push off the hard work of developing difficult social skills and to instead dive deeper into solitary time, honing their skills in their nonsocial areas of interest.

It's tough for parents, teachers, and mentors of talented children to know how to best support them. If talented kids devote too much time to their obsessive interests, then they put themselves at risk for becoming more socially isolated and will not practice handling social skills that are integral to maintain social connectedness. On the other hand, encouraging nerdy kids to "be more like the other kids" risks discouraging their uniqueness and depriving them of what makes them happiest. There are no easy answers here, but it's possible that these two scenarios are not diametrically opposed.

Talented kids may find it harder to make friends with a wide variety of children, but once they find like-minded kids they can be social while being able to immerse themselves in what they love. This does not necessarily mean that a talented artist needs to find other artists of similar talent, but they do need to find people who will push their boundaries and who will understand the unusual types of support one needs while trying to pursue ideas that sound outlandish to most people. Prodigious achievements are rarely accomplished in a social vacuum.

If people are gifted, but not awkward, then the prescription for nurturing those gifts is relatively straightforward. I went to Brooklyn College to visit with Jennifer Drake, who is a leading researcher of children who are gifted in the visual arts. She said that kids who are gifted in painting or drawing tend to not be socially awkward and the task is finding ways for them to nurture their talents. Low levels of arts funding in schools make it hard for gifted artists to find the resources they need through typical coursework.

Although gifted artists may not want to pursue an artistic career, they still feel a rage to master their inherent abilities and they are frustrated when that motivation cannot find an outlet. Parents often have to seek out summer programs or community opportunities where their kids can find other gifted artists who understand their way of thinking and who can push them to further develop their skills or inspire new ideas. When I asked Professor Drake about what parents should do, she responded with an emphatic, "Don't push them."

I thought this was particularly good advice in an age of hypercompetitive parenting, in which some parents try to compete based on their children's accomplishments. Gifted kids have already achieved a high level of excellence for their age and they are naturally motivated to master their area of talent. Parents have to keep in mind that kids or adult kids with a rage to master are probably at the brink of what could be a healthy level of drive and focus, which means that pushing them could drive up their intensity to a level that overheats their engine.

Talented kids need meaningful relationships with mentors and supportive peers who get them. They need to be able to rely upon loyal relationships for guidance and support just like anyone else, but they also need mentors and peers who get them. One of the most helpful things parents, teachers, or coaches of talented kids can do is to put those kids in positions to find like-minded peers or mentors. This may involve seeking out programs for gifted kids at schools and summer programs hosted by universities for high-achieving youth. These brief immersion experiences at conferences or institutes, or through other extracurricular activities, puts talented kids in a position to be with people who are interested in the same things they are, who move at the same brisk pace. Professor Winner remarked, "The most important impact this has on kids is socially because they find other kids like themselves and they realize that they're not alone."

Being True to Yourself and Fitting In

AFTER I GAVE my first lecture about awkwardness and giftedness there was a question-and-answer session. The first question came from a soft-spoken young man who bravely stood up and asked, "What happens if you are awkward, but you have average ability?" The social cues surrounding the situation suggested that he was not posing a hypothetical question as an academic exercise, rather he was asking a matter-of-fact question about how he should proceed. The convenient conclusion is to say that awkward people always harbor exceptional ability, but it's the kind of rah-rah self-help oversimplification that is not only untrue, but also unhelpful. Even though awkwardness and giftedness show significant overlap, they are far from perfectly correlated. Some people are awkward and gifted and some people are awkward with normal levels of ability. I replied with a non-rhetorical question: "I wonder about people's remarkable potential, regardless of their level of ability, that arises from doing what they love with an obsessive energy, sharp focus, and tireless persistence."

It's natural for the best of us to wonder whether we have the ability to achieve our goals, but the research findings pertinent to this question suggest that ability may be less important than people assume. Consider the extent to which graduate school performance is predicted by the Graduate Record Examination (GRE), which is used as a measure of raw scholastic ability. In a meta-analysis of more than seventeen hundred studies, Nathan Kuncel and his colleagues found that GRE scores were accurate predictors for a little more than 30 percent of graduate students' subsequent grade-point averages and performance ratings from faculty. While 30 percent is a significant amount, the finding also implies that there is plenty of room for other factors such as grit, confidence, or social support to elevate one's performance.

When people think about striving toward their ambitious long-term goals, I think the question is not so much about whether they have enough raw ability, but rather how they can leverage their unique dispositions to achieve their ambitious aspirations. For awkward people, two distinctive characteristics are their spotlighted focus and obsessive interests.

When I entered graduate school at the University of Minnesota, I overheard conversations among classmates discussing their near-perfect GRE scores or perfect undergraduate grades and I knew that by these metrics it would be foolish for me to try to compete with their raw intellectual firepower. In fact, it would have been foolish for me to compete at all because the reality was that there was plenty of success to go around for everyone and so I resolved to do the same thing I had always done to adapt to a new situation: I turned my spotlighted attention on one challenge at a time, determined to eventually understand how the parts came together.

Awkward individuals' spotlighted focus makes their perspective sharp and vivid. Although they miss the bigger picture at times, they may see details that others miss, details that could provide inspiration for a novel approach. For example, improv ac-

tors call small, aberrant details during a scene the "unusual thing."
It's something another actor does that is a little atypical, maybe
a shirttail that has come untucked or a slight hesitation in their
speech, but this unusual thing becomes the foothold for them to
launch the scene in unexpected directions. There are small hic-
cups in technology that might spark innovative breakthroughs,
outliers in science to guide other scientists to groundbreaking discoveries, or unusual sounds in a city that can inspire novel music
compositions.

Awkward people also like to understand how details can be organized in a systematic way. While awkward people can be frustrated
by their difficulty in spotting social conventions, their bottom-up
view gives them an opportunity to question whether the accepted
way of doing things is the best way. Although they should pick their
battles, they are good at seeing inefficiencies in systems and are
naturals at thinking about how to build a better system.

The other advantage awkward people have is their obsessive
interest. Behind every scientific breakthrough or Olympic gold
medal are thousands of mundane hours spent peering into a mi-
croscope or years of swimming laps at four-thirty in the morning.
While most people would find this repetition mind-numbingly
boring, awkward people's obsessive interest confers an intrinsic
pleasure and the persistent energy necessary to trudge through
thousands of tiny details and endure repeated trial and error to
achieve many long-term goals.

So the same spotlighted focus and obsessive energy that makes
awkward people uncomfortable in social situations are the same
qualities that can drive their push toward remarkable achievements. As I have alluded to earlier in the book, being awkward
is a trade-off. I find it interesting to wonder what one would pick
if given the choice, a disposition that allows one to see the bigger picture and easily navigate social life or a spotlighted focus

that gives one an advantageous intensity, but that makes social life less intuitive. I don't think that there is one that is better than the other, but understanding the differences is important for both awkward and non-awkward people alike because when diverse mind-sets combine, the results can be truly extraordinary.

10

GROUNDBREAKING INNOVATION

Our first lessons about extraordinary achievement are about outcasts who accomplish superhuman feats in the face of impossible odds. As kids we hear bedtime stories about the Little Engine That Could or a red-nosed reindeer who used the thing that made him an outcast to save Christmas for everyone. Many grade school kids devour stories about superheroes who are capable of specific abilities. Heroes are secretive about their superpowers and are usually known to most people by their awkward alter egos. There's the mild-mannered Clark Kent who becomes a Superman, the weak boy Steve Rogers who turns into Captain America, or the nerdy David Banner who morphs into the Incredible Hulk.

Teens want more angst in their stories. They love the paradox in genres like the *X-Men* that feature superheroes whose unique powers make them societal outcasts until the world is reminded that these same abnormalities are essential to saving the world. Most tales of heroism follow what American scholar Joseph Campbell called the hero's journey. Campbell found that heroes begin with a vague understanding about their special abilities and try to distance themselves from those abilities until a wise mentor comes along who helps the heroes understand them and how to

channel them for good. The heroes are exiled or depart from the
world they have known to a distant land where they hone their
abilities. During this training period, they encounter like-minded
people with whom they collectively resolve to take on a seemingly
impossible challenge.

The hero's journey embedded in superhero tales is not just
childish imagination. Many of the professional icons adults admire
and try to emulate have life stories that follow the same path laid
out in the hero's journey: people from humble beginnings who
found a hidden power within themselves, suffered numerous setbacks trying to do good, but ultimately triumphed by bravely har-
nessing their abilities to overcome improbable odds. There is the
Silicon Valley lore about Bill Gates dropping out of school and
building Microsoft from his parents' garage or Steve Jobs, who
was exiled by the board of directors at Apple but returned to make
Apple into the most valuable company in the world.

One of the interesting qualities about our fictional heroes and
real-life heroes is that many of them have a distinctive awkward
quality about them. Sometimes it appears as though they overcome their awkwardness to become successful, or they succeed
despite their awkwardness, but in modern stories people find
something captivating and inspiring about those who feel like they
do not fit in, but who harness their unusual strengths and find the
courage to persist through tremendous adversity on their way to
accomplishing prodigious feats.

It might seem unlikely that so many people who reach prodigious heights share the same story. After all, someone might argue
that the journey is irrelevant because the outcome is the same
regardless of whether someone awkwardly pushed toward a goal
or charmed his or her way to the top. Maybe people resonate with
the awkward hero because that's the narrative arc that best ap-
proximates people's real-life journeys toward prodigious goals. We
will see that the research results from studies of extraordinary

achievement happen to mirror all of the adversity and extraordinary possibility found in fictional tales about the hero's journey.

The Future Perfect

TALENTED PEOPLE CAN be perfectionistic about their interests. Once their rage to master is ignited, they become intent on learning everything they can and work tirelessly to hone their skills. In most fields or disciplines, there are structured procedures and systematic steps laid out for novices and intermediates. Math and science are very rule-governed; solo physical activities like tennis or ballet rely on practicing well-known fundamentals; and even creative domains like drawing follow rules about perspective and music comes from well-practiced scales. Awkward people find pleasure in deliberate practice and they enjoy seeing measurable results from their persistent efforts. The early, systematic steps needed to learn a craft are like candy for the awkward mind.

If talented people were fully satisfied by systematically moving along these well-defined paths from novice to expertise, then they would find life to be much easier. But talented people tend to choose areas of interest characterized by vast possibilities. Even in systematic disciplines like science or mathematics, it's impossible for the elite performers to achieve perfection on a regular basis because the upside is limitless. Science and math are defined by rules and methods, but there are an infinite number of ways those rules and methods can combine, which means that new questions and possibilities are always being raised. In creative endeavors like painting or fiction writing, there are even broader possibilities and pressure to generate work that explores uncharted territory.

Talented people find this kind of limitless possibility exhilarating when it comes to their interests. Most top scientists will admit that they prefer to push for new discoveries instead of replication, advanced mathematicians are most driven by unsolved proofs, and elite athletes want to push beyond the existing standards of excellence. Once talented kids find something they love, the intensity and focus of their spotlighted attention has a way of illuminating unique possibilities.

Once someone discovers new possibilities, they have to set their sights on a long-term goal to achieve. At a young age, talented people think differently about the future, and you can hear it in the way they speak about their aspirations. Most kids talk about the future in the simple future tense, which implies an isolated act that will occur. For example, someone using the simple future tense would say, "I will be a great chemistry student," or "I will go swim later today." But talented children are more likely to use a rarely used tense called the future perfect, which conveys that something will occur, but only after other things occur.

"If I do a better job of showing my work, then I may become a better chemistry student," or "I will get up at five A.M. to do my chores, then I can go swimming." It's a subtle but important grammatical variation that reflects an unusual amount of intellectual complexity for children. Prodigious children recognize the details along the way to lofty goals that are farther down the road.

For people who are beset by a rage to master, there's a natural tension in their narrative. This tension is drawn between their perfectionistic nature and their desire to achieve outcomes that are nearly impossible to perfect. If one spends too much time thinking about the impossibility of an outcome it's debilitating, but talented people tend to start along their paths by putting their heads down and shining their spotlighted focus on following a path of detailed goals one step at a time.

The Comfort of Expertise

EXPERTS DEVELOP KNOWLEDGE and skills that are superior to those of the average person in their field. Experts have vast knowledge, they think about problems at a deeper level of analysis, and they are faster at implementing effective solutions. They show an insatiable curiosity for knowledge in their field, they have an unusual ability to store this information in their memory, and they use this vast store of knowledge to see connections between the elements of complex problems.

Experts can have a calming presence on groups when the group faces steep challenges. The cool execution that experts display under duress is a paradox for people who know them well because experts have restless minds. When giftedness researchers look at what type of person is most likely to attain expertise, they find that they are those who have a razor-sharp focus and are prone to becoming obsessive about their work.

We want doctors, airline pilots, financial planners, and commanders-in-chief who are experts at what they do because the costs of poor choices carry heavily weighted consequences. Experts do not have to be told what to do, they see what needs to be done and they take effective action to thoroughly solve problems. Given the outsize value of expertise, it's no surprise that our educational culture aims to develop expertise and companies devote extensive resources to recruiting or developing expertise.

Organizations are increasingly interested in assessing their students' or employees' progress toward expertise with metrics. Public schools' funding levels rely on their students' performance on standardized tests. Business schools increasingly emphasize coursework about assessing return-on-investment, how employees contribute to the quarterly bottom line with quantifiable metrics about their daily or weekly performance.

One of the advantages of metrics is that they force organizations to use future-perfect language to define their goals. Organizations have to clearly define what they want in the long run, but also need to specify the essential steps to reach those lofty goals. When metrics work well, people know what they are expected to do, they are more consistent about meeting those expectations, and they are fairly rewarded.

Metrics can be a powerful tool for setting standards for expertise, but when organizations focus too narrowly on measurable results they can create a culture that limits and frustrates their highest potential members. Talented students will shoot for straight-A grades, work to build a long resume for entry to top schools, and practice to maximize their performance on standardized tests. Talented young employees will work tirelessly to master the tasks prescribed by the evaluation plans, whether that's becoming a whiz at Excel or someone who is capable of developing more efficient work flow.

Once their growing expertise eventually pushes them to the tail end of the bell curve, in this confined space they begin to grow restless. When people driven by a rage to master feel like they have been expert for too long, they appear agitated in the confines of well-defined organizational criteria, like petulant children who have been in their car seat for too long. Talented people love challenges and many of them see expertise as a state that is fun for a few weeks and then they need something new to tackle. But their restlessness can feel like discontent to an outsider and raise concerns about whether the talented person can ever be happy.

Winning the Innovation Lottery

DEAN SIMONTON IS a distinguished professor of psychology from the University of California, Davis, who has spent decades studying talent and prodigious achievement. Simonton has found that many talented individuals do not see expertise as an end point, but rather as a stop along the way to other destinations. Talented people aspire to groundbreaking innovations that will redefine their field or challenge existing standards of excellence. Examples of groundbreaking innovation are easy to see in hindsight, such as Sergey Brin and Larry Page's vision for a website called Google .com, Lin-Manuel Miranda's Broadway play *Hamilton*, or the way Bill and Melinda Gates have thought about philanthropy. These innovators not only contributed creative ideas that were valuable, but fundamentally shifted their fields and sometimes changed our cultural fabric.

To maximize the potential of their most talented members, organizations can start by posing the question, What are talented people trying to master? While most people are focused on expertise, talented individuals' focus is oriented elsewhere. They see expertise as a necessary step, but it's a checkpoint along the way as they rage to find groundbreaking innovations. It's a venerable aspiration, but even the most talented individuals find that innovative ideas are tough to come by and getting people to buy a worthwhile innovation presents a whole different set of challenges.

Simonton has found that groundbreaking innovations are often the product of people combining existing concepts or ideas in unusual ways. All of us have random combinations of ideas, but most of the time these combinations result in nothing useful or original. Sometimes the iterations of random collisions between ideas running around someone's head produces a winning combination, which is the first step to affecting groundbreaking innovations. Although breakthroughs are never guaranteed, Simonton's research findings can help us be methodical about increasing our odds of finding useful and innovative ideas.

Someone trying to unlock innovative discoveries is like someone trying to get into a safe that holds valuable information. Imagine the safe you are trying to crack has an electronic keypad and the code to the safe has two buttons, a two-digit code, and the numbers cannot be repeated. That safe would be easy to crack because there are only two possible combinations (1 and 2 or 2 and 1). If you needed to crack a three-button safe with a three-digit code, then that would be a little harder because there would be six possible combinations. But the number of combinations grows exponentially, which means that once there are more than three buttons the safe becomes much harder to crack. A safe with five buttons and a five-digit code produces 120 possible combinations and a twelve-digit code with twelve buttons yields more than 479 million combinations. When people try to figure out how to combine multiple facts and ideas to solve a problem, the sheer number of possible combinations of those facts and ideas can make the problem extremely difficult to crack.

People striving for groundbreaking innovation need to constantly be mindful about striking a balance between complexity versus simplicity. If they consider too few factors they may not have an opportunity to generate the right combination of ideas, but considering too many ideas can make the task too complex to solve. Simonton finds that talented people intentionally seek out ideas that appear tangential to their primary area of interest because they understand that diverse ideas are the fuel for innovative combinations.

Consider artificial intelligence computers that are built to combine data and ideas and evaluate the value of millions of possible combinations. Artificial intelligence machines are overly rational or systematic, which is why computer scientists intentionally program them to introduce random information into the process. In the same way, talented people need to find a systematic way to introduce new experiences and ideas that fall outside of their core areas of interest and that might seem illogical at first glance.

A classic example of combinatorial innovation comes from Steve Jobs, who was an abrasive brand of awkward. As a young man Jobs decided to attend calligraphy classes at College of the Redwoods, which seems like an endeavor unrelated to someone on a path to technological innovation. But Jobs recalled in a commencement speech at Stanford University years later that learning the nonlinear rules of calligraphy, such as the nonlinear aesthetics of unequal spacing between letters, helped inspire Jobs's emphasis on beautiful design. Apple's innovation home runs with elegant design helped drive their meteoric rise and changed the role of technology in most people's daily lives.

Later, when Jobs became the majority shareholder at Pixar, he met Ed Catmull, another prodigious innovator who merged two divergent disciplines. As a kid, Catmull had a passionate interest in animated films, but he decided to pursue a more practical route at the University of Utah, where he majored in computer engineering. In the 1970s, Catmull studied with Ivan Sutherland, who was one of the leading trailblazers in computer graphics, and this experience inspired collisions between his interest in animation and computer science. Catmull had a novel idea to create a movie animated by computer instead of the traditional hand-drawn method. The outcome was a revolutionary method of animated storytelling that was brought to life in Academy Award–winning Pixar films. The innovation also influenced other fields like gaming, which have introduced beautiful graphics and compelling story lines as an integral part of their products.

Although innovation often comes through the collision of diverse ideas, sometimes it comes from simply being willing to look at an existing field with a different perspective. Michael Lewis captured this type of detail-oriented innovative thinking in his book *The Big Short*, which is a true story about a rogue group of financial experts who foresaw the looming housing credit bubble in the mid-2000s. The awkward force was strong with these rogue investors, and their awkward nature oriented their attention toward details instead of the big picture. While the rest of the financial community saw mortgage securities that had been rated "AAA" (high quality, low risk), Lewis's awkward protagonists trained their spotlighted focus on the thousands of risky subprime loans in these mortgage-backed securities.

With obsessive energy they marched through details that failed to capture other people's attention. As they began to combine these details they discovered a stark reality: the U.S. economy was on the verge of a crash that would happen when home owners inevitably began to default on their subprime mortgages. In 2009 when their prophecy came to fruition, this awkward bunch of rogue investors captured returns in excess of a billion dollars as the rest of the financial world went south. Their breakthrough came from a willingness to see a stark truth composed of a million tiny details.

The timing of groundbreaking innovation is random or what Simonton calls a stochastic process. Sometimes people reach valuable combinations early in their process, like lottery balls that happen to fall into place for someone who bought their first lottery ticket. Talented people typically labor for years or decades if they do have a breakthrough moment and the hard truth is that even among talented people who strive for groundbreaking innovation, most will never realize their vision. Professor Winner and others find that the most common outcome for talented kids is expertise, which makes them remarkable contributors to their organizations.

Even if someone manages to discover the right combination of ideas, he needs to hope that the world is ready to adopt a different way of doing things, then she needs to effectively communicate her innovation to a broad audience. For the awkward innovator, this can be the biggest challenge of all.

During our discussion about talent, I have focused on awkward people's obsessive interests, but of course social challenges are also an important part of the awkward disposition. For awkward innovators who stall when they need to communicate their ideas to others, it's like they finally cracked the code for the safe that holds the innovative idea, and then discover that there is a second safe inside the first safe. Many awkward people find that effec-tively communicating their idea can be harder than discovering a scientific breakthrough or inventing the product.

Awkward people can hope that the value of their innovations is readily apparent to everyone else, but that's almost never the case. In business start-ups, consider all of the stakeholders who need to buy into an innovative idea for those start-ups to survive. Investors, employees, regulators, and of course customers need to be convinced that an idea is valuable enough to get behind. Henry Blodget wrote in a 2013 *Business Insider* article that the chances of a start-up succeeding could be estimated from data provided by Y Combinator, one of Silicon Valley's most prestigious incuba-tors for start-ups. Blodget estimates that less than 10 percent of Y Combinator start-ups are successful within five years, which is a staggering percentage considering that less than 5 percent of start-ups are accepted into Y Combinator in the first place.

In the world of books, even the most talented authors can spend decades waiting for publishers or audiences to resonate with the message they are trying to communicate. A few examples of well-known authors' initial rejections from publishing houses include Stephen King's thirty rejections for his first novel, *Carrie*; J. K. Rowling's first *Harry Potter* novel was rejected twelve times; *Gone with the Wind* was rejected thirty-eight times; and C. S. Lewis accumulated a staggering eight hundred rejections during the course of his literary career.

We could continue down this glum path of insurmountable odds, but I'll try to refrain from going on in too much detail for too long. I think these examples can inspire something other than de-moralization. The most interesting question to ask is, "Why would these people keep trying to succeed?" The narratives we hear about the .00001 percent of people who achieve groundbreaking innovation are inspiring, but for the majority of people passion-ately pursuing a new way of doing things, the reality is that their path is so difficult and so long that continuing down the path can seem unreasonable or downright foolish to others.

But what if someone was built to survive in exactly this type of treacherous environment? What if someone's gaze was not trained on the insurmountable odds, but rather directed elsewhere, trained intently on the small chances of creating something extraordinary? Someone would need to enjoy systematically marching through the thousands or millions of ideas, possess an unusual passion for the work, and repeatedly try combinations in the face of failure. It would also help if they had a razor-sharp focus so as not to become distracted from the work and a natural tendency to pay only passing attention to the criticisms of the doubters and the haters. When it comes to taking on visions with the odds stacked against me, I like my chances with an awkward person or two by my side.

Imperfect Brilliance

ALL OF US need to be inspired. We need stories like the fictional tales of superheroes overcoming evil or real-life heroes rising against tremendous odds because they inspire hope and remind us about what is possible through character strengths like persistence and bravery. But if you look closely at the details of the hero's arc, there are valuable details about the challenges of realizing prodigious achievements in real life.

In heroic tales, talent is a mixed blessing. Protagonists are usually loners whose differences make it harder for them to fit in and they have trouble figuring out how to do more good than harm with their abilities. In most stories, the complications that accompany unique ability inevitably present protagonists with a tempting choice to relinquish their talent.

Awkward people who also possess a tremendous amount of talent will tell you that they would sacrifice some of their intellectual or creative abilities if they could more easily fit in with others. Not once have I heard one of my awkward students or awkward clients say otherwise. Unique abilities can actually make it harder for people to find their place to belong and their obsessive energy can easily spin out of control. Talented people can become so narrowly focused and intensely driven in their careers that their personal lives and the people in them slowly fade away. Talent also inspires visions of one day achieving groundbreaking innovation, but the odds are small that anyone will ever achieve that kind of breakthrough. The world can handle only so many revolutions at once.

Talented people tend to be perfectionistic, but the lives of talented people are far from perfect. It's not to say that their circumstances are worse than anyone else's or that they deserve a disproportionate amount of empathy, but rather, it's helpful for all of us when we recognize that everyone's struggles are different and are open to understanding these unique challenges.

In high school, even though I no longer sat next to Kellie Kimpton, I continued taking Spanish classes. My Spanish teacher, Mr. Martinez, was my favorite teacher and he taught me a great deal. One of the most valuable lessons he imparted to me was how to think about what was going on around me. Mr. Martinez taught me how to conjugate verbs in the present tense to describe what is happening at the moment, the simple future to describe what would happen, and the future perfect to describe what would happen before another thing happened. Mr. Martinez also taught us about a tense that we do not formally use in English. The past imperfect allows you to communicate something that happened in the past as the result of an ongoing, habitual action that may have spanned months or years.

When someone achieves something extraordinary, what we see in this era of well-manicured social media posts and two-minute

YouTube video are end points. We see the trophy held, the key-
note speech, the selfie of someone looking fancy and put together.
When we witness these moments, there is a tendency to engage in
what psychologists call a hindsight bias, which is essentially when
people say, "I knew it all along, I knew that she would win a cham-
pionship one day," or "I knew from the first day I met him that he
would win a lifetime achievement award. It was inevitable." But if
someone has risen to heights where they have challenged the status quo, then it's almost always because they labored for years, in
the least glorious circumstances imaginable, to push their talents
to higher levels.

There are times during the years it takes to accrue the knowledge and practice necessary to achieve at high levels that people can look, for lack of a more diplomatic word, foolish. Talented
people can appear foolish to others because those who become
innovative have a propensity for experimentation and it's not a
perfect science. So they try things that fail miserably and when
they do it can be so bewildering to others who try to understand
what would motivate someone to try something so outlandish. To
others, the talented person in the making will look at times like
they have lost their minds.

The talent we observe during groundbreaking moments is a
highly concentrated version of what happens when people apply
unwavering drive to an already exceptional level of ability. But the
road to prodigious achievement is not a straight line; in fact people
spend a tremendous amount of time literally spinning themselves
in circles as they look for new routes or new ideas. The scientist
who spins her head around a problem during late nights in her
laboratory or the ballerina who stays after practice because she
is determined to improve her pirouette, these people are making
the sacrifices and putting in the extra effort necessary to get somewhere no one has been before. We would do well as a society not

to glorify talent, but rather to nurture talented kids with a realistic perspective about the potential and pitfalls they might anticipate.

My Spanish class with Mr. Martinez was a small group of ten students and we were an unusually tight-knit bunch. When Mr. Martinez taught us the past imperfect, he did something that was both innovative and meaningful while setting up our class conversation using the past imperfect. He asked us to talk about something a friend or family member had accomplished, something remarkable that was a result of their persistent efforts from the past. My classmates shared surprisingly personal stories.

Some students talked about family members who were the first to graduate from college or friends who had overcome tough home environments. Others talked about the sacrifices their immigrant parents had made to give their kids better opportunities in life. None of the stories was the same, but they were all inspiring tales about people who had reached new heights based on their life experience, and by doing so, lifted up those around them through their sheer determination.

The ten students in that class seemed to represent the main social groups of most high schools in the United States, including the head cheerleader, a football star, a punk rocker with purple hair, and an awkward person or two. We looked like a high school movie cliché. What I realized in that moment was that once we got past the surface, there were common aspirations and fears that ran through each person's narrative. There was something about speaking of people we admired in the past imperfect that made us recognize how much other people had continually sacrificed to kindly help us along in life.

From my perspective, I also realized that my classmates' stories were built on a bedrock of meaningful details, small, but significant acts that their loved ones performed over the course of years. When people became emotional, it was when they recalled habitual details like a mother waking up every morning at four-thirty for seventeen years to provide for her children or an older sibling who patiently helped a dyslexic student for years until she learned to read at grade level.

Through the shared wisdom in that classroom, I saw with brilliant clarity that the beauty of our social relationships is not about social awkwardness or social skill, but rather comes from our kind attention to thousands of social details.

Authors develop a relationship with their books. I know that sounds strange, but even the most systematic authors will tell you that books take on a life of their own. Authors try to communicate their ideas through pages of a manuscript. Months later when they revisit those pages to begin the editing process, the book offers new perspectives that were not apparent to the authors who created those pages. It's like the relationship people have with a city where they once lived. When they return to their beloved city and familiar places that are full of nostalgia, there is something about the collision of the familiarity from one's past life with one's present life that creates new insights.

As I started the previous chapter, I started looping back to earlier chapters I had not read in months. Doing so stirred an unusual degree of self-reflection within me. As I read about my Mr. Fuji wrestling fiasco, my mouthful of Kellie Kimpton's hair on the dance floor, or my memories about a friend who has passed, I reexperienced the gravitas of an awkward disposition that I had spent so much of my life trying to unload, but also felt new insights about how my awkwardness had shaped my life for the better.

In the end, life has worked out well. I have been blessed with a generous and nurturing group of friends and family, who remained loyal through my most awkward stretches. My family and mentors have helped me pursue a career that I find challenging and that allows me to absorb myself in systematic investigations about broad topics such as what makes romantic relationships work or the advantages that might result from being someone who is socially awkward. In matters of work and play, I feel grateful for how everything has turned out.

I'm not entirely sure why my life has worked out so well. I can think about the ways that pro-social attitudes or how my deliberate practice to meet minor social expectations eventually turned into social proficiency, but I do not understand my social life as a smooth, flowing narrative. Awkward people make sense of things with a bottom-up process, which means that realizations happen abruptly for them, like a chemical reaction that reaches a threshold for changing colors or igniting in an explosion. Awkward people are prone to being surprised, which can manifest as rude awakenings when outcomes are bad or as a magical event when outcomes are good.

When I first embarked on this book, my friend Andie once asked me if I wished that I had not been awkward. It was a thought-provoking question, one that I contemplated for quite some time, but eventually I realized that I am largely grateful for my awkwardness. Although there have been many instances when I dearly wish that social life was more intuitive and I am guilt-ridden by the times my awkwardness has caused trouble for other people, I also think that being awkward can be humbling and I think that it can instill a particular kind of empathy for others who do not fit the traditional societal mold.

Awkward people often feel like the social world is too chaotic to be systemized, but we have seen throughout this book that social science can help us unearth some reasonable and predictable social rules. The scientific method helps bring order to chaos, allows us to see relationships between ideas, and even helps us to predict what might happen. The social science we have suggests that awkward people have a spotlighted focus that shines narrowly and brightly on specific areas of interest. Awkward individuals default to focusing on their specific areas of interest, which tend to be nonsocial interests, and this means that they are prone to missing social cues that are obvious to others. When awkward people's behaviors deviate from minor social expectations, others interpret those deviations as small signs that someone might not be on board with the collective goals and values of the group and that's where the trouble begins.

But the science of why we're awkward can also be applied to help awkward people think about where to intentionally train their gaze in social situations, tells us why social graces are an important mechanism to master, and provides a rough road map about how likable people think about social life. My hope is that the data and theory available at this point might provide a structure for awkward individuals who are looking for some traction and rough maps for navigating social life. Social science can never tell a certain person exactly how to handle every situation, but it can provide some guidance for people to craft their own path that is necessarily unique to each individual.

Awkward people do not need to become popular or maintain dozens of friendships. The happiest people focus on forging a handful of gratifying social ties as the centerpiece of their lives. Awkward people need to devote the same concentrated focus to their social relationships that they would give to their work or other areas of nonsocial interest. When people are mutually committed to being fair, kind, and loyal, then the psychological weight of their ties grows exponentially, and it exerts the kind of gravitational pull necessary to keep awkward people passionately pursuing groundbreaking innovation in a stable orbit.

Awkward people are not better than anyone else, they are simply different. Although they may have abilities or dispositions that give them great potential in some areas, awkward individuals are challenged by social situations that come naturally to most people. Awkward people do not deserve some sort of special treatment, but they can certainly benefit from some patience, an open-minded approach to their quirks, and support for the things they want to achieve in life. It's the same thing that any of us want, awkward or not.

The theories and scientific findings we have reviewed in the previous chapters give us a way to understand why people are awkward and how they can redirect their attention to better understand and manage social situations. But logic and theory only take one so far. "If-then" rules about how to handle various social situations and generally accepted rules of etiquette are still subject to unpredictability because they are being applied to humans, who are variable in nature. In human interactions, one plus one does not always equal two and combining two elements does not always produce the same compound. It's this variability in the human condition that makes people maddening and wonderful.

The history of psychology suggests that there are many routes to a meaningful and happy life and there's good reason to be suspicious of anyone who espouses a one-size-fits-all approach to social or emotional fulfillment. But one of the most consistent findings in psychology is that a meaningful and happy life is strongly associated with the quality of people's social relationships.

I see now that the best things in life have come from the unpredictable and subtle acts of kindness and loyalty that have far exceeded anything I could have reasonably imagined. When I have had the presence of mind to purposefully direct my spotlighted attention toward important details about other people, I have found that I am pulled toward a sense of belonging that delightfully pushes the limits of my emotional capacity.

While the unpredictable elements of social life can be frustrating for me, the most meaningful moments in my life have involved people acting in unpredictable ways. Life is full of people who defy our expectations, whether parents with remarkable patience, a teacher who helps you to see clearly, the kind words of a Spanish girl, a friend who embodies the power of being pro-social, or a teacher who helps you see the future in a new way. When we set our sharp focus on these remarkable people who grace our lives, when we appreciate the ways they exceed our expectations in the most unexpected ways, that's when we begin to see in brilliant detail how awesome this life can be.

ACKNOWLEDGMENTS

Thanks to my agent, Laurie Abkemeier, for "getting me," and for her generous support and direction. I have been lucky to have three insightful editors, Deb Brody, Cara Bedick, and Cassie Jones, who expanded my perspective throughout the evolution of this book.

Thank you to my parents for their patience, persistence, faith, and abundant wisdom.

I am indebted to hundreds of researchers whose research findings provided the scientific foundation for this book. There are countless others to thank for their sharp ideas and generous support. A few of these remarkable friends and colleagues include Pat, Amy, Andy, Ashley, Hedy, Elliott, Sarah, Jeff, Jill, Kellie, Kate, Pippa, Aimee, Marina, Andrea, Lauren, Ellen, Jen, Kristen, and Jennifer.

BIBLIOGRAPHY

1: What Does It Mean to Be Awkward?

Anderson, Owen. *Running Science*. Human Kinetics, 2013. Harvard.

Back, Mitja D., Stefan C. Schmukle, and Boris Egloff. "A closer look at first sight: Social relations lens model analysis of personality and interpersonal attraction at zero acquaintance." *European Journal of Personality* 25, no. 3 (2011): 225–38.

Baumeister, Roy F., and Mark R. Leary. "The need to belong: desire for interpersonal attachments as a fundamental human motivation. "*Psychological bulletin* 117, no. 3 (1995): 497.

Berscheid, Ellen. "Love in the fourth dimension." *Annual review of psychology* 61 (2010): 1–25.

Berscheid, Ellen, and Hilary Ammazzalorso. "Emotional experience in close relationships." *Blackwell handbook of social psychology: Interpersonal processes* (2001): 308–30.

Diener, Ed, and Martin E.P. Seligman. "Very happy people." *Psychological science* 13, no. 1 (2002): 81–84.

Douglas, Mary. *Purity and danger: An analysis of concepts of pollution and taboo*. Routledge, 2003.

Farooqi, I. Sadaf, and Stephen O'Rahilly. "Genetics of obesity in humans." *Endocrine reviews* 27, no. 7 (2006): 710–18.

Glaser, Ronald, and Janice K. Kiecolt-Glaser. "Stress-induced immune dysfunction: implications for health." *Nature Reviews Immunology* 5, no. 3 (2005): 243–51.

Maslow, Abraham Harold. "A theory of human motivation." *Psychological review* 50, no. 4 (1943): 370.

Naumann, Laura P., Simine Vazire, Peter J. Rentfrow, and Samuel D. Gosling. "Personality judgments based on physical appearance." *Personality and Social Psychology Bulletin* (2009).

Quail, Christine. "Nerds, geeks, and the hip/square dialectic in contemporary television." *Television & New Media* 12, no. 5 (2011): 460–82.

Richard, Annette E., and Renee Lajiness-O'Neill. "Visual attention shifting in autism spectrum disorders." *Journal of clinical and experimental neuropsychology* 37.7 (2015): 671–87.

Schawbel, Dan. 2016. "The Multi-Generational Job Search Study 2014 | Millennial Branding-Gen-Y Research & Management Consulting Firm." Accessed August 7. http://millennialbranding.com/2014/multi-generational-job-search-study-2014/.

Shalev, Sharon. "Solitary confinement and supermax prisons: A human rights and ethical analysis." *Journal of Forensic Psychology Practice* 11, no. 2–3 (2011): 151–83.

Wagner, Dylan D., William M. Kelley, and Todd F. Heatherton. "Individual differences in the spontaneous recruitment of brain regions supporting mental state understanding when viewing natural social scenes." *Cerebral Cortex* 21, no. 12 (2011): 2788–96.

"What Singles Want: Survey Looks at Attraction, Turnoffs." 2016. *USA Today*. Accessed August. http://www.usatoday.com/story/news/nation/2013/02/04/singles-dating-attraction-facebook/1878265/.

2: Is There Anything Wrong With Being Awkward?

Asperger, Hans. "Die Autistischen Psychopathen im Kindesalter." *European Archives of Psychiatry and Clinical Neuroscience* 117, no. 1 (1944): 76–136.

Baron-Cohen, Simon, Sally Wheelwright, Richard Skinner, Joanne Martin, and Emma Clubley. "The autism-spectrum quotient (AQ): Evidence from asperger syndrome/high-functioning autism, males and females, scientists and mathematicians." *Journal of autism and developmental disorders* 31, no. 1 (2001): 5–17.

Gernsbacher, Morton Ann, Michelle Dawson, and H. Hill Goldsmith. "Three reasons not to believe in an autism epidemic." *Current directions in psychological science* 14, no. 2 (2005): 55–58.

Haslam, N., E. Holland, and Peter Kuppens. "Categories versus dimensions in personality and psychopathology: a quantitative review of taxometric research." *Psychological medicine* 42, no. 05 (2012): 903–20.

Ingram, David G., T. Nicole Takahashi, and Judith H. Miles. "Defining autism subgroups: a taxometric solution." *Journal of autism and developmental disorders* 38, no. 5 (2008): 950–60.

Kanner, Leo. "Early infantile autism." *The Journal of Pediatrics* 25, no. 3 (1944): 211–17.

Lyons, Viktoria, and Michael Fitzgerald. "Did Hans Asperger (1906–1980) have Asperger Syndrome?" *Journal of autism and developmental disorders* 37, no. 10 (2007): 2020–21.

Singer, Emily. "Diagnosis: redefining autism." *Nature* 491, no. 7422 (2012): S12-S13.

3: Looking for Some Sweet Skills

Adolphs, Ralph, Michael L. Spezio, Morgan Parlier, and Joseph Piven. "Distinct face-processing strategies in parents of autistic children." *Current Biology* 18, no. 14 (2008): 1090–93.

Anticevic, Alan, Grega Repovs, Gordon L. Shulman, and Deanna M. Barch. "When less is more: TPJ and default network deactivation during encoding predicts working memory performance." *Neuroimage* 49, no. 3 (2010): 2638–48.

Baron-Cohen, Simon, Sally Wheelwright, Jacqueline Hill, Yogini Raste, and Ian Plumb. "The 'Reading the Mind in the Eyes' test revised version: A study with normal adults, and adults with Asperger syndrome or high-functioning autism." *Journal of child psychology and psychiatry* 42, no. 2 (2001): 241–51.

Baron-Cohen, Simon, Howard A. Ring, Sally Wheelwright, Edward T. Bullmore, Mick J. Brammer, Andrew Simmons, and Steve C.R. Williams. "Social intelligence in the normal and autistic brain: an fMRI study." *European Journal of Neuroscience* 11, no. 6 (1999): 1891–98.

Besner, Derek, Evan F. Risko, Jennifer A. Stolz, Darcy White, Michael Reynolds, Shannon O'Malley, and Serje Robidoux. "Varieties of Attention: Their Roles in Visual Word Identification." *Current Directions in Psychological Science* 25, no. 3 (2016): 162–168.

Diaz, B. Alexander, Sophie Van Der Sluis, Sarah Moens, Jeroen S. Benjamins, Filippo Migliorati, Diederick Stoffers, Anouk Den Braber et al. "The Amsterdam Resting-State Questionnaire reveals multiple phenotypes of resting-state cognition." *Frontiers in human neuroscience* 7 (2013): 446.

Di Martino, Adriana, Kathryn Ross, Lucina Q. Uddin, Andrew B. Sklar, F. Xavier Castellanos, and Michael P. Milham. "Functional brain correlates

of social and nonsocial processes in autism spectrum disorders: an activation likelihood estimation meta-analysis." *Biological psychiatry* 65, no. 1
(2009): 63–74.

Di Martino, Adriana, Zarrar Shehzad, Clare A.M. Kelly, Amy Krain Roy,
Dylan G. Gee, Lucina Q. Uddin, Kristin Gotimer, Donald F. Klein, F.
Xavier Castellanos, and Michael P. Milham. "Autistic traits in neurotyp-
ical adults are related to cingulo-insular functional connectivity." *The
American journal of psychiatry* 166, no. 8 (2009): 891.

Dunbar, Robin I.M., Anna Marriott, and Neil D.C. Duncan. "Human conver-
sational behavior." *Human Nature* 8, no. 3 (1997): 231–46.

Dunbar, Robin I.M., and Susanne Shultz. "Evolution in the social brain."
Science 317, no. 5843 (2007): 1344–47.

Ekman, Paul, Wallace V. Friesen, and Phoebe Ellsworth. *Emotion in the human
face: Guidelines for research and an integration of findings.* Elsevier, 2013.

Fox, Kieran C.R., R. Nathan Spreng, Melissa Ellamil, Jessica R. Andrews-
Hanna, and Kalina Christoff. "The wandering brain: Meta-analysis of
functional neuroimaging studies of mind-wandering and related spontaneous thought processes." *Neuroimage* 111 (2015): 611–21.

Hall, Judith A., and Marianne Schmid Mast. "Sources of accuracy in the empathic accuracy paradigm." *Emotion* 7, no. 2 (2007): 438.

Hahamy, Avital, Marlene Behrmann, and Rafael Malach. "The idiosyncratic
brain: distortion of spontaneous connectivity patterns in autism spectrum
disorder." *Nature neuroscience* 18, no. 2 (2015): 302–309.

Ingersoll, Brooke, Christopher J. Hopwood, Allison Wainer, and M. Brent
Donnellan. "A comparison of three self-report measures of the broader
autism phenotype in a non-clinical sample." *Journal of autism and developmental disorders* 41, no. 12 (2011): 1646–157.

Krueger, Joachim, Jacob J. Ham, and Kirsten M. Linford. "Perceptions of behavioral consistency: Are people aware of the actor-observer effect?"*Psychological Science* 7, no. 5 (1996): 259–64.

Lieberman, Matthew. *Social: Why Our Brains Are Wired to Connect.* Broadway Books (2013).

Lieberman, Matthew D. "Social cognitive neuroscience." *Handbook of social
psychology* (2010).

Mar, Raymond A., Malia F. Mason, and Aubrey Litvack. "How daydreaming
relates to life satisfaction, loneliness, and social support: the importance
of gender and daydream content." *Consciousness and cognition* 21, no. 1
(2012): 401–407.

McCann, Joanne, and Sue Peppé. "Prosody in autism spectrum disorders: a critical review." *International Journal of Language & Communication Disorders* 38, no. 4 (2003): 325–50.

Mead, Margaret. *Sex and temperament in three primitive societies.* Vol. 370. New York: Morrow, 1963.

Ryan, Nicholas P., Cathy Catroppa, Richard Beare, Timothy J. Silk, Louise Crossley, Miriam H. Beauchamp, Keith Owen Yeates, and Vicki A. Anderson. "Theory of mind mediates the prospective relationship between abnormal social brain network morphology and chronic behavior problems after pediatric traumatic brain injury." *Social cognitive and affective neuroscience* 11, no. 4 (2016): 683–92.

Pesquita, Ana, Timothy Corlis, and James T. Enns. "Perception of musical cooperation in jazz duets is predicted by social aptitude." *Psychomusicology: Music, Mind, and Brain* 24, no. 2 (2014): 173.

Pinsky, Robert. *The sounds of poetry: A brief guide.* Macmillan, 1999.

Rutherford, Mel D., Simon Baron-Cohen, and Sally Wheelwright. "Reading the mind in the voice: A study with normal adults and adults with Asperger syndrome and high functioning autism." *Journal of autism and developmental disorders* 32, no. 3 (2002): 189–94.

Spencer, M. D., R. J. Holt, L. R. Chura, J. Suckling, A. J. Calder, E. T. Bullmore, and S. Baron-Cohen. "A novel functional brain imaging endophenotype of autism: the neural response to facial expression of emotion." *Translational psychiatry* 1, no. 7 (2011): e19.

Spezio, Michael L., Ralph Adolphs, Robert S.E. Hurley, and Joseph Piven. "Analysis of face gaze in autism using 'Bubbles.'" *Neuropsychologia* 45, no. 1 (2007): 144–51.

Tickle-Degnen, Linda, and Robert Rosenthal. "The nature of rapport and its nonverbal correlates." *Psychological inquiry* 1, no. 4 (1990): 285–93.

Yucel, G. H., A. Belger, J. Bizzell, M. Parlier, R. Adolphs, and J. Piven. "Abnormal neural activation to faces in the parents of children with autism." *Cerebral Cortex* (2014): bhu147.

4: Emotions Make Me Feel Funny

Baron-Cohen, Simon, Howard A. Ring, Edward T. Bullmore, Sally Wheelwright, Chris Ashwin, and S.C.R. Williams. "The amygdala theory of autism." *Neuroscience & Biobehavioral Reviews* 24, no. 3 (2000): 355–64.

Baron-Cohen, Simon, Sally Wheelwright, Jacqueline Hill, Yogini Raste, and Ian Plumb. "The 'Reading the Mind in the Eyes' test revised version: A study with normal adults, and adults with Asperger syndrome or high-functioning autism." *Journal of child psychology and psychiatry* 42, no. 2 (2001): 241–51.

Darwin, Charles. *The expression of the emotions in man and animals.* Vol. 526. University of Chicago Press, 1965.

Feinberg, Matthew, Robb Willer, and Dacher Keltner. "Flustered and faithful: embarrassment as a signal of prosociality." *Journal of personality and social psychology* 102, no. 1 (2012): 81.

Fredrickson, Barbara L. "Positive emotions broaden and build." *Advances in experimental social psychology* 47 (2013): 1–53.

Harker, LeeAnne, and Dacher Keltner. "Expressions of positive emotion in women's college yearbook pictures and their relationship to personality and life outcomes across adulthood." *Journal of personality and social psychology* 80, no. 1 (2001): 112.

Isen, Alice M., Kimberly A. Daubman, and Gary P. Nowicki. "Positive affect facilitates creative problem solving." *Journal of personality and social psychology* 52, no. 6 (1987): 1122.

Izard, Carroll E. "Basic emotions, natural kinds, emotion schemas, and a new paradigm." *Perspectives on psychological science* 2, no. 3 (2007): 260–280.

Markram, Kamila, and Henry Markram. "The intense world theory–a unifying theory of the neurobiology of autism." *Frontiers in human neuroscience* 4 (2010).

Markram, Kamila, Tania Rinaldi, Deborah La Mendola, Carmen Sandi, and Henry Markram. "Abnormal fear conditioning and amygdala processing in an animal model of autism." *Neuropsychopharmacology* 33, no. 4 (2008): 901–12.

Tangney, June Price, and Ronda L. Dearing. *Shame and guilt.* Guilford Press, 2003.

Tangney, June Price, Jeff Stuewig, and Debra J. Mashek. "Moral emotions and moral behavior." *Annual review of psychology* 58 (2007): 345.

5: Unlocking the Minds of Likable People

Baron-Cohen, Simon, Alan M. Leslie, and Uta Frith. "Does the autistic child have a 'theory of mind'?" *Cognition* 21, no. 1 (1985): 37–46.

Berndt, Thomas J. "Friendship quality and social development." *Current directions in psychological science* 11, no. 1 (2002): 7–10.

Cook, Clayton R., Kirk R. Williams, Nancy G. Guerra, Tia E. Kim, and Shelly Sadek. "Predictors of bullying and victimization in childhood and adolescence: A meta-analytic investigation." *School Psychology Quarterly* 25, no. 2 (2010): 65.

Csikszentmihalyi, Mihaly. *Flow: The psychology of optimal experience.* Vol. 41. New York: HarperPerennial, 1991.

Demaray, Michelle Kilpatrick, and Christine Kerres Malecki. "Importance ratings of socially supportive behaviors by children and adolescents." *School Psychology Review* 32, no. 1 (2003): 108–31.

Freud, Sigmund. "The development of the sexual function." *Standard edition* 23 (1940): 152–56.

Frith, Chris, and Uta Frith. "Theory of mind." *Current Biology* 15, no. 17 (2005): R644–R645.

Gliga, Teodora, Atsushi Senju, Michèle Pettinato, Tony Charman, and Mark H. Johnson. "Spontaneous belief attribution in younger siblings of children on the autism spectrum." *Developmental psychology* 50, no. 3 (2014): 903.

Gini, Gianluca, and Tiziana Pozzoli. "Association between bullying and psychosomatic problems: A meta-analysis." *Pediatrics* 123, no. 3 (2009): 1059–65.

Gini, Gianluca, Paolo Albiero, Beatrice Benelli, and Gianmarco Altoè. "Does empathy predict adolescents' bullying and defending behavior?." *Aggressive behavior* 33, no. 5 (2007): 467–76.

Gottman, John M., and Robert W. Levenson. "Marital processes predictive of later dissolution: behavior, physiology, and health." *Journal of personality and social psychology* 63, no. 2 (1992): 221.

Happé, Francesca, and Uta Frith. "The weak coherence account: detail-focused cognitive style in autism spectrum disorders." *Journal of autism and developmental disorders* 36, no. 1 (2006): 5–25.

Lejuez, C. W., Derek R. Hopko, Ron Acierno, Stacey B. Daughters, and Sherry L. Pagoto. "Ten year revision of the brief behavioral activation treatment for depression: revised treatment manual." *Behavior modification* 35, no. 2 (2011): 111–61.

Losh, Molly, and Joseph Piven. "Social-cognition and the broad autism phenotype: identifying genetically meaningful phenotypes." *Journal of Child Psychology and Psychiatry* 48, no. 1 (2007): 105–12.

Moore, Chris. "Fairness in children's resource allocation depends on the recipient." *Psychological Science* 20, no. 8 (2009): 944–48.

Rand, David G., Corina E. Tarnita, Hisashi Ohtsuki, and Martin A. Nowak. "Evolution of fairness in the one-shot anonymous Ultimatum Game." *Proceedings of the National Academy of Sciences* 110, no. 7 (2013): 2581–86.

Seyfarth, Robert M., and Dorothy L. Cheney. "The evolutionary origins of friendship." *Annual review of psychology* 63 (2012): 153–77.

Shetgiri, Rashmi. "Bullying and victimization among children." *Advances in pediatrics* 60, no. 1 (2013): 33.

Tager-Flusberg, Helen. "On the nature of linguistic functioning in early infantile autism." *Journal of Autism and Developmental Disorders* 11, no. 1 (1981): 45–56.

Tellegen, Auke, and Gilbert Atkinson. "Openness to absorbing and self-altering experiences ('absorption'), a trait related to hypnotic susceptibility." *Journal of abnormal psychology* 83, no. 3 (1974): 268.

Van de Cruys, Sander, Kris Evers, Ruth Van der Hallen, Lien Van Eylen, Bart Boets, Lee de-Wit, and Johan Wagemans. "Precise minds in uncertain worlds: Predictive coding in autism." *Psychological review* 121, no. 4 (2014): 649.

6: Nurturing Awkward Children

Baron-Cohen, Simon, Emma Ashwin, Chris Ashwin, Teresa Tavassoli, and Bhismadev Chakrabarti. "Talent in autism: hyper-systemizing, hyper-attention to detail and sensory hypersensitivity." *Philosophical Transactions of the Royal Society B: Biological Sciences* 364, no. 1522 (2009): 1377–83.

Constantino, John N., and Richard D. Todd. "Autistic traits in the general population: a twin study." *Archives of general psychiatry* 60, no. 5 (2003): 524–30.

Dunbar, Robin I.M. "Coevolution of neocortical size, group size and language in humans." *Behavioral and brain sciences* 16, no. 04 (1993): 681–94.

Greenberg, Jeff, Tom Pyszczynski, Sheldon Solomon, Abram Rosenblatt, Mitchell Veeder, Shari Kirkland, and Deborah Lyon. "Evidence for terror management theory II: The effects of mortality salience on reactions to those who threaten or bolster the cultural worldview." *Journal of personality and social psychology* 58, no. 2 (1990): 308.

Gopnik, Alison. "Scientific thinking in young children: Theoretical advances, empirical research, and policy implications." *Science* 337, no. 6102 (2012): 1623–127.

Happé, Francesca, J. Briskman, and Uta Frith. "Exploring the cognitive phenotype of autism: weak 'central coherence' in parents and siblings of children with autism: I. Experimental tests." *Journal of child psychology and psychiatry* 42, no. 3 (2001): 299–307.

Weil, Elizabeth. "Mary Cain Is Growing Up Fast." *New York Times*, March 4, 2015. http://www.nytimes.com/2015/03/08/magazine/mary-cain-is-growing-up-fast.html.

7: THE AWKWARDNESS OF MAKING FRIENDS

Alkon, Amy. *Good Manners for Nice People Who Sometimes Say F°ck*. St. Martin's Griffin, 2014.

Cacioppo, John T., and Stephanie Cacioppo. "Social relationships and health: The toxic effects of perceived social isolation." *Social and personality psychology compass* 8, no. 2 (2014): 58-72.

Clark, D. Matthew T., Natalie J. Loxton, and Stephanie J. Tobin. "Declining loneliness over time: Evidence from American colleges and high schools." *Personality and Social Psychology Bulletin* 41, no. 1 (2015): 78-89.

Haidt, Jonathan. "The new synthesis in moral psychology." *Science* 316, no. 5827 (2007): 998-1002.

Ivcevic, Zorana, and Nalini Ambady. "Personality impressions from identity claims on Facebook." *Psychology of Popular Media Culture* 1, no. 1 (2012): 38.

Jobe, Lisa E., and Susan Williams White. "Loneliness, social relationships, and a broader autism phenotype in college students." *Personality and Individual Differences* 42, no. 8 (2007): 1479–89.

Khosla, Aditya, Atish Das Sarma, and Raffay Hamid. "What makes an image popular?" In *Proceedings of the 23rd international conference on World wide web*, pp. 867–76. ACM, 2014.

Kruger, Justin, and Epley, Nicholas. "Egocentrism Over E-Mail: Can We Communicate as Well as We Think?" *Journal of personality and social psychology* 89, no. 6 (2005): 925-936.

McPherson, Miller, Lynn Smith-Lovin, and Matthew E. Brashears. "Social isolation in America: Changes in core discussion networks over two decades." *American sociological review* 71, no. 3 (2006): 353-375.

Pew Research Center, March, 2014, "Millennials in Adulthood: Detached from Institutions, Networked with Friends."

Putnam, Robert D. "Bowling alone: America's declining social capital." *Journal of democracy* 6, no. 1 (1995): 65-78.

United Kingdom Mental Health Foundation. 2010, "The Lonely Society"

Williams, Alex. "The Emily Posts of the Digital Age." *New York Times*, March 31, 2013., 1–10, Academic Search Premier, EBSCOhost (accessed January 15, 2016).

Wrzus, Cornelia, Martha Hänel, Jenny Wagner, and Franz J. Neyer. "Social network changes and life events across the life span: A meta-analysis." *Psychological bulletin* 139, no. 1 (2013): 53.

8: Dating and Sex are So Awkward

Byers, E. Sandra, Shana Nichols, Susan D. Voyer, and Georgianna Reilly. "Sexual well-being of a community sample of high-functioning adults on the autism spectrum who have been in a romantic relationship." *Autism* 17, no. 4 (2013): 418–33.

Coontz, Stephanie. *Marriage, a history: How love conquered marriage*. Penguin, 2006.

Feeney, Brooke C. "The dependency paradox in close relationships: accepting dependence promotes independence." *Journal of personality and social psychology* 92, no. 2 (2007): 268.

Holt-Lunstad, Julianne, Timothy B. Smith, Mark Baker, Tyler Harris, and David Stephenson. "Loneliness and social isolation as risk factors for mortality: a meta-analytic review." *Perspectives on Psychological Science* 10, no. 2 (2015): 227–37.

Mintah, Kojo. "I Cannot See It in Their Eyes: How Autism Symptoms Hamper Dating." PhD diss., Carleton University, Ottawa, 2014.

Moore, Monica M. "Human nonverbal courtship behavior—a brief historical review." *Journal of sex research* 47, no. 2–3 (2010): 171–80.

Pew Research Center, March 2014, "Millennials in Adulthood: Detached from Institutions, Networked with Friends."

Pollmann, Monique M.H., Catrin Finkenauer, and Sander Begeer. "Mediators of the link between autistic traits and relationship satisfaction in a non-clinical sample." *Journal of autism and developmental disorders* 40, no. 4 (2010): 470–78.

9: Practically Prodigious

Achter, John A., David Lubinski, and Camilla Persson Benbow. "Multipotentiality among the intellectually gifted: 'It was never there and already it's vanishing.'" *Journal of Counseling Psychology* 43, no. 1 (1996): 65.

Borkenau, Peter, and Anette Liebler. "Convergence of stranger ratings of personality and intelligence with self-ratings, partner ratings, and measured intelligence." *Journal of Personality and Social Psychology* 65, no. 3 (1993): 546.

Centers for Disease Control and Prevention. Developmental Milestones. (January 14, 2016). http://www.cdc.gov/ncbddd/actearly/milestones/.

Simonton, Dean Keith. "Creativity: Cognitive, personal, developmental, and social aspects." *American psychologist* 55, no. 1 (2000): 151.

Sternberg, Robert J. "Implicit theories of intelligence, creativity, and wisdom." *Journal of personality and social psychology* 49, no. 3 (1985): 607.

Terman, Lewis Madison. "Genetic studies of genius. Mental and physical traits of a thousand gifted children" (1925).

Vital, Pedro M., Angelica Ronald, Gregory L. Wallace, and Francesca Happé. "Relationship between special abilities and autistic-like traits in a large population-based sample of 8-year-olds." *Journal of Child Psychology and Psychiatry* 50, no. 9 (2009): 1093–1101.

Winner, Ellen. "The origins and ends of giftedness." *American psychologist* 55, no. 1 (2000): 159.

Winner, Ellen. *Gifted children: Myths and realities*. Basic Books, 1997.

10: Groundbreaking Innovation

Baron-Cohen, Simon, Emma Ashwin, Chris Ashwin, Teresa Tavassoli, and Bhismadev Chakrabarti. "Talent in autism: hyper-systemizing, hyper-attention to detail and sensory hypersensitivity." *Philosophical Transactions of the Royal Society B: Biological Sciences* 364, no. 1522 (2009): 1377–83.

Baron-Cohen, Simon, Sally Wheelwright, Amy Burtenshaw, and Esther Hobson. "Mathematical talent is linked to autism." *Human nature* 18, no. 2 (2007): 125–31.

Ruthsatz, Joanne, and Jourdan B. Urbach. "Child prodigy: A novel cognitive profile places elevated general intelligence, exceptional working memory and attention to detail at the root of prodigiousness." *Intelligence* 40, no. 5 (2012): 419–26.

Simonton, Dean Keith. "Scientific creativity as constrained stochastic behavior: the integration of product, person, and process perspectives." *Psychological bulletin* 129, no. 4 (2003): 475.

Winner, Ellen. "The origins and ends of giftedness." *American psychologist* 55, no. 1 (2000): 159.

ABOUT THE AUTHOR

TY TASHIRO, PhD, is the author of *The Science of Happily Ever After*. His work has been featured in the *New York Times,* the *Washington Post,* Time.com, TheAtlantic.com, and on NPR and SiriusXM Stars radio. He received his doctorate in psychology from the University of Minnesota, has been an award-winning professor at the University of Maryland and University of Colorado, and has addressed TED@NYC, Harvard Business School, MIT's Media Lab, and the American Psychological Association. He lives in New York City.